DRAKE FOSTER

21 Habits of Highly Sensitive and Empowered People

Navigating Life as an HSP

Copyright © 2025 by Drake Foster

All rights reserved. No part of this publication may be reproduced, stored or transmitted in any form or by any means, electronic, mechanical, photocopying, recording, scanning, or otherwise without written permission from the publisher. It is illegal to copy this book, post it to a website, or distribute it by any other means without permission.

First edition

Part 1: Foundation of Sensitive Strength

Habit 1: Understanding Your Sensitive Nature

Deep within each highly sensitive person lies an extraordinary gift, a finely tuned awareness that perceives the subtle threads weaving through existence. This heightened perception shapes every interaction, every moment, and every breath of daily life.

There's a profound truth about sensitive people that often get overlooked in our busy world. The very trait that many see as a weakness, that deep, penetrating awareness of everything around you, is actually a remarkable gift. It's not something to overcome or suppress. Rather, it's a sophisticated perceptual system that allows you to experience life with extraordinary depth and nuance. Think about what happens when sunlight streams through your window in the morning. Where others may note that it's bright outside, you perceive an entire symphony of sensory information. You notice the subtle interplay of light and shadow, the gentle warmth on your skin, and perhaps even the way the quality of light hints at the weather to come. This isn't being "too sensitive", it's having access to a richer, more textured experience of reality.

Your sensitivity functions like a finely tuned instrument. Consider a master violinist's Stradivarius; its extraordinary sensitivity to pressure and temperature isn't a flaw; it's precisely what allows it to produce such exquisite music. Similarly, your heightened awareness enables you to detect and respond to subtle environmental variations that others might miss entirely. Throughout each day, you encounter countless moments that others might pass by without notice. The slight shift in a friend's tone reveals their unspoken worry. The almost imperceptible change in air pressure that precedes a storm. The underlying currents of tension or harmony in a group conversation. By acknowledging these perceptions rather than dismissing them, you begin to recognize them as valuable data points about your world.

When you feel overwhelmed in a crowded restaurant, you're not failing to cope, you're simultaneously processing multiple streams of sensory information. Your system is picking up on dozens of conversations, the clatter of dishes, the movement of servers, the various aromas, and the shifting social dynamics. It's like having a high-definition camera in a world where most people use basic point-and-shoot models. The richness of detail you perceive isn't a malfunction, it's a higher level of functioning that requires its own special kind of care and attention. The path forward isn't about becoming less sensitive. It's about understanding and honoring these traits as valuable aspects of who you are. This understanding becomes the foundation for everything that follows: how you arrange your environment, how you manage your energy, and how you engage with others. When you stop fighting against your sensitive nature and start working with it, you begin to discover its true power as a guide through life's complexities.

This journey of understanding marks the beginning of a profound transformation. Each step forward carries the potential for greater awareness, deeper connections, and more authentic living. The path ahead is clear, it leads toward embracing your sensitivity as the extraordinary gift it truly is.

The Journey of Sensitive Awareness

When you walk into a room, your nervous system acts like an exquisitely calibrated instrument, registering changes and patterns that most would overlook. A slight tension in your shoulders might be your first warning about an approaching deadline. That flutter in your stomach could detect unspoken tension in a meeting before anyone else notices it. These physical responses aren't random, they represent an advanced warning system honed through millions of years of human evolution. Your energy moves through the day like a river, with natural peaks and valleys that demand respect. Some mornings bring crystal clarity when your mind feels sharp and ready to tackle complex challenges. Other mornings ask for a gentler approach, a slower engagement with the world. These fluctuations aren't character flaws or signs of weakness, they represent your body's natural rhythm responding to countless environmental and internal factors. Consider how your body demonstrates remarkable wisdom in signaling stress. Perhaps your jaw clenches during difficult conversations, or your digestion changes under pressure. Your sleep might become lighter, or certain foods suddenly seem less appealing. These stress signatures serve as valuable indicators, pointing toward needed adjustments before overwhelm sets in. By tracking these responses, clear patterns emerge that can guide your decisions about environments, relationships, and commitments.

Each sensitive person carries a unique constellation of comfort signals. Your body might find peace in nature, while another sensitive person feels most at ease in quiet indoor spaces. Certain textures might feel soothing to you, while others create discomfort. These preferences aren't arbitrary; they reflect deep wisdom about your needs and boundaries. Reading these comfort signals provides a reliable compass for navigating daily life. Sleep patterns reveal crucial information about your overall well-being. As a sensitive person, you may experience sleep differently, taking longer to transition from day to night or requiring specific conditions for rest. These patterns aren't problems to fix but rather essential aspects of your sensitivity to understand and honor. When you track your sleep, valuable insights emerge. Certain evening activities promote better rest, while others disrupt it. This knowledge enables you to create conditions that support rather than hinder your natural sleep rhythms. Your body constantly adapts to changing circumstances, but your sensitive system responds more quickly and intensely to these shifts. Weather changes might trigger physical responses. New environments require more adjustment time. These adaptations aren't weaknesses, they reflect an exquisitely responsive system working to maintain balance. Understanding these adaptation needs allows for better planning and self-care. Instead of pushing through discomfort, you can honor your body's need for gradual transitions and adequate adjustment periods.

This deep understanding of your physical and emotional signals forms a crucial foundation for sensitive living. Each noticed signal, each honored need, and each respected boundary strengthens the connection between body and awareness. This growing understanding enables increasingly refined navigation of daily life, transforming your sensitivity from what might have felt like a liability into the remarkable gift it truly represents.

The Path of Recognition

Throughout human history, those individuals who could detect subtle changes in their environment, who could sense the shift in tribal dynamics or spot the predator's movement in the undergrowth, were the ones who survived. And we are their descendants, carrying that exquisite machinery of perception in our modern minds. But here's where it gets really interesting, which is absolutely crucial: In our contemporary society, we've pathologized this gift. We tell sensitive people they're "too much" or "too intense" when, in fact, they're carrying forward an ancestral wisdom that we desperately need. It's like telling a master violinist they're too attuned to subtle variations in pitch; it completely misses the point. The patterns these individuals recognize, how a room's energy shifts when someone enters, and how specific environments feel fundamentally unsafe while others promote flourishing aren't arbitrary, subjective experiences. They're sophisticated readings of complex social and environmental dynamics that our conscious minds haven't yet learned to articulate fully. And that's precisely what makes them so valuable.

When a sensitive person feels drained after being in a crowd, that's not weakness; it's their nervous system processing an enormous amount of social information. It's like running sophisticated software on a computer; of course, it requires more energy. And understanding this transforms the entire framework of how we view sensitivity. Recognizing these patterns isn't just about personal comfort, it's about survival and meaning itself. Because in a world that's increasingly artificial and disconnected from our evolutionary heritage, these sensitive individuals serve as canaries in the coal mine of human experience. They tell us something profound about what we need as a species to flourish. And that's why dismissing these experiences or trying to numb them away with medication or distraction isn't just ineffective, it's practically a crime against consciousness itself. We need these sensitive souls. We need their insights, warnings, and profound understanding of the human condition. Because without them, we risk losing touch with the very mechanisms that have kept our species alive and thriving for millennia.

The Power of Awareness

In a busy restaurant scenario, your nervous system isn't just being "overwhelmed." Instead, it's performing an incredibly sophisticated feat of parallel processing. Your brain simultaneously processes multiple audio streams, including conversations, kitchen noise, music, and ambient sounds, while analyzing complex visual data like movement patterns, facial expressions, and spatial relationships. At the same time, it's integrating environmental sensations such as temperature changes, air currents, and scent molecules, all while monitoring social dynamics, group interactions, emotional undercurrents, and power dynamics. This isn't weakness, it's extraordinary computational power. Imagine running dozens of complex programs on a computer simultaneously. Of course, it requires more processing power and energy. The same principle applies to your neural networks.

The radar system metaphor is particularly apt, but let's deepen it. Like a modern radar system, sensitivity operates on multiple frequencies simultaneously. Just as radar can detect variations in weather patterns, track moving objects, and analyze atmospheric conditions all at once, your sensitivity allows you to process emotional frequencies by picking up subtle shifts in mood and meaning. You monitor environmental frequencies by detecting changes in physical space and atmosphere while tracking social frequencies by reading group dynamics and interpersonal energies. This multi-frequency awareness isn't random or chaotic. It's a highly evolved system that served crucial survival functions throughout human history. Our ancestors, who could detect subtle environmental changes, read social undercurrents, and sense impending dangers, were more likely to survive and pass on these traits. In our modern context, this awareness becomes even more valuable. In an increasingly complex social world, the ability to read subtle cues and process multiple layers of information simultaneously isn't just helpful; it's essential for navigating relationships, professional environments, and social structures.

The key transformation occurs when you shift from seeing these experiences as overwhelming to recognizing them as valuable data points. Each sensation, each emotional response, and each moment of overwhelm contains important information about your personal boundaries and needs, the dynamics of your environment, the emotional states of those around you, potential threats or opportunities, and the overall health of your social ecosystem. By developing this meta-awareness, this ability to observe and understand your own sensitivity patterns, you gain access to more information about yourself and your environment. This isn't just about coping with sensitivity; it's about harnessing its power as a sophisticated information-gathering system. Moreover, this awareness allows you to develop more nuanced and effective strategies for managing your energy and attention. Instead of trying to suppress or ignore your sensitivity, you can learn to calibrate your exposure to different environments, develop a precise understanding of your personal thresholds, create sophisticated strategies for processing and integrating information, and use your sensitivity as a tool for deeper understanding and connection. In essence, awareness transforms sensitivity from a perceived liability into a powerful asset, one that enables deeper understanding, more meaningful connections, and more effective navigation of our complex social world.

Building the Foundation

Just as a musician with perfect pitch can detect subtle variations in tone that others might miss, your heightened sensitivity allows you to perceive nuances in your environment that many cannot. This isn't a flaw, it's a specialized capability that requires proper training and care to fully utilize. The process of careful observation serves multiple purposes. First, it helps create a detailed map of your personal response patterns. When you notice that a crowded coffee shop drains your energy while a quiet bookstore helps you recharge, you gather vital data about your nervous system's optimal operating conditions. This information becomes the foundation for making informed decisions about how to structure your daily life.

The documentation process is particularly powerful because it moves these experiences from the realm of subjective feeling into objective observation. Instead of thinking, "I'm too sensitive because I get overwhelmed at parties," you might note, "After 90 minutes in social gatherings with more than ten people, I notice my energy levels declining and my ability to focus decreasing." This shift in perspective transforms vague feelings into actionable insights. Consider how a master sommelier develops their wine-tasting abilities. They don't try to dull their sensitive palate, instead, they learn to catalog and understand the subtleties they can detect. Similarly, sensitive individuals benefit from developing a refined understanding of their perceptual abilities rather than trying to suppress them.

The conformity trap deserves special attention. Many sensitive people have internalized the message that their natural responses are somehow wrong or excessive. This internalized judgment often leads to a destructive cycle: feeling overwhelmed, pushing through anyway, experiencing exhaustion, and then feeling guilty about needing recovery time. Breaking this cycle requires understanding that sensitivity isn't a character flaw to overcome but rather a trait to work with intelligently. Think of it like having a high-performance vehicle. You wouldn't expect a Formula 1 car to operate like a standard sedan, it requires specific conditions, careful maintenance, and skilled handling to perform optimally. Similarly, a sensitive nervous system needs appropriate care and conditions to function at its best.

The path forward involves developing what we might call "sensitivity literacy", a deep understanding of your unique operating parameters. This includes recognizing early warning signs of overstimulation, understanding your optimal recovery methods, and identifying the environments and activities that allow you to thrive rather than just survive. This foundation-building phase isn't about finding quick fixes or temporary coping mechanisms. Instead, it's about creating a sustainable way of living that honors your natural traits while allowing you to engage effectively with the world. It's about moving from a stance of apology and accommodation to one of informed self-advocacy and authentic expression.

The Nature of Sensitivity, Intersection of Neural Activity and Lived Experience

Deep sensitivity creates an intricate dance between our internal world and external surroundings. Every moment brings waves of information: textures, sounds, emotions, and energies flow through our awareness like water through a stream. This heightened perception reshapes daily experiences. A piece of music might trigger goosebumps, or a friend's subtle tone shift could spark immediate concern. The world becomes rich with meaning as our system processes each detail with remarkable depth. Such intense awareness brings both gifts and challenges. Walking into a room, sensitive individuals might instantly grasp complex social dynamics or notice environmental factors affecting everyone's mood. These insights emerge naturally from an innate ability to absorb and process information at multiple levels.

Our nervous systems operate like sophisticated instruments, constantly gathering and interpreting data from our surroundings. We notice it immediately when something disrupts this delicate balance, whether it's harsh lighting, emotional tension, or environmental stressors. Rather than dismissing these signals, we can learn to trust them as valuable guidance. This deep processing reveals patterns others might overlook. A subtle shift in someone's energy could signal an approaching conflict. An inexplicable sense of discomfort might point toward an unhealthy situation. We access a wealth of information about our world by honoring these perceptions instead of doubting them. Understanding this aspect of ourselves opens new possibilities. Instead of fighting against our sensitive nature, we can embrace it as a source of wisdom and insight. Every reaction and every response provides valuable information about our environment and relationships. This knowledge guides us toward choices that support our well-being and enhance our connections with others. The key lies in recognizing sensitivity's inherent value. Everything changes when we stop viewing it as a weakness and start seeing it as a sophisticated information-processing system. We discover that our reactions make perfect sense, given the depth at which we experience life. This realization transforms self-doubt into self-understanding, creating space for genuine growth and acceptance.

Embracing the Journey

The journey of understanding sensitivity mirrors the gradual unfolding of a new perspective. When we first begin exploring these traits, we often carry the weight of past misunderstandings. Society's messages about "toughening up" or "not being so sensitive" create deep grooves in our thinking, leading us to question our natural responses to the world around us. Let's explore what happens as we start to shift this perspective. At first, we might notice small things, such as how certain environments leave us feeling energized while others drain our resources. We begin to pay attention to the wisdom in our responses rather than pushing them away. Each observation adds another piece to our understanding. Over time, patterns emerge that show us the intelligence behind our sensitivity. Those moments of overwhelm in crowded spaces aren't random; they signal our system's need to process complex social information carefully. The deep emotional responses to art or nature reveal our capacity for profound connection and meaning-making.

This growing awareness naturally leads to changes in how we structure our lives. Instead of forcing ourselves to endure draining situations, we learn to create spaces that support our natural way of being. This might mean establishing quiet morning routines that set us up for success or designing our living spaces to provide the right balance of stimulation and calm. Relationships transform as well through this process of understanding. As we recognize the validity of our needs, we become better equipped to communicate them to others. We learn to express our boundaries not as limitations but as necessary guidelines for maintaining our well-being and showing up fully in our connections with others.

The beauty of this journey lies in its ripple effects. As we develop a more nuanced understanding of our sensitivity, we often discover new depths in our interactions with the world. Our capacity for empathy, creativity, and insight expands. We begin to trust our system's subtle signals, using them as guidance rather than seeing them as obstacles to overcome. This shift doesn't happen overnight. It unfolds gradually, requiring patience with ourselves as we unlearn old patterns and develop new ways of being. Each step forward in understanding our sensitivity opens new possibilities for living more authentically and effectively in the world.

The Bridge to Transformation

The transformation of sensitivity from perceived weakness to recognized strength represents a fundamental shift in self-understanding. When we start viewing sensitivity as a sophisticated form of perception, its true value emerges. Our nervous system processes information with remarkable depth, creating insights that shape how we move through the world. This shift begins at the level of decision-making. Instead of second-guessing our reactions, we learn to decode them. That subtle unease about a situation often contains valuable information about misaligned values or hidden problems. The immediate resonance with certain people or places can guide us toward environments where we naturally thrive. These intuitive signals become reliable guides rather than inconvenient feelings to suppress. In relationships, this understanding creates space for authentic connection. We naturally gravitate toward deeper connections when we recognize our need for meaningful exchanges rather than surface-level interaction. Our ability to sense underlying emotions and unspoken dynamics allows us to respond with greater understanding and empathy. This depth of perception helps build trust and intimacy in our relationships. Professional life transforms through this lens of understanding as well. Rather than forcing ourselves into environments that drain our energy, we can seek or create situations that harness our natural strengths. Our capacity for deep processing and attention to detail becomes valuable in roles requiring careful analysis or emotional intelligence. Sensing subtle shifts in group dynamics can enhance leadership and collaboration.

The path forward unfolds through small, consistent acknowledgments of our true nature. Each time we honor our need for quiet reflection rather than pushing through overwhelm, we strengthen our self-trust. When we communicate our boundaries clearly instead of accommodating them at our own expense, we build confidence in our perceptions. This journey requires sustained courage, the kind that manifests in everyday choices rather than grand gestures. It takes courage to leave a gathering when we sense our energy depleting, even if others seem fine. It requires bravery to structure our lives around our actual needs rather than conforming to external expectations. Yet each small act of honoring our sensitivity builds momentum toward lasting transformation. Understanding emerges gradually through experience and reflection. As we collect evidence of how our sensitivity serves us and others, doubt gives way to certainty. We begin to trust the wisdom of our responses and recognize them as valuable guidance for navigating life's complexities. This growing self-trust becomes the foundation for authentic living and meaningful contribution to the world around us.

The Path Ahead

Understanding sensitivity opens up a new way of moving through the world. The journey ahead unfolds naturally as we learn to work with our perceptive nature rather than against it. Each experience adds depth to our understanding, teaching us how sensitive traits enrich our lives and relationships. Our responses to situations begin to make more sense. What once felt like random overwhelm reveals itself as helpful information about our surroundings. We start noticing clear signals, certain environments consistently support our well-being while others deplete it. These insights help us choose where and how to spend our energy.

The process transforms challenging situations into opportunities for growth. Social gatherings that once felt draining become easier to navigate as we understand our needs. We learn when to step away for quiet moments and how to return refreshed. This rhythm of engagement and recovery becomes natural, allowing us to participate more fully in life while honoring our sensitive nature. Past experiences take on new meaning through this lens of understanding. Times we felt overwhelmed or out of place now make perfect sense; our system was simply processing more information than most people around us. This realization helps release old shame or self-judgment about being "too sensitive". The future opens up possibilities as we align our choices with our true nature. Work becomes more satisfying when we choose roles that value our perceptive abilities. Relationships deepen as we express our needs clearly and attract people who appreciate our depth of understanding. Even everyday activities feel different when approached with awareness of our sensitivity.

Moving forward doesn't mean the path will always be smooth. There will still be challenging moments and situations that test our understanding. But now, these challenges feel different, they become opportunities to refine our awareness rather than proof of weakness. Each difficult situation teaches us something valuable about ourselves and how to navigate our sensitivity more effectively. This journey leads to a profound shift in self-perception. Instead of trying to change or suppress our sensitive traits, we discover how to use them wisely. Life becomes more prosperous and more meaningful as we embrace our natural way of experiencing the world. The path ahead isn't about becoming someone different, it's about growing into who we truly are.

Tomorrow's Promise

Recognizing sensitivity's true nature opens up remarkable possibilities for growth and fulfillment. We discover their inherent wisdom when we stop viewing our perceptive traits as something to overcome. This understanding creates space for natural evolution. Much like a flower opening toward sunlight, our authentic nature emerges when given the right conditions. Each person's journey unfolds in its own time. The initial steps might feel small, perhaps noticing how certain environments affect your energy, or recognizing when you need time alone to process experiences. These observations lay the groundwork for deeper understanding. As patterns emerge, you begin to trust the intelligence behind your responses to the world around you.

Sensitivity brings unique gifts that enrich both personal experience and relationships with others. Your ability to notice subtle shifts in emotion allows for deeper connections. The way you process experiences thoroughly leads to a more nuanced understanding. Even your need for quiet reflection serves an essential purpose, allowing you to integrate information and experiences more completely. The path forward involves learning to work with these traits rather than against them. Instead of pushing through overwhelm, you might create regular periods for recovery and integration. Rather than forcing yourself to endure draining situations, you can design your environment to support your natural way of being. These adjustments aren't about limitations; they're about creating conditions where you can fully express your capabilities.

Future chapters will explore practical approaches for thriving as a sensitive person. You'll discover ways to maintain your energy while engaging fully with life. You'll learn how to communicate your needs effectively and create boundaries that protect without isolating. Most importantly, you'll understand how to leverage your sensitivity as a source of insight and connection. This journey begins a profound shift in how you experience life. Each step forward brings new insights and possibilities. As you embrace your sensitive nature, you'll find yourself moving through the world more easily and authentically. The path ahead leads toward a fuller expression of who you truly are, someone uniquely equipped to experience life's depth and richness. This transformation doesn't require becoming someone different. Instead, it involves recognizing and nurturing qualities that have always been present within you. Your sensitivity isn't a weakness to overcome but a sophisticated system of perception waiting to be fully understood and expressed. The journey ahead holds the promise of deeper understanding, richer experiences, and more meaningful connections, all emerging naturally as you embrace your true nature.

Reading Your Inner Compass

Your body constantly processes information from your environment. These signals manifest in various ways, perhaps a slight tension in your shoulders when someone enters a room or a flutter in your stomach during a challenging conversation. Rather than random sensations, these physical responses represent your nervous system's sophisticated communication of important information. When we tune into these bodily signals, we begin to recognize patterns. The tightness in your chest might appear before particularly stressful situations, acting as an early warning system. A feeling of expansiveness and ease in certain environments signals places where your nervous system feels safe and supported. Over time, these physical cues become reliable indicators of what serves your well-being and what might drain your energy. Understanding these signals requires patience and practice. Initially, you might only notice strong physical reactions, the racing heart during conflict or the exhaustion after a crowded event. As your awareness develops, more subtle signals emerge. You start recognizing the slight shift in your breathing when someone's words don't match their tone or the small release of tension when you enter a genuinely welcoming space.

Your body's wisdom often manifests before conscious thought catches up. That inexplicable urge to leave a situation or the immediate sense of trust with certain people stems from your system processing countless subtle cues simultaneously. Trusting these physical insights can lead to better decision-making and stronger boundaries. This bodily awareness also helps in managing energy levels. You can take protective action before reaching complete exhaustion by noticing early signs of overwhelm, perhaps a slight headache or difficulty focusing. Similarly, recognizing signals of well-being helps identify activities and environments that genuinely support your sensitive nature.

The body's messages become particularly valuable in relationships. Physical sensations often reveal truths about interactions that might otherwise go unnoticed. The subtle tension during certain conversations, or the natural ease felt with specific people, provides valuable information about relationship dynamics and personal boundaries. Think of this inner compass as a sophisticated guidance system, continuously gathering and interpreting data to help navigate life's complexities. As you develop trust in these physical signals, decision-making becomes more transparent and aligned with your needs. This more profound connection with your body's wisdom represents a powerful tool for living authentically as a sensitive person.

The Symphony of Signals, From the Basic Physical Responses to More Complex Patterns of Awareness

Think about your body as an intricate network of sensors constantly gathering information from your surroundings. These sensors don't just detect noticeable changes; they pick up subtle shifts in atmosphere, energy, and social dynamics that many people might miss entirely. This heightened awareness stems from the way sensitive nervous systems process information more deeply and thoroughly than average. When you enter a new environment, your body immediately begins processing multiple streams of information. Your skin might register slight temperature changes or air movement. Your ears pick up both unmistakable sounds and background noises that others filter out. Your nervous system responds to the social energy and emotional atmosphere. All these inputs combine to create immediate physical responses that serve as valuable feedback about your environment. These physical signals often appear in specific patterns. In challenging environments, you might notice tension starting in your shoulders, then moving to your neck and finally causing shallow breathing. Understanding these patterns helps you recognize situations that might become overwhelming before they actually do. Similarly, environments that support your well-being often create a cascade of positive physical responses, starting with deeper breathing, followed by relaxed muscles and increased energy.

Your body's responses become particularly meaningful in social situations. That subtle stomach tightness during a conversation might alert you to underlying tension before it becomes evident to others. A feeling of expansion in your chest could signal genuine connection and safety with certain people. These physical cues often process social information faster than your conscious mind can analyze it. The key to working with these signals lies in understanding their progression. Early warning signs usually start subtly, maybe a slight change in breathing or a minor muscle tension. If these initial signals go unnoticed, they typically intensify, becoming more obvious and more challenging to manage. Recognizing and responding to early signals helps prevent overwhelming situations and supports better self-regulation.

Over time, paying attention to these bodily responses creates a sophisticated guidance system for navigating life. You learn which environments support your nervous system and which ones require more careful energy management. This understanding allows you to make choices that honor your sensitivity while still engaging fully with the world around you. This bodily wisdom represents an evolutionary advantage, allowing sensitive individuals to detect and respond to environmental changes quickly. Rather than seeing these responses as inconvenient or excessive, we can understand them as valuable information that helps us navigate our world more effectively and make choices that support our well-being.

The Energy Equation

Energy is a dynamic resource that follows natural cycles throughout each day. For sensitive people, these cycles tend to be more pronounced because their nervous systems process information more intensely. Just as a high-performance engine uses more fuel than a standard one, a sensitive nervous system requires more energy to handle its deeper level of information processing. These energy patterns connect directly to how our bodies interact with our environment. During peak energy times, our system efficiently processes multiple streams of information, sounds, emotions, social dynamics, and physical sensations. We might feel alert, focused, and capable of handling complex situations. However, this heightened processing gradually depletes our energy reserves, much like running multiple computer programs drains its battery. Low-energy periods are essential, allowing our system to restore and integrate all the information we've gathered. Our body signals its need for quieter activities and reduced stimulation during these times. These signals might include difficulty concentrating, increased physical tension, or a strong desire for solitude. Understanding these signals helps us recognize when we need to shift into recovery mode.

The timing of these cycles varies among individuals. Some sensitive people experience their highest energy in the early morning when the world feels quieter and less demanding. Others find their peak energy during evening hours when daily pressures have subsided. The key lies in observing your personal patterns without judgment, noting when you naturally feel more capable of handling stimulation and when you need recovery time. Working with these natural rhythms transforms productivity and well-being. Instead of pushing through low-energy periods with caffeine or willpower, we can structure our days to match our natural cycles. This might mean scheduling essential meetings or complex tasks during high-energy times while reserving administrative work or quiet reflection for lower-energy periods. Understanding these patterns also helps in managing social energy. Large gatherings or intense conversations might best be scheduled during peak energy times when our system can better handle multiple inputs. Recovery periods can include activities that restore our energy, perhaps spending time in nature, engaging in creative pursuits, or simply being alone in a quiet space.

This awareness of energy patterns leads to more effective self-care strategies. We can implement supportive practices throughout the day rather than waiting until we're completely exhausted. Small breaks, quiet moments, or brief meditation periods can help maintain our energy levels and prevent complete depletion. By honoring these natural energy cycles, sensitive individuals can maintain more stable energy levels throughout the day while fully engaging in their work and relationships. This understanding transforms what might once have felt like limitations into guidelines for creating a more sustainable and satisfying way of living.

Stress Signatures

Physical stress responses emerge from our autonomic nervous system's attempt to protect us. When we encounter challenging situations, our body activates various protective mechanisms. These reactions appear in consistent patterns, what we might call our personal stress signatures. Some people experience digestive changes first, while others notice sleep disruption or muscle tension as their initial warning signs. Understanding how stress manifests in our bodies requires careful attention to subtle changes. Consider digestion as an example. Under stress, our digestive system might slow down or speed up, leading to appetite or food preferences changes. These shifts occur because our nervous system diverts energy toward managing perceived threats, affecting how we process nutrients.

Sleep patterns offer another window into our stress levels. During periods of heightened stress, many sensitive individuals notice changes in their sleep architecture. They might take longer to fall asleep, experience more vivid dreams, or wake up more frequently. These changes reflect our nervous system remaining vigilant even during rest periods. Muscle tension provides obvious stress signals. Under pressure, specific muscle groups tend to hold tension in predictable ways. Some people carry stress in their shoulders and neck, while others notice jaw clenching or lower back tightness. These physical responses often appear before we consciously recognize feeling stressed. Temperature sensitivity and energy fluctuations can also signal rising stress levels. Many sensitive individuals notice they become more reactive to temperature changes when stressed or experience unusual hot or cold sensations. Energy levels might fluctuate more dramatically, with sudden drops in stamina or unexpected bursts of restless energy.

We can identify our stress patterns by tracking these physical responses over time. This awareness allows us to recognize early warning signs and take protective action before stress becomes overwhelming. We might notice that certain work situations consistently trigger shoulder tension or that specific social dynamics lead to digestive disruption. This understanding enables more effective stress management strategies. Rather than waiting until stress accumulates to an uncomfortable level, we can respond to early physical signals with appropriate self-care measures. This might mean taking short breaks when we notice muscle tension building or adjusting our schedule when sleep patterns begin to shift.

The body's stress signatures provide valuable guidance for creating sustainable lifestyles. By honoring these physical messages and adjusting accordingly, we can maintain better balance and prevent the accumulation of chronic stress. This attention to our body's wisdom helps us navigate challenges while protecting our long-term well-being.

The Comfort Constellation

Our nervous system maintains an ongoing dialogue with our environment, constantly evaluating safety and comfort. When we encounter conditions that support our well-being, our body responds with distinct physical signals. Our breathing naturally deepens, muscles soften, and the digestive system functions smoothly. These physical responses indicate environments where our nervous system can operate optimally. Consider how this process works in natural settings. For many sensitive individuals, time in nature triggers a cascade of comfort responses. The rhythmic sound of waves or rustling leaves helps regulate our breathing. Natural light supports our circadian rhythms. The diverse but predictable sensory input of outdoor spaces provides stimulation without overwhelming our system. Our body expresses this alignment through physical ease, relaxed shoulders, steady heart rate, and improved digestion. Indoor environments also generate clear comfort signals. Some people feel their nervous system settle in spaces with soft lighting and minimal noise. Others notice their body relaxes in rooms with specific colors or arrangements. These responses stem from our system's need for environmental conditions that support optimal functioning. Our body communicates through physical signs of ease when these needs are met. Texture sensitivity plays a crucial role in comfort. Our skin processes a constant stream of sensory information about our immediate environment. Certain fabrics or surfaces might promote physical relaxation, while others trigger tension or discomfort. These reactions provide valuable information about creating supportive environments, from choosing clothing to selecting furniture.

Understanding our comfort signals helps refine decision-making. When considering new situations or environments, we can consider our body's immediate responses. A subtle feeling of expansion in the chest might indicate alignment with our needs. Conversely, persistent muscle tension or disrupted breathing patterns could signal the need for adjustments or boundaries. These physical comfort indicators extend to social situations and relationships. Our body often recognizes supportive connections before our conscious mind catches up. We might notice easier breathing around certain people or a natural relaxation of facial muscles in particular social settings. These responses help guide us toward relationships and communities that genuinely support our well-being. Learning to trust these comfort signals represents a vital step in self-care. Rather than dismissing physical responses as oversensitivity, we can view them as valuable guidance from our nervous system. This understanding allows us to create environments and choose activities that genuinely support our sensitive nature, leading to more sustainable and satisfying ways of living.

Sleep as a Barometer

Sleep functions differently for those with heightened sensitivity because their nervous systems process information more intensely throughout the day. This deeper processing requires more thorough rest and recovery time. When a sensitive person has difficulty sleeping, it often indicates their nervous system needs additional support to transition from the active state of daytime to the quiet state needed for rest. The transition period between wakefulness and sleep holds particular importance. Many sensitive people need a longer "wind-down" phase as their system processes the day's experiences. This extra time allows the nervous system to gradually shift from its alert daytime state to a calmer one, supporting sleep. Understanding this need helps explain why rushing into bed after a busy evening often leads to restless nights.

Environmental factors play a crucial role in sleep quality for sensitive individuals. The bedroom temperature, ambient noise levels, texture of bedding, and even subtle changes in air quality can significantly impact sleep. These aren't mere preferences; they reflect the body's need for specific conditions that support optimal rest. When these conditions align with our needs, the nervous system can more easily enter and maintain sleep states. Evening routines become especially significant because they help prepare the sensitive nervous system for rest. Activities that support this transition might include gentle movement, quiet reflection time, or activities that help process the day's experiences. Conversely, certain activities can disrupt this preparation, such as exposure to bright screens, emotionally charged conversations, or intense mental stimulation, often making it harder for sensitive systems to sleep.

Sleep quality also provides valuable feedback about our daily choices. If particular activities or situations consistently lead to disrupted sleep, it might indicate these experiences require more energy than we realize to process. This information helps us make more informed decisions about how we structure our days and manage our energy. Understanding our personal sleep patterns enables us to create more supportive bedtime practices. Some sensitive individuals discover they need complete darkness to sleep well, while others might require white noise to mask environmental sounds. Some find that certain evening activities consistently promote better rest, perhaps reading, gentle stretching, or meditation. These aren't universal solutions but rather personal discoveries about what helps our unique system prepare for rest.

Sleep patterns can also reveal when we need to adjust our daily routines or boundaries. Persistent sleep difficulties might indicate we're taking on too much during our waking hours or need more time to process experiences. This awareness helps us make choices that better support our overall well-being, leading to more sustainable daily rhythms and improved sleep quality. By viewing sleep as a barometer of well-being rather than a problem to solve, we can use this information to create lifestyle patterns that better support our sensitive nature. This understanding allows us to work with our natural rhythms rather than against them, leading to more restful nights and more energized days.

The Dance of Adaptation

Our bodies maintain an ongoing dialogue with the environment, continuously adjusting various systems to maintain balance. This adaptation process occurs more rapidly and intensely for sensitive individuals because their nervous systems process environmental information more thoroughly. When the weather shifts, for instance, sensitive bodies might immediately begin adjusting temperature regulation, blood flow, and energy distribution to accommodate the change. These swift adaptations serve an important evolutionary purpose. Having a system that quickly responds to environmental changes allows for better survival and functioning. However, this responsiveness requires energy and attention. When a sensitive person enters a new environment, their body begins processing multiple information streams, temperature, air quality, sound levels, social dynamics, and more. This simultaneous processing explains why new situations often feel more demanding for sensitive individuals.

The adaptation process follows distinct patterns. Initially, the body might respond with heightened alertness as it assesses the new conditions. This can manifest as increased heart rate, shallow breathing, or heightened sensory awareness. Following this initial response, the system makes subtle adjustments, perhaps shifting blood flow, adjusting muscle tension, or modifying energy distribution. Finally, if conditions remain stable and feel safe, the body gradually moves toward a more balanced state. Understanding these adaptation needs changes how we approach transitions. Rather than expecting immediate comfort in new situations, we can recognize that our bodies need time to process and adjust to changed conditions. This might mean arriving early to important events, taking breaks during periods of change, or creating buffer zones between activities to allow for proper adaptation.

Environmental shifts mainly highlight these adaptation processes. Changes in weather patterns, seasonal transitions, or moves to new locations can trigger comprehensive physical responses. These might include shifts in energy levels, sleep patterns, digestion, or temperature regulation. Rather than viewing these responses as problematic, we can understand them as our body's sophisticated way of maintaining balance in changing conditions.

Social situations also require significant adaptation energy. Entering new social environments involves processing complex interpersonal dynamics, which can trigger various physical responses as our system assesses and adapts to the social landscape. This explains why many sensitive individuals need recovery time after social engagements, even enjoyable ones.

The key to working with these adaptation needs is creating supportive transition conditions. This might mean developing routines that help ease environmental changes, like having specific practices for weather transitions or creating familiar elements in new spaces. It could also involve building in adequate time for adaptation when planning activities or travel. Sensitivity individuals can better support their body's natural processes by understanding and honoring these adaptation needs. This awareness leads to more effective self-care strategies and allows fuller participation in life's various activities while maintaining physical and emotional well-being.

Building Body Trust

Our body constantly communicates with us through physical sensations, emotions, and subtle shifts in our internal state. However, many of us have learned to override these signals, often due to external pressures or beliefs that our needs are somehow excessive. This disconnect develops gradually; each time we push through exhaustion, ignore physical discomfort or dismiss our need for quiet time, we weaken our ability to hear and trust our body's wisdom.

Rebuilding body trust begins with simple awareness. We start by noticing physical sensations without immediately trying to change or judge them. When we feel tension in our shoulders, we first acknowledge the sensation instead of pushing through or attempting to relax. This basic recognition helps reestablish the connection between our conscious awareness and our body's communication system. The process deepens as we begin validating our physical experiences. When our body signals discomfort in a crowded space, we accept this as legitimate information rather than dismissing it as oversensitivity. This validation process helps our nervous system recognize that we're listening and taking its signals seriously. Over time, this creates a positive feedback loop; as we honor our body's messages, it communicates more clearly and reliably.

Learning to interpret body signals requires patience and practice. Different sensations often carry specific meanings; a tight chest might signal emotional overwhelm, while stomach tension could indicate boundary violations. As we pay attention to these patterns, we develop a more nuanced understanding of our body's language. This growing comprehension helps us respond more effectively to our needs. The impact of rebuilding body trust extends beyond physical comfort. When we consistently honor our body's signals, we make better decisions about relationships, work environments, and daily activities. Our body often recognizes situations that align with our well-being before our conscious mind catches up. That subtle sense of ease around certain people, or the instant tension in specific environments, provides valuable guidance about what truly supports our growth and happiness.

This restored connection also helps regulate our energy levels more effectively. Instead of pushing until exhaustion forces us to stop, we learn to recognize and respond to earlier signs of fatigue. This might mean taking breaks during intense activities, adjusting our schedule to include recovery time, or setting boundaries around energy-demanding situations. By responding to these signals earlier, we prevent the deep depletion that often leads to lengthy recovery periods.

The process of rebuilding body trust transforms our relationship with sensitivity itself. Rather than seeing our physical responses as limitations to overcome, we recognize them as sophisticated guidance systems. This shift in perspective allows us to work with our sensitivity instead of against it, leading to more authentic and sustainable ways of living. As trust in our body's wisdom grows more substantial, we discover an increasingly reliable internal compass for navigating life's complexities. This restored connection helps us create lives that genuinely support our well-being while allowing us to share our unique gifts with the world.

The Power of Prevention

Prevention works by recognizing and responding to early warning signs before they become fully exhausted. Our bodies communicate through a progression of increasingly urgent signals. The earliest signs might be subtle: a slight change in breathing, minor muscle tension, or a slight shift in energy levels. These initial signals often appear long before we reach a state of overwhelm, giving us time to make adjustments if we learn to notice them. Understanding this progression transforms how we approach daily activities. Consider what happens during social gatherings. Instead of waiting until exhaustion forces us to leave, we can notice early signs of energy depletion. Perhaps our attention starts to wander, or we find it harder to follow conversations. By recognizing these subtle shifts, we can make choices that protect our energy, step outside for fresh air, find a quieter corner, or decide to leave while we still feel relatively balanced. The same principle applies to work environments. Our bodies often signal mounting stress through small changes in physical comfort. We might notice our posture becoming tense, our eyes straining more easily, or our thoughts becoming less focused. These early warnings allow us to adjust our work patterns, take short breaks, change tasks, or modify our environment before stress accumulates to uncomfortable levels.

This preventive approach mainly helps with emotional processing. Sensitive individuals often absorb and process emotions deeply, both on their own and with others. By noticing early signs of emotional saturation, perhaps a tightening in the chest or a feeling of heaviness, we can take steps to process these feelings before they become overwhelming. This might mean scheduling quiet time, engaging in movement practices, or seeking supportive conversations.

Environmental factors also benefit from preventive attention. Instead of enduring uncomfortable conditions until they trigger strong reactions, we can notice subtle signs of discord between our needs and our surroundings. This awareness allows us to adjust lighting, noise levels, or air quality before these factors significantly impact our well-being. Creating sustainable daily rhythms requires understanding our personal patterns of escalation. Some people might first notice physical signs of strain, while others might experience cognitive or emotional signals. By mapping these patterns, we can develop personalized strategies for maintaining balance. This might include regular check-ins with our body throughout the day, scheduled breaks during intense periods, or specific practices that help us reset when we notice early warning signs.

The shift from crisis management to prevention transforms our relationship with sensitivity. Instead of viewing our sensitive nature as a source of inevitable overwhelm, we begin to see it as a sophisticated early warning system. This perspective allows us to work with our sensitivity rather than against it, creating more sustainable and enjoyable ways of engaging with the world. This preventive approach ultimately leads to more consistent energy levels and greater resilience. When we honor our body's early signals, we avoid the extreme cycles of depletion and recovery that often characterize sensitive experiences. This steadier state allows us to participate more fully in life while maintaining our physical and emotional well-being.

Moving Forward with Awareness

Our body's communication system operates continuously, providing detailed information about our needs and environmental responses. These physical messages emerge from our nervous system's sophisticated ability to process multiple information streams simultaneously. When we learn to recognize and interpret these signals, we gain access to a remarkable guidance system for navigating life's complexities. Understanding these physical messages requires a nuanced awareness of our body's language. Consider how this works in practice: Our system might signal the need for rest through a sequence of increasingly noticeable cues. Perhaps we first experience subtle changes in concentration or slight physical tension. As we continue engaging with demanding situations, these signals typically intensify; our muscles might become more obviously tense, our breathing more shallow, and our thoughts less focused. Learning to recognize these patterns at their earliest stages allows us to respond before reaching states of significant depletion.

This growing awareness transforms how we approach daily activities. Rather than pushing through discomfort until we reach exhaustion, we can make adjustments based on early physical feedback. When our body signals increasing tension during a social gathering, we might take short breaks or find quieter spaces. If our system indicates mounting stress during work, we can modify our environment or schedule brief recovery periods. These responsive adjustments help maintain more stable energy levels throughout our days. The relationship between physical signals and boundaries becomes significant. Our body often recognizes when situations or relationships strain our well-being before our conscious mind fully processes this information. That subtle chest tightening during certain interactions, or the persistent muscle tension in specific environments provides valuable guidance about where we need to establish or maintain clearer boundaries. Creating sustainable daily rhythms requires ongoing attention to these physical messages. Each time we notice and honor our body's signals, we strengthen our ability to interpret this internal guidance system accurately. This might mean adjusting our schedule when we notice signs of fatigue, modifying our environment when we sense increasing tension or seeking a quiet time when our system indicates the need for processing and integration.

This deepening body awareness gradually transforms our relationship with sensitivity itself. Instead of viewing our physical responses as inconvenient reactions to manage, we recognize them as sophisticated feedback mechanisms that guide us toward more aligned ways of living. This shift in perspective allows us to work with our sensitive nature rather than against it, creating lives that genuinely support our well-being while allowing us to share our unique gifts with the world. The path forward involves developing this body awareness through consistent attention and respect for our physical experiences. As we strengthen this connection, we discover increasingly refined ways to navigate daily life, making choices that honor our sensitivity while enabling full participation in meaningful activities and relationships.

The Sensory Symphony

The nervous system continuously processes an intricate stream of sensory inputs from our environment. Every moment brings multiple layers of information, sounds at various frequencies and volumes, visual stimuli ranging from subtle light changes to bold movements, tactile sensations from temperature shifts to texture variations, and complex combinations of scents and tastes. For sensitive individuals, this processing occurs with particular depth and intensity. This heightened sensory processing creates a rich and nuanced experience of the world. Consider what happens when you walk into a coffee shop. While others might notice the general ambiance, a sensitive person processes numerous distinct elements simultaneously. The complex aroma profile of coffee breaks down into distinct notes: earthy, fruity, and roasted. The soundscape includes not just obvious conversations but also the rhythm of the espresso machine, the subtle hum of refrigeration units, and the way these sounds reflect off different surfaces. Visual input encompasses both obvious movements and subtle changes in lighting, while the skin registers air temperature variations and the textures of surfaces.

This depth of sensory processing serves essential purposes. Individuals who could detect subtle environmental changes often had survival advantages throughout human evolution. They could notice approaching weather changes, sense potential dangers through slight environmental shifts, and pick up on important social cues through minimal signals. In our modern context, this sensitivity allows for a deeper appreciation of experiences and a more nuanced understanding of environments. However, managing this constant influx of sensory information requires significant neural resources. Our brains must continuously process, filter, and integrate multiple input streams. This explains why sensitive individuals often need more time to process experiences and may require regular periods of reduced stimulation. It's not about being overwhelmed by individual sensations but rather about managing the cumulative effect of processing multiple inputs simultaneously and deeply. Understanding this sensory processing helps explain why specific environments feel more challenging than others. Spaces with competing sensory inputs, like fluorescent lighting, background noise, and strong scents, require more energy to process and integrate. Conversely, environments with harmonious sensory elements often feel more supportive because they create less demanding processing requirements.

This awareness of sensory processing can guide us in creating more supportive environments. We might choose natural lighting over fluorescent, opt for spaces with good acoustic properties, or select clothing and furniture based on how their textures affect our nervous system. These aren't merely preferences but rather responses to our system's need for manageable sensory input. The key lies in recognizing that this deep sensory processing represents a sophisticated way of experiencing and understanding the world. Rather than seeing it as a limitation to overcome, we can appreciate how it enables us to notice subtle details, appreciate nuanced experiences, and gather rich information about our environment. This perspective transforms our relationship with sensitivity from one of management to one of appreciation and skillful navigation. Understanding this sensory symphony helps us create lives that honor our need for balanced sensory input while allowing us to engage with the world's rich tapestry of experiences fully. This knowledge enables us to make choices that support our well-being while benefiting from the unique insights our sensitive nature provides.

The Sound Landscape

Sound is constantly in our lives, engaging our nervous system in complex ways that many people might not consciously notice. For sensitive individuals, sound processing occurs deeper; the brain analyzes the obvious noises and subtle variations in tone, rhythm, and layering. This heightened processing means that sounds that others might easily filter out remain present in conscious awareness. Consider how this works in a typical office environment. While someone might adapt to the general background noise, a sensitive person's nervous system continues processing multiple acoustic layers: the low-frequency hum of computers, the subtle variations in colleagues' typing rhythms, the distant conversations that carry through walls, and the way different sounds reflect off various surfaces. Each element requires neural resources to process, even when we're not consciously focusing on them.

Our auditory system evolved to remain alert to environmental changes, as sound often provided crucial survival information for our ancestors. This evolutionary heritage explains why sudden sounds can trigger immediate physiological responses, changes in heart rate, muscle tension, or breathing patterns. This alerting system operates with particular intensity for sensitive individuals, responding to smaller variations in the acoustic environment. Understanding personal sound sensitivity patterns helps create more sustainable daily routines. Some people might find specific frequency ranges particularly challenging, perhaps the high-pitched whine of fluorescent lights or the low rumble of ventilation systems. Others might struggle more with unpredictable or chaotic sound patterns, like those in busy public spaces. Recognizing these patterns lets us choose when and how to engage with different acoustic environments.

The timing of sound exposure also plays a crucial role. Our nervous system's capacity to process acoustic information often varies throughout the day. Morning hours might bring greater tolerance for complex sound environments, while evening hours might require more acoustic calm to support the transition toward rest. Understanding these temporal patterns helps in scheduling activities that involve different sound levels.

Creating supportive acoustic environments involves multiple strategies. Sound-dampening materials can help reduce environmental noise, while white noise machines might help mask unpredictable sounds that trigger alerting responses. Strategic use of noise-canceling headphones during focused work periods can provide relief from demanding acoustic environments. These aren't just comfort measures but tools for effectively managing neural resources.

The relationship between sound and energy levels deserves particular attention. Extended exposure to complex acoustic environments often requires significant energy for processing, even when the individual sounds aren't particularly loud. This explains why many sensitive people feel drained after spending time in acoustically busy environments, even if they weren't consciously bothered by the noise. Understanding this connection helps plan adequate recovery time after exposure to demanding sound environments. By developing awareness of how different sounds affect our system, we can create daily routines that better support our auditory processing needs. This might mean scheduling quiet periods throughout the day, choosing workspaces with favorable acoustic properties, or using sound-modifying tools strategically. These choices aren't about avoiding sound entirely but rather about creating sustainable ways to engage with our acoustic environment while maintaining our well-being.

Illuminating Understanding

Light profoundly influences our physiological functioning through multiple pathways. When light enters our eyes, it triggers complex responses in our nervous system that go far beyond simple vision. For sensitive individuals, these responses tend to be more pronounced and nuanced. Light exposure's quality, intensity, and timing can significantly impact everything from energy levels to cognitive function to physical comfort.

Natural light works differently from artificial light in how it affects our system. Sunlight contains a full spectrum of wavelengths that our bodies have evolved to process over millions of years. When natural light enters our eyes, it helps regulate our circadian rhythms, hormone production, and various metabolic processes. Sensitive individuals often notice how their energy levels and mood shift with changes in natural light, perhaps feeling more alert on bright mornings or calmer during the gentle light of dawn and dusk. Artificial lighting presents particular challenges because it often lacks the full spectrum present in natural light. Fluorescent lights, for example, typically produce light in specific wavelength peaks rather than the smooth spectrum of sunlight. For sensitive individuals, this can manifest as eye strain, headaches, or a general sense of discomfort that builds throughout the day. LED lighting, while more energy-efficient, can create similar issues if not carefully chosen to mirror natural light patterns. Screen light deserves special attention because of its unique properties. Digital devices emit blue-enriched light that can be particularly stimulating to our nervous system. Sensitive individuals might notice how evening screen exposure affects their sleep patterns or how certain screen brightness levels create physical discomfort. Understanding these effects helps in developing strategies for screen use, such as adjusting brightness settings or using blue light filters at appropriate times.

The timing of light exposure plays a crucial role in how it affects our system. Our bodies expect certain light patterns throughout the day, with brightness and spectral composition changing from morning to evening. When artificial lighting disrupts these natural patterns, it can affect our circadian rhythms and energy levels. Sensitive individuals often benefit from aligning their light exposure more closely with natural patterns, using brighter light in the morning and dimmer, warmer light in the evening. Creating supportive lighting environments involves understanding personal light sensitivity patterns. Some people might find they're particularly affected by overhead lighting, while others might be more sensitive to flickering or certain color temperatures. This awareness allows for targeted adjustments, perhaps using task lighting instead of overhead lights, choosing bulbs with specific color temperatures, or positioning workspaces to maximize natural light exposure.

The relationship between light and energy levels becomes significant in daily planning. Extended exposure to challenging lighting conditions can drain energy reserves, even if we're not consciously aware of the strain. Understanding this connection helps in structuring activities and environments to support rather than deplete our resources. This might mean scheduling demanding tasks during periods of optimal lighting or creating spaces with variable lighting options for different needs. By developing awareness of how different types of light affect our system, we can create environments that better support our well-being. Simple lighting adjustments can significantly impact comfort and functionality throughout the day. These changes aren't just about avoiding discomfort; they're about creating conditions that allow us to function at our best while honoring our sensitive nature.

The Touch Dimension

Touch represents one of our most fundamental ways of interacting with the world. Our skin contains millions of receptors that constantly send information about pressure, temperature, texture, and movement to our brain. This sensory system operates with heightened precision for sensitive individuals, processing tactile information more intensely and thoroughly than average. How clothing interacts with our skin is an excellent example of how touch sensitivity manifests. Each fabric creates a unique sensory pattern, the way it moves against the skin, how it responds to body temperature, its weight, and pressure distribution. Sensitive individuals process these sensations more profoundly and continuously throughout the day. A shirt tag that others might barely notice could create ongoing distraction because the nervous system continues to process that sensation rather than filtering it out.

Temperature and pressure sensitivity often intertwine with touch processing. Sensitive individuals might notice subtle changes in air temperature against their skin or respond more intensely to different levels of physical pressure. This explains why some people find weighted blankets deeply comforting while others experience them as overwhelming; the pressure sensation that soothes one person's nervous system might overstimulate another's.

Physical space and touch boundaries become particularly important because of this heightened processing. When someone stands too close, a sensitive person's system must process not just the emotional aspects of personal space violation but also the actual sensory information, changes in air movement, subtle temperature variations, and potential light touch sensations. Understanding these responses helps explain why maintaining comfortable physical boundaries becomes crucial for managing sensory input. Texture sensitivity often extends beyond clothing to affect interactions with the entire environment. The feel of furniture surfaces, floor textures, or different materials used in daily activities all create sensory experiences that require processing. This explains why sensitive individuals might have strong preferences about things others consider minor; the texture of a chair fabric or the feel of different writing implements can significantly impact comfort and focus.

Creating supportive environments requires understanding personal patterns of touch sensitivity. This might involve choosing clothing based on how different fabrics feel after hours of wear, not just initial comfort. It could mean selecting furniture and bedding that provide appropriate texture and pressure stimulation levels. Even seemingly small choices like the type of towels used or the texture of soap can affect overall sensory comfort throughout the day. The impact of touch sensitivity on energy levels deserves careful attention. Prolonged exposure to uncomfortable tactile sensations requires continuous energy for processing, even when we're not consciously focusing on them. Understanding this connection helps explain why specific environments or activities might feel particularly draining, even if they're not obviously challenging in other ways.

By developing awareness of how different tactile experiences affect our system, we can create environments that better support our sensory needs. This understanding allows us to make more informed choices about clothing, furniture, and daily activities. Rather than viewing these preferences as inconvenient sensitivities, we can recognize them as important aspects of creating conditions that allow us to function at our best. These adjustments and awareness help transform touch sensitivity from a potential source of discomfort into an opportunity for creating more supportive and comfortable daily experiences. Understanding and honoring these sensory needs enables better energy management and overall well-being.

Scent Stories

The olfactory system connects directly to areas of our brain involved with memory and emotion, which explains why scents can trigger such immediate and powerful responses. For sensitive individuals, this processing occurs with particular intensity. Our nervous system detects and analyzes subtle variations in aromas that others might not consciously register, creating a rich but potentially overwhelming sensory experience. When we encounter a scent, our brain processes it through multiple pathways simultaneously. The first pathway involves immediate physical reactions, such as changes in breathing patterns, heart rate, or muscle tension in response to different aromas. The second pathway connects to our emotional processing centers, triggering memories and feelings associated with particular scents. For sensitive individuals, both these pathways operate with heightened activity. Understanding personal scent responses requires careful attention to patterns. Some aromas might consistently promote relaxation, perhaps the fresh scent of pine trees or the gentle aroma of lavender. Other scents, such as artificial fragrances or cleaning products, might trigger tension or discomfort. These reactions aren't arbitrary but rather reflect our nervous system's learned associations and natural protective responses.

The cumulative effect of scent exposure deserves particular attention. While a single aromatic element might seem manageable, sensitive individuals often process multiple scent layers simultaneously. In an office environment, this might include cleaning products, personal care items worn by colleagues, food odors, and building materials. Each of these scents requires neural resources to process, even when we're not consciously focusing on them. Creating supportive environments involves understanding how different scents affect our system throughout the day. Morning sensitivity to aromas might differ from evening sensitivity. Certain scents might feel energizing during active periods but overwhelming during rest times. This awareness helps in planning when and how to encounter different aromatic environments.

Managing unexpected scent encounters requires developing specific strategies. This might include having access to fresh air, carrying personal items that provide olfactory comfort, or having techniques for managing breathing when encountering challenging aromas. These aren't just coping mechanisms but rather tools for maintaining sensory balance. The relationship between scent processing and energy levels provides essential insights. Extended exposure to challenging aromas requires significant energy for processing, even when the scents aren't particularly strong. Understanding this connection helps explain why specific environments feel more draining than others and guide us in planning appropriate recovery periods.

We can create environments that better support our nervous system's needs by developing awareness of our scent processing patterns. This might involve choosing fragrance-free products, using natural aromatics thoughtfully, or designing spaces with good ventilation. These choices allow us to manage our olfactory input while fully engaging with our environment. This understanding transforms our relationship with scent sensitivity from one of avoidance to one of conscious navigation. Rather than seeing heightened scent awareness as a limitation, we can appreciate it as another dimension of our sophisticated sensory processing system, using this awareness to create more supportive and enjoyable daily experiences.

Environmental Mastery

The broader environment affects us through multiple interconnected channels, creating what we might consider an environmental conversation with our nervous system. Temperature, air movement, spatial layout, lighting quality, acoustic properties, and countless other factors combine to influence how our body functions and feels. For sensitive individuals, this environmental dialogue occurs with particular intensity and nuance.

Temperature regulation provides an excellent example of this complex interaction. Our bodies constantly work to maintain optimal internal temperature, but this process requires energy and resources. When environmental temperature falls outside our comfort range, our system must work harder to maintain balance. Sensitive individuals often notice these temperature effects more acutely because their nervous system processes these changes more thoroughly. A room that feels slightly warm to others might trigger significant discomfort as their body works harder to maintain homeostasis. Air quality creates another crucial dimension of environmental interaction. Our bodies process numerous aspects of air quality simultaneously, such as humidity levels, particulate content, air movement patterns, and chemical composition. Sensitive individuals might notice subtle changes in these factors that others overlook. Poor ventilation might manifest as difficulty concentrating or unexplained fatigue before others become aware of air quality issues. This heightened awareness serves as an early warning system but also requires more careful attention to creating supportive air environments. Spatial arrangement affects us through multiple sensory channels. How a space is organized influences how we move through it, how sound travels within it, and how light interacts with different surfaces. Sensitive individuals often process these spatial relationships more deeply, leading to stronger responses to different arrangements. A cluttered space might create more tension because the nervous system must constantly process and navigate around multiple objects. Conversely, a well-organized space with clear pathways might feel immediately calming because it requires less processing energy.

Understanding personal environmental responses requires careful observation over time. You might notice that specific spaces consistently support better focus or energy levels while others create subtle strain. These patterns aren't random but rather reflect how different environmental combinations affect your nervous system. Perhaps rooms with natural light and good air circulation consistently feel more supportive, or spaces with particular acoustic properties help maintain better energy levels throughout the day. Creating supportive environments involves managing multiple factors simultaneously. This might mean adjusting temperature and air movement patterns, organizing spaces to reduce visual complexity, or choosing materials that create better acoustic properties. While controlling every environmental factor is impossible, understanding which elements most strongly affect your system helps prioritize the most important adjustments. The concept of environmental mastery extends beyond physical spaces to understand how different environments affect your energy levels over time. Some environments might feel manageable for short periods but create a cumulative strain with extended exposure. Others might require initial adjustment but then support sustained comfort and functionality. This awareness helps in planning how to structure time in different environments and when to schedule recovery periods. By developing a deeper understanding of how environments affect us, we can make more informed choices about where and how we spend our time. This might mean choosing workspaces with better environmental qualities, creating designated recovery spaces at home, or developing strategies for managing challenging environments when they can't be avoided. These choices aren't about limiting our engagement with the world but rather about creating conditions that allow us to function at our best while honoring our sensitive nature.

Creating Sanctuary

Establishing environments that support rather than drain sensitive systems becomes essential for daily functioning. Think of sanctuary creation as designing spaces that allow your nervous system to rest and recalibrate truly. Our nervous system constantly processes information from our environment, sounds, lights, textures, temperatures, and social dynamics. For sensitive individuals, this processing occurs with particular depth and intensity. Creating a sanctuary provides essential opportunities for the nervous system to reduce its processing load and restore its resources.

Physical sanctuary spaces serve multiple important functions. First, they provide predictable sensory conditions that your system doesn't need to monitor and assess continuously. When you enter a space where lighting, sound levels, temperature, and air quality remain consistently comfortable, your nervous system can relax its vigilance. This relaxation directs energy toward restoration rather than constant environmental processing. The design of sanctuary spaces requires careful attention to individual sensory needs. Consider how different elements affect your system. Perhaps natural light helps regulate your energy levels, while artificial lighting creates strain. Maybe certain textures promote relaxation while others trigger tension. Understanding these personal patterns helps create spaces that genuinely support your nervous system rather than just following general design principles. Temporal boundaries play an equally crucial role in creating sanctuary. Think of these as protected periods when you can fully honor your sensitivity needs. This might mean scheduling regular quiet periods throughout your day, allowing transition between activities, or setting aside specific times for sensory recovery. These temporal boundaries help prevent the accumulation of sensory overload that can lead to exhaustion.

The concept of a portable sanctuary deserves special attention because we can't always control our environment. This might involve items that help modify sensory input, perhaps noise-canceling headphones, sunglasses, or comfortable clothing layers. It could also include having strategies for creating mini-sanctuaries in different settings, like finding quiet corners in busy spaces or establishing calming routines that can be performed anywhere. Understanding transition needs becomes particularly important when moving between different sensory environments. Your nervous system requires time to adjust when shifting from quiet to stimulating spaces or vice versa. Creating transition rituals helps manage these shifts more effectively. This might involve taking a few minutes of quiet time before entering busy environments or having decompression routines after leaving stimulating situations. Sanctuary creation also involves understanding your energy patterns throughout the day. Some people need more sanctuary time in the morning to prepare for daily activities, while others require more recovery periods in the evening. Recognizing these patterns helps design daily schedules that support rather than strain your sensitive system.

The social aspect of sanctuary creation requires careful consideration. This might mean communicating your needs to family members or roommates, establishing clear boundaries around your sanctuary spaces, or creating a shared understanding about quiet times. While these conversations can feel challenging, they're essential for maintaining the integrity of your sanctuary spaces. Developing this comprehensive approach to sanctuary creation builds a foundation for sustainable living as a sensitive person. Rather than constantly adapting to environments that drain your energy, you create spaces and rhythms supporting your natural processing of the world. This allows you to engage more fully in life's activities while maintaining your well-being.

The Art of Adaptation

Sensory adaptation is developing sophisticated skills, similar to how an athlete trains for different conditions. Just as athletes gradually build their capacity through consistent practice, sensitive individuals can develop their ability to handle various sensory situations. This doesn't mean becoming less sensitive, instead, it means becoming more skilled at managing sensory input.

The first key to successful adaptation is understanding your sensory patterns in detail. Notice how your system responds to different types of input throughout the day. For instance, you might discover that your tolerance for noise varies significantly depending on factors like time of day, overall energy levels, or the presence of other sensory challenges. This detailed understanding helps you predict and prepare for challenging situations. Building sensory tolerance works best through gradual exposure combined with effective recovery strategies. Consider how you might slowly increase your comfort with busier environments. You might start with short visits to moderately stimulating places during quiet times, then gradually extend the duration or intensity as your system develops better coping mechanisms. The key here is maintaining a balance, pushing gently at your edges while ensuring adequate recovery time.

Recovery strategies play a crucial role in successful adaptation. Think of recovery not as avoiding stimulation entirely but as actively supporting your nervous system's natural regulation processes. This might involve creating specific routines that help your system reset after challenging experiences. For example, you might develop a sequence of activities that help you transition from high-stimulation environments to calmer states, perhaps starting with gentle movement, followed by quiet time in a familiar space.

Environmental modifications represent another important aspect of adaptation. Rather than accepting environments as fixed, look for ways to adjust them to support your needs better. This might involve simple changes like adjusting lighting, using sound-dampening materials, or rearranging spaces to create better flow. The goal isn't to eliminate all challenging aspects but to create conditions that allow you to engage more effectively. Understanding the cumulative effects of sensory input helps plan more sustainable daily routines. Consider how different activities and environments affect your sensory load throughout the day. This awareness allows you to sequence activities more effectively, perhaps scheduling more demanding sensory experiences when your system is fresh and reserving quieter activities for times when you need to restore balance.

The concept of sensory pacing becomes particularly important in this context. Think of your capacity for handling sensory input as a renewable but limited resource. By carefully pacing your exposure to different types of sensory challenges, you can maintain better overall function. This might mean alternating between more and less demanding activities or building in regular periods for sensory recovery throughout your day. Developing this skillful approach to sensory management transforms daily life from a series of overwhelming challenges into a more nuanced dance with your environment. You begin recognizing patterns, anticipating needs, and responding more effectively to various sensory situations. This doesn't mean you'll never feel overwhelmed, but rather that you'll have better tools for managing challenges when they arise. Remember that adaptation is an ongoing process that develops over time. Each experience provides new information about your sensory needs and responses, helping you refine your strategies and build greater capacity for engaging with the world while honoring your sensitive nature.

Balanced Engagement

Sensory engagement operates on a spectrum rather than as a simple on-off switch. Our nervous system constantly adjusts how much information it processes from our environment. For sensitive individuals, understanding this spectrum allows for more nuanced choices about how to engage with different situations. Consider how this works in social gatherings. Some moments might call for full sensory engagement, perhaps during meaningful conversations or special celebrations where you want to experience the richness of the event fully. Other times might benefit from gentle filtering, like using strategic positioning in a room to moderate sound levels or taking short breaks to prevent sensory overload. This selective engagement allows participation while maintaining energy levels.

The key to successful, balanced engagement lies in understanding your personal processing patterns. Notice how different levels of sensory input affect your system over time. You might discover that certain types of engagement energize you, perhaps the sensory richness of nature or the focused intensity of creative work. Other situations might require more careful management, like busy urban environments or loud social events. This understanding helps guide choices about when to embrace full sensory experiences and when to implement protective strategies. Developing this balanced approach requires attention to timing and context. Some days, your nervous system might handle more intense sensory experiences with ease, while other times, it needs more protection. Factors like overall energy levels, recent demands on your system, and current stress levels all influence your capacity for sensory engagement. Learning to read these internal conditions helps make better choices about engaging with different situations.

Protection strategies work best when viewed as tools for enabling engagement rather than barriers to experience.

Think of them as ways to modulate sensory input to manageable levels. This might involve using physical tools like noise-reducing earphones or sunglasses or behavioral strategies like positioning yourself in less stimulating parts of a space. These approaches don't disconnect you from experiences but help you engage more sustainably.

The concept of selective attention plays a vital role in balanced engagement. By directing your attention, you can choose which sensory aspects of an environment to engage with fully and which to filter more heavily. This skill develops with practice and allows for richer participation in chosen activities while managing the overall sensory load. Understanding the natural rhythms of engagement and recovery helps create more sustainable patterns. Just as physical exercise requires periods of rest for optimal performance, sensory engagement benefits from regular recovery periods. These aren't signs of weakness but rather necessary components of healthy functioning for sensitive nervous systems.

This balanced approach transforms how sensitive individuals can participate in life. Instead of feeling overwhelmed by sensitivity or trying to suppress it, you can work with your natural processing style to create rich, meaningful experiences. This might mean engaging fully in chosen activities while building in recovery time or finding creative ways to modify environments that allow for comfortable participation. Finding this balance is an ongoing process that evolves with experience and changing circumstances. Each situation provides opportunities to refine your understanding of engaging with the world in ways that honor both your sensitivity and your desire for full participation in life.

The Path of Integration

Sensory integration develops gradually through an increased understanding of how our nervous system processes information. Think of it as learning to work with a sophisticated instrument. At first, the complexity of sensory processing might feel overwhelming, like trying to play a complex piece of music before understanding the instrument. As we develop a better awareness of how our system responds to different inputs, we begin to work more skillfully with our sensitivity rather than fighting against it. Understanding sensory integration starts with recognizing that sensitivity serves essential life functions. Our heightened awareness lets us notice subtle environmental changes, pick up on important social cues, and deeply process experiences. These capabilities evolved for good reasons; they help us navigate complex environments and respond appropriately to changing conditions. The goal isn't to reduce these capabilities but to develop better skills for managing the information they provide.

The process of integration involves learning to modulate our responses to sensory input. Consider how this works in practice: When entering a busy environment, instead of becoming immediately overwhelmed, we might notice our initial sensory responses and adjust our engagement accordingly. This could mean positioning ourselves where we can better manage sound levels, taking short breaks when needed, or using other strategies we've developed through experience. These aren't avoidance behaviors but rather skilled responses that allow us to participate while maintaining our well-being. Confidence grows through the successful navigation of challenging situations. Each time we effectively manage a complex sensory environment, we add to our repertoire of successful strategies. We learn that while certain situations might require careful attention to our needs, they don't have to limit our participation in life. This growing confidence allows us to engage more fully in chosen activities while maintaining awareness of our sensory needs.

The development of sensory integration skills changes how we approach daily life. Instead of viewing certain situations as inherently overwhelming, we see them as experiences requiring specific management strategies. This might mean planning ahead for challenging environments, having reliable recovery practices in place, or knowing how to modify situations to suit our needs better. These skills transform our relationship with our sensitivity from one of limitation to one of informed navigation. Understanding our personal patterns plays a crucial role in this integration process. We learn to recognize early signs of sensory overload, identify which environments support or challenge our system, and understand how different factors affect our processing capacity. This knowledge allows us to make more informed choices about how to engage with various situations while maintaining our balance.

The freedom that comes with better sensory integration manifests in multiple ways. Knowing we have strategies to manage sensory challenges, we might be more willing to try new experiences. Social situations become more enjoyable as we learn to balance engagement with necessary breaks. Work environments can be more manageable as we implement effective strategies for managing sensory input throughout the day. This integration process leads to a more nuanced understanding of our sensitivity. Rather than seeing it as something to overcome, we recognize it as a fundamental aspect of processing information about the world. This acceptance and practical management skills create a foundation for more authentic and sustainable ways of living. Integration represents an ongoing journey rather than a final destination. As we encounter new situations and challenges, we continue to refine our understanding and develop more sophisticated strategies for working with our sensitivity. This continuous growth process allows us to engage more fully with life while honoring our unique way of experiencing the world.

The Inner Architecture of Processing

The sensitive mind operates like an intricate information processing system, simultaneously taking in experiences through multiple channels. While everyone processes sensory input and experiences, sensitive individuals engage with this information at a deeper and more nuanced level. This heightened processing creates rich mental landscapes where subtle connections emerge between seemingly unrelated elements. Consider how this processing works in everyday situations. When entering a new environment, a sensitive person's mind doesn't just register the obvious features; it creates complex webs of association and meaning. The quality of light might trigger memories of similar experiences, while subtle sounds could prompt emotional responses or intellectual insights. These layered processes happen automatically, creating a rich tapestry of understanding that goes beyond surface-level perception. This deep processing extends to emotional experiences as well. When encountering situations that stir feelings, sensitive individuals often process the primary emotion, its subtle variations, and broader implications. A moment of joy might be experienced alongside awareness of its transient nature, while sadness might come with deeper insights into human connection. This emotional depth creates opportunities for profound understanding but also requires more time and energy to process fully.

The way meaning emerges from these processing patterns deserves special attention. Rather than forming quick conclusions, sensitive minds often simultaneously hold multiple possibilities, allowing deeper patterns to emerge. This might mean taking longer to form opinions or make decisions, not from indecision but from a natural tendency to process information more thoroughly and consider subtle implications. Time plays a crucial role in this processing architecture. Sensitive individuals often need more time to integrate experiences fully. This isn't a limitation but rather a reflection of the depth at which their minds engage with information. Quick responses might feel incomplete or superficial because the natural processing rhythm requires time for all the layers of meaning to emerge and connect. Understanding these processing patterns helps explain why sensitive people often need quiet time for reflection. These periods aren't about escaping but rather about allowing the mind to complete its natural processing cycles. During these times, connections form between different experiences, insights emerge, and deeper understanding develops. This integration process is essential to how sensitive minds make sense of their experiences.

The relationship between processing patterns and creativity often becomes particularly evident. The ability to notice subtle connections and hold multiple perspectives simultaneously can lead to unique insights and innovative solutions. However, this creative potential requires honoring the natural rhythm of sensitive processing rather than rushing to conclusions or actions. Learning to work with these processing patterns rather than against them transforms daily experience. Instead of feeling overwhelmed by the depth of processing, sensitive individuals can create conditions that support their natural way of engaging with information. This might mean allowing more time for important decisions, creating space for regular reflection, or finding ways to capture insights as they emerge.

Understanding inner processing architecture helps sensitive individuals navigate life more effectively while maintaining their natural depth of engagement. Rather than trying to speed up or simplify their processing, they can learn to honor its complexity while finding practical ways to manage its demands in daily life.

The Information Landscape

The sensitive mind naturally explores information through multiple layers simultaneously. When encountering new ideas or experiences, it doesn't just catalog surface details but instinctively searches for deeper patterns and meanings. This might mean noticing how a new concept connects to seemingly unrelated areas of knowledge or sensing emotional undertones in factual information that others might process more mechanically. Time moves differently in this deep processing space. What others might quickly sort through and file away, sensitive minds naturally examine from various angles, allowing connections and implications to emerge gradually. This thoroughness isn't about being slow; it reflects a natural tendency to engage with information's full complexity rather than settle for quick categorization. The way meaning develops through this process often surprises others. While some might reach immediate conclusions, sensitive individuals typically hold space for multiple interpretations to coexist. This openness allows subtle patterns to surface that might otherwise go unnoticed. A seemingly simple piece of information might reveal unexpected connections to past experiences, emotional insights, or creative possibilities.

Our minds create intricate webs of association as we process information. Reading about a scientific concept might trigger connections to art, personal experiences, or philosophical ideas. Watching a film could spark insights about human nature that extend far beyond the actual plot. These spontaneous connections often lead to unique perspectives and creative breakthroughs. However, this depth of processing requires careful management of information flow. When too much information arrives simultaneously, our system can feel overwhelmed trying to process everything at its natural depth. Understanding this tendency helps us create better conditions for learning and integration, perhaps breaking complex information into smaller portions or allowing more time for processing essential concepts. The gifts of this processing style become particularly evident in problem-solving situations. The ability to notice subtle patterns and hold multiple perspectives often leads to innovative solutions that others might miss. Yet accessing these insights requires honoring our need for thorough processing rather than rushing to conclusions.

Working skillfully with this deep processing tendency transforms how we engage with information. Instead of fighting against our natural thoroughness or feeling overwhelmed by it, we can create conditions that support our way of understanding. This might mean allowing extra time for important decisions, finding ways to capture emerging insights, or creating quiet spaces for processing complex information. This approach to information isn't better or worse than faster processing styles; it's simply different and brings its own unique advantages and challenges. By understanding and working with these natural patterns, we can better access their benefits while managing their demands on our system.

The Emotional Depths

Sensitive people experience emotions like light passing through a prism. What others might feel as a single emotional tone breaks into multiple subtle shades of feeling. For instance, when encountering a moving piece of art, the initial response might branch into appreciation for its beauty, resonance with the artist's intention, sadness for life's impermanence, and joy at the human capacity for creation. Each of these emotional threads carries its own significance and requires its own processing time. Our emotional responses often arrive with physical sensations that add another layer of experience. A moment of connection might bring warmth to the chest, while concern for others could create a subtle tension in the shoulders. These physical manifestations aren't separate from emotional experience but rather part of how our sensitive system processes feeling states in their full complexity.

Learning to navigate these emotional waters requires developing a sophisticated understanding of personal patterns. We might notice how certain situations reliably trigger particular emotional cascades or how different feelings move through our system in characteristic ways. This knowledge helps us anticipate and work with emotional responses rather than being caught off guard by their intensity. The depth of emotional processing often means we need more time to integrate experiences fully. Where others might quickly move on from an emotional event, our system naturally continues exploring its implications and meanings. This isn't a flaw but rather reflects our natural tendency to process experiences thoroughly. Understanding this need for integration time helps us create space for emotional processing without judgment. Empathy flows naturally from this depth of emotional experience. Having felt feelings so thoroughly ourselves, we often sense subtle emotional shifts in others or pick up on unspoken emotional undercurrents in situations. While this capacity for empathy can enrich relationships and understanding, it also requires clear boundaries to prevent emotional overwhelm.

Our emotional depth brings particular gifts in understanding human experience. The ability to sense and process subtle feelings often leads to insights about motivation, relationship dynamics, or the deeper meanings behind surface behaviors. These insights emerge from thinking about situations and fully feeling their emotional textures. Working skillfully with emotional depth involves developing trust in our feelings and responses while maintaining perspective on them. Rather than seeing intense emotions as problems to solve, we can learn to appreciate them as valuable information about our interaction with the world. This might mean allowing space for feelings to move through us while knowing they don't define us. Understanding these emotional patterns transforms how we navigate daily life. Instead of fighting against emotional intensity or trying to dull it, we can work with our natural emotional responsiveness as a sophisticated guidance system. This awareness helps us make choices that honor both our sensitivity and our need for sustainable emotional engagement with life.

Social Processing Architecture

Social situations present sensitive minds with multiple streams of information flowing simultaneously. During conversations, we process not just the spoken words but also subtle shifts in tone, micro-expressions, body language changes, and emotional undercurrents. Our system naturally registers these layers even in casual interactions, creating a rich but potentially overwhelming flow of social data. This depth of processing shapes how we engage in social situations. Quick exchanges that others might handle casually often require more internal processing time as our system works to integrate all the information received. We might notice subtle contradictions between someone's words and their nonverbal signals or pick up on underlying emotional dynamics that affect group interactions.

The energy requirements of this processing deserve particular attention. Each social interaction involves significant neural resources as our system tracks and makes sense of multiple information streams. Understanding these energy patterns helps explain why some social situations feel more demanding than others. A one-on-one conversation in a quiet setting might flow naturally, while a group interaction in a busy environment requires much more processing energy. Social timing often works differently for sensitive individuals because of this thorough processing. We need more time to formulate responses as we integrate multiple layers of information and consider subtle implications. This isn't about being slow but reflects our natural tendency to process social information more comprehensively before responding.

Creating sustainable social patterns requires understanding our unique processing style. This might mean scheduling recovery time after socially demanding events, choosing environments that support more precise communication, or finding ways to engage that match our natural processing rhythm. Rather than forcing ourselves into standard social patterns, we can develop approaches that work with our processing needs. The gifts of this processing depth often emerge in close relationships. Our ability to notice subtle shifts in others' emotional states or understand unspoken dynamics can create opportunities for a deeper connection. However, accessing these gifts requires honoring our need for processing space rather than pushing ourselves to engage more quickly or superficially.

Learning to work with these processing patterns transforms how we approach social situations. Instead of seeing our need for processing time as a limitation, we can recognize it as part of how we create meaningful connections. This understanding helps us make choices about social engagement that support our relationships and well-being. This awareness enables the creation of more sustainable social rhythms. We may engage more fully in selected social situations while building inadequate recovery time. We might develop strategies for managing more challenging social environments or find ways to communicate our needs to others who are important to us.

The Time Dimension

The sensitive mind processes experiences like a master artisan working with complex materials, giving each element the attention it requires for proper integration. When facing decisions or changes, our system naturally explores multiple layers of meaning and potential implications. What might seem like a simple choice to others often unfolds into more profound questions about values, long-term effects, and subtle consequences. Processing time isn't about passive waiting but active integration. During these periods, our minds weave together various strands of information, emotional responses, practical considerations, intuitive insights, and past experiences. This thorough processing often leads to more nuanced understanding and better-considered decisions, but it requires respecting its natural rhythm rather than rushing to conclusions.

Daily rhythms are of particular importance because of how our processing works. Moving too quickly from one activity to another can leave our system struggling to complete its natural integration cycle. Like trying to read a complex book while constantly being interrupted, rushed transitions often mean losing valuable insights that emerge through thorough processing. Creating sustainable daily patterns means understanding our temporal needs. This might involve scheduling buffer time between meetings to process social interactions, allowing quiet moments throughout the day for integration, or setting aside specific times for deeper reflection. These aren't luxuries but necessary components of how our system makes sense of experiences. Understanding these temporal patterns helps explain why certain situations are more challenging. When life demands quick decisions or rapid transitions, we might feel internal resistance not from unwillingness to engage but from our system's natural need for adequate processing time. Recognizing this helps us develop strategies for managing situations that require faster responses while still honoring our processing needs.

Working with rather than against these temporal needs transforms how we approach life's challenges. Instead of feeling pressured to match others' pace, we can develop rhythms that support our natural processing style. This might mean starting important projects earlier to allow for thorough consideration or creating space for integration after significant experiences. The benefits of thorough processing become particularly evident in complex situations. Our ability to notice subtle connections and consider multiple perspectives often leads to more comprehensive solutions or deeper insights. However, accessing these benefits requires protecting the time needed for our natural processing rhythm to unfold. This understanding of temporal needs enables the creation of more sustainable life patterns. Rather than constantly pushing against our natural processing rhythm, we can structure our lives to support it. This transformed relationship with time allows us to engage more fully with life while maintaining our well-being and accessing the unique benefits of our sensitive nature.

Decision-Making Architecture

Our minds naturally examine possibilities from numerous angles, weaving together practical realities, gut feelings, and deep-seated values. While others might reach quick conclusions, our awareness catches subtle implications that require further exploration. A seemingly straightforward choice about changing jobs, for instance, might unfold into considerations about life purpose, relationship dynamics, and long-term growth opportunities. This comprehensive evaluation serves an essential purpose; it helps prevent overlooking crucial aspects that could affect outcomes. Yet it also means recognizing when analysis becomes excessive. Some choices flow naturally from clear inner guidance, while others benefit from methodical consideration of each element. The way we process options often reveals itself through physical and emotional signals. A path that aligns with our authentic needs might bring a sense of expansion or relief, while misaligned choices could trigger subtle tension or unease. These internal responses offer valuable guidance when we learn to interpret them accurately.

Creating effective decision-making strategies means understanding our natural tendencies. Rather than forcing quick answers under pressure, we might develop methods supporting thorough evaluation while maintaining momentum. This could involve setting aside dedicated reflection periods, discussing possibilities with trusted advisors, or capturing insights as they emerge over time. The challenge lies in balancing depth with practicality. Not every choice requires extensive analysis; learning to distinguish between decisions that need comprehensive exploration and those that can be made more directly helps prevent decision paralysis while honoring our need for thoroughness.

These insights transform how we handle life's crossroads. Instead of viewing our careful consideration as indecision, we recognize it as a valuable process that often leads to more sustainable choices. This understanding allows us to create decision-making approaches that work with our natural tendencies rather than against them. The rewards of this measured approach often become apparent in retrospect. Choices made through careful consideration tend to align better with our core values and long-term well-being. By respecting our need to examine decisions thoroughly, we develop greater trust in our ability to navigate life's complexities while maintaining alignment with our authentic selves.

The Integration Dance

Mental processing weaves multiple threads of insight; analytical thoughts merge with instinctive reactions, while emotional wisdom blends with sensory awareness. Picture a musician hearing not just individual notes but simultaneously experiencing the entire composition, the melody, harmony, rhythm, and emotional resonance. Similarly, sensitive minds naturally combine different channels of understanding into rich, layered experiences. When encountering new situations, our awareness captures both obvious and subtle elements. A business meeting might register as more than just exchanging information; we notice interpersonal dynamics, unspoken tensions, environmental factors, and emerging possibilities. This natural depth brings valuable insights but requires skillful management to prevent overload.

Learning which experiences deserve full attention helps create sustainable patterns. Critical conversations or important decisions might benefit from allowing our complete processing capacity to engage. Routine tasks or simple interactions might need a lighter touch, preserving energy for matters that truly require depth. The skill lies in recognizing different processing needs as they arise. Sometimes our system signals that quick decisions serve best, perhaps when choosing lunch or handling familiar tasks. Other times, an inner knowing suggests slowing down to explore all aspects of a situation, particularly when dealing with relationships or life-changing choices.

This balanced approach transforms how we handle daily challenges. Rather than feeling overwhelmed by constant deep processing or trying to rush through everything, we develop fluid responses that match each situation's needs. Like an experienced dancer who knows when to move quickly or slowly, we learn to adjust our processing rhythm to life's changing demands. The beauty of this integration appears in moments when different forms of understanding align naturally. Analytical clarity combines with emotional wisdom and bodily knowing to create responses that feel both thoughtful and authentic. These moments of harmony show how our processing depth can serve rather than hinder us when we work with its natural patterns.

Building Processing Wisdom

A sophisticated understanding emerges as we study our mental patterns. Some environments naturally support clear thinking, perhaps quiet spaces with natural light and minimal distractions. Other situations might fragment our attention, requiring more energy to maintain focus and process information effectively. Recognizing these patterns helps create conditions that enhance rather than inhibit our natural processing abilities. Managing information flow becomes an art form. Like a skilled curator selecting pieces for an exhibition, we learn to choose which inputs deserve deep attention and which can receive lighter processing. This selective engagement prevents mental exhaustion while allowing thorough consideration of truly important matters.

The relationship between timing and processing clarity reveals itself through experience. Morning hours might bring sharper analytical abilities for some, while others find evening times more conducive to deep thinking. Understanding these rhythms enables scheduling activities when our processing capacity naturally aligns with specific tasks. Environmental design plays a crucial role in supporting effective mental function. Creating spaces that minimize unnecessary sensory input while providing appropriate stimulation helps maintain optimal processing conditions. This might involve adjusting lighting, managing sound levels, or organizing physical spaces to reduce cognitive load.

Social situations require particular attention because they often present complex processing demands. Recognizing when we need breaks for integration or when certain social contexts overtax our system helps maintain better balance. This awareness leads to more sustainable ways of engaging with others while honoring our processing needs. The courage to advocate for suitable conditions grows with this understanding. Rather than attempting to force ourselves into environments or schedules that consistently disrupt our processing, we can express needs clearly and seek adjustments when possible. This self-advocacy stems not from preference but from recognizing genuine requirements for effective functioning. Working skillfully with our processing style transforms potential challenges into opportunities for deeper understanding. Instead of viewing thorough processing as an obstacle, we recognize it as a valuable tool for gaining insights and making well-considered decisions.

The Flow State

When activities match our processing rhythm, a remarkable shift occurs. Instead of struggling to manage input or adjust our pace, we enter a state where attention flows naturally and deeply. Like a river finding its proper channel, our mental energy moves smoothly when conditions support rather than restrict our natural way of engaging with experiences. The gateway to this state opens through understanding personal patterns. Some activities naturally invite deeper immersion, perhaps creative work, meaningful conversations, or focused problem-solving. During these moments, our thorough processing becomes an asset, allowing us to notice subtle connections and explore layered meanings that might otherwise remain hidden. Environmental factors play a vital role in sustaining engagement. The right balance of stimulation, neither too much nor too little, helps maintain focused attention without strain. This means different things at different times: sometimes a quiet space for deep concentration, other times gentle background activity that helps maintain focus.

Timing influences how easily we access these optimal states. Certain periods naturally support deeper engagement, perhaps early morning hours for some or the quiet evening for others. Understanding these temporal patterns helps schedule activities when our processing style naturally aligns with the task at hand. Creating conditions that support flow means paying attention to transition periods. Moving too quickly between activities can disrupt our processing rhythm while allowing proper time for shifts helps maintain smoother engagement. This understanding transforms how we structure our days, building in space for natural transitions rather than forcing abrupt changes.

The benefits extend beyond individual tasks to shape our overall approach to life. New possibilities emerge when we stop fighting our thorough processing style and instead, learn to work with it. Complex problems become opportunities for insight, challenging situations invite deeper understanding, and daily experiences take on richer meaning. This alignment with natural processing patterns creates more sustainable ways of engaging with the world. Instead of exhausting ourselves trying to match others' rhythms, we can find our own pace that allows for both deep engagement and proper integration of experiences.

The Path Forward

The journey involves constant refinement and discovery. Yesterday's strategies need adjustment as circumstances change, while new situations reveal previously unknown aspects of our processing style. This ongoing exploration leads to increasingly nuanced ways of handling life's complexities. Creating supportive environments becomes more intuitive as understanding deepens. We learn to recognize which conditions enhance our natural abilities and which create unnecessary strain. This knowledge extends beyond physical spaces to include temporal and social environments, knowing when to engage deeply, when to step back, and how to maintain boundaries that protect our processing needs.

The fundamental transformation occurs in how we view our sensitivity itself. What once might have felt like limitations reveal themselves as sophisticated tools for understanding and engaging with the world. Our thorough processing brings insights others might miss, while our depth of experience enables a richer appreciation of life's subtle moments. This shift in perspective opens new approaches to challenges. Instead of trying to override our natural tendencies, we learn to harness them effectively. Complex situations become opportunities to apply our natural depth of processing, while more uncomplicated matters benefit from our attention to detail.

Moving forward means developing this understanding while remaining flexible about how it manifests. Each day brings opportunities to refine our awareness and adjust our strategies. This ongoing process transforms our relationship with sensitivity from management to appreciation and skilled application. The path ahead involves both personal discovery and practical application. As we understand our processing patterns better, we can create increasingly effective ways to engage with the world while honoring our authentic nature. This journey leads to better functioning and fuller expression of our unique gifts and perspectives.

The Architecture of Sensitive Strength

The sensitive nervous system operates like a finely tuned instrument, capable of detecting and processing subtle variations that others might miss entirely. This heightened awareness creates opportunities for deeper understanding and more nuanced responses to situations. When we recognize this sophistication, what might appear as overwhelming sensitivity reveals itself as exceptional perceptive ability. Our capacity for thorough processing enables remarkable pattern recognition. Where others might notice only surface connections, sensitive minds naturally explore deeper relationships between ideas, experiences, and observations. This ability leads to innovative solutions and creative insights from seeing seemingly unrelated elements interweave.

Emotional depth brings particular gifts for understanding human experience. The ability to sense subtle emotional currents and process feelings thoroughly often leads to more profound empathy and more authentic connections. This emotional intelligence serves in personal relationships and any situation requiring an understanding of human dynamics. Physical sensitivity provides sophisticated feedback about environments and situations. Our bodies often recognize important information before conscious awareness catches up. This early warning system helps us navigate challenges more effectively and make better decisions about which situations support or drain our energy. The natural thoroughness of sensitive processing creates advantages in complex situations. While quick decisions have their place, many important life choices benefit from the careful consideration sensitive individuals naturally bring. This depth of processing often leads to more sustainable solutions and better-considered outcomes. Creative thinking flows naturally from sensitive perception. Observing subtle connections and holding multiple perspectives simultaneously often generates unique insights and innovative approaches. This creativity emerges not just in artistic expression but in problem-solving and understanding complex systems.

Understanding these inherent strengths transforms how sensitive individuals can engage with the world. Instead of trying to suppress or work around sensitivity, we can learn to harness its natural advantages while managing its demands skillfully. This shift in perspective opens new possibilities for contributing our unique gifts while maintaining personal well-being. This recognition of sensitive strength doesn't deny the challenges of heightened sensitivity. Rather, it places those challenges in proper context as natural aspects of operating with greater perceptive capacity. Working with rather than against these traits allows their benefits to emerge more fully.

Natural Gifts Unveiled

Sensitive awareness reveals hidden dimensions of reality that others might overlook. A tremor in someone's voice signals emotional truth beneath casual words. Atmospheric shifts forecast weather changes long before clouds gather. Silent dynamics in groups shape outcomes more powerfully than spoken agreements. Each perception flows naturally, offering guidance through life's subtle currents.

Instinctive pattern recognition shapes how attuned minds process experience. During social interactions, slight changes in posture or breathing reveal deeper meanings beneath surface conversations. Meetings unfold through intricate webs of relationship and influence, visible in countless small gestures. Such multilayered understanding emerges from natural processing depth.

Environmental signals communicate through myriad channels: shadows dance across walls, sound waves bounce off surfaces, and air pressure shifts imperceptibly. Rich details paint complete pictures of spaces and situations, creating sophisticated maps for navigation. Such comprehensive awareness enables skillful movement through both physical and social landscapes.

Beneath apparent simplicity lies profound complexity. While quick judgments might suffice for some, attuned minds naturally explore deeper currents of meaning. Such thoroughness is a sophisticated information-gathering system, enabling fully informed decisions and actions.

Professional environments clearly highlight such capabilities. Emerging challenges or opportunities often become apparent long before obvious signs appear. Group dynamics reveal themselves through subtle interaction patterns. Advanced awareness allows proactive responses to developing situations.

Natural settings especially illuminate such gifts. Light, sound, motion and stillness combine sensory symphonies that inform and restore. Beyond mere pleasure, such experiences demonstrate how heightened perception enriches understanding of life's nuanced dimensions.

Navigating complexity requires sophisticated tools. Rather than missing crucial details or reaching hasty conclusions, sensitive processing naturally gathers rich information that enables nuanced and effective responses to unfolding situations.

Pattern Recognition Excellence

Keen pattern recognition shapes how attuned minds process information and experience. Intricate connections reveal themselves naturally, weaving apparently separate events into meaningful insights. Market fluctuations mirror social dynamics, hinting at emerging trends. Casual conversations unexpectedly illuminate current situations months later. Each observation adds depth to an evolving map of understanding.

Holistic comprehension flows from this natural ability to spot relationships across different domains. Where linear thinking might miss crucial links, sensitive awareness grasps the subtle threads connecting disparate elements. A shift in office dynamics could signal broader organizational changes. Weather patterns might parallel social movements, suggesting deeper cultural currents at work.

Intuitive understanding emerges through this sophisticated processing system. Rather than relying solely on logical analysis, attuned minds perceive situations through multiple channels simultaneously. Body language aligns with spoken words, or reveals contradictions. Group energy shifts forecast coming changes before formal announcements arrive.

Professional environments particularly benefit from such perceptive abilities. Market trends become clearer when viewed through multiple lenses. Consumer behavior, cultural shifts, and economic patterns all interweave to suggest future directions. Team dynamics reveal themselves through countless small signals that combine to create accurate predictions of project outcomes.

Social situations illuminate this gift for pattern recognition. Complex relationship dynamics unfold like intricate dances, each movement carrying meaning beyond its apparent significance. Past experiences connect with present moments unexpectedly, offering guidance through similar situations.

Creative insights often spring from this ability to perceive unexpected connections. Solutions emerge by linking previously unrelated concepts. Innovation flows naturally when seemingly separate ideas suddenly reveal their hidden relationships. Such breakthrough moments demonstrate how pattern recognition transforms overwhelming input into valuable understanding.

Mastery develops as recognition abilities sharpen through experience. What begins as vague perception grows into clear insight. Confidence builds as pattern recognition repeatedly proves its worth in navigating life's complexities. Each confirmed observation strengthens trust in this natural gift for understanding life's subtle interconnections.

The Power of Deep Processing

Processing depth creates a remarkable foundation for understanding life's complexities. When encountering new situations, sensitive minds naturally explore multiple layers, examining practical details while also considering broader implications, emotional resonance, and subtle relationship dynamics. Rather than skimming the surface, each experience receives careful attention that reveals its full significance.

Complex challenges particularly highlight the value of thorough processing. While quick solutions might address immediate symptoms, sensitive analysis often uncovers root causes and systemic patterns. A workplace conflict viewed superficially might seem like a simple personality clash. Yet deeper examination could reveal underlying structural issues, communication gaps, or competing needs that require more comprehensive solutions.

Time spent in thorough consideration serves an important purpose. Just as rushing natural processes rarely yields optimal results, allowing space for complete processing enables better outcomes. Ideas need time to develop fully, implications must be explored carefully, and subtle factors deserve proper attention. This natural thoroughness leads to more sustainable decisions and effective actions.

Innovative solutions often emerge through this multilayered approach to understanding. When examining situations from various angles, unexpected connections appear. Problems that seemed intractable from one perspective might reveal novel solutions when viewed through different lenses. The ability to hold multiple viewpoints simultaneously while processing deeply creates opportunities for creative breakthroughs.

Decision-making benefits particularly from processing depth. Rather than reacting to surface pressures, sensitive minds naturally consider long-term implications and subtle consequences. Financial choices get examined not just for immediate impact but for their effects on relationships, values, and future possibilities. Career decisions incorporate both practical factors and deeper questions of meaning and purpose.

Leadership situations showcase how processing depth creates advantages. Understanding team dynamics requires looking beyond obvious behaviors to grasp underlying motivations and unspoken needs. Strategic planning benefits from careful consideration of multiple scenarios and subtle influencing factors. The ability to process situations thoroughly while maintaining forward momentum becomes invaluable in guiding groups effectively.

Mastering this natural thoroughness transforms it from a potential source of delay into a powerful tool for navigation. Experience teaches when situations require full processing depth and when lighter consideration suffices. This discernment enables strategically processing depth while maintaining practical momentum through daily life.

Intuitive Intelligence

Keen instincts guide sensitive people through life's challenges. Quick feelings about a situation aren't random; they come from noticing small details others miss. Years of watching and learning create a deep well of knowledge that helps make sense of new experiences quickly. When something feels off about a situation, there's usually a good reason. Maybe you noticed tiny changes in how people act or picked up on subtle shifts in the mood of a place. Your mind puts these pieces together faster than conscious thought, warning you through feelings rather than words. Learning to trust these natural instincts makes life easier. At first, you might doubt these quick insights or try to ignore them. But over time, you'll likely find your gut feelings are right more often than not. The more you pay attention to these instincts and check if they're accurate, the better they become at steering you well.

This natural wisdom shows up clearly in relationships. You might sense when someone needs support before they say anything, or know when to give others space. These feelings come from unconsciously noticing small changes in tone, expression, and body language that signal what others are experiencing.

Work situations also benefit from this kind of understanding. A project might feel like it needs more attention, or a meeting's direction may seem off track. These impressions often come from automatically spotting patterns you've seen before, your mind recognizes signs of potential issues early, letting you address them before they grow.

The key is finding a balance between quick feelings and careful thinking. Not every gut reaction needs immediate action. Taking time to understand why something feels important helps sort out which instincts to follow right away and which ones need more thought. This creates a practical way to use your natural sensitivity while staying grounded in reality. Over time, working with these instincts becomes natural. Instead of seeing quick feelings as something to doubt, you learn to value them as part of your mind's sophisticated way of understanding the world. This creates more confidence in navigating life's challenges while staying true to your sensitive nature.

Depth as Advantage

Looking deeply at things brings real advantages in life. When others might rush past important details, sensitive people naturally take time to understand situations fully. This careful attention leads to better insights and more thoughtful responses.

In relationships, deep processing helps build stronger connections. You might notice small changes in how someone speaks or acts that signal they need support. Understanding the subtle feelings behind what people say creates more meaningful conversations. Instead of just responding to words, you grasp the deeper meaning behind them.

Work situations improve when someone can spot potential problems early. Your natural way of thinking deeply about things helps prevent issues before they grow bigger. You might notice that a project needs adjusting or that team members need different kinds of support. This foresight makes work flow more smoothly.

Creative work especially benefits from deep processing. You naturally explore different angles and meanings when making art, writing, or solving problems. Your mind uniquely connects ideas, leading to fresh solutions and original expressions. The ability to see subtle shades of meaning helps create work that touches people more deeply.

Research and analysis become more complete through thorough engagement. Instead of accepting surface explanations, you naturally dig deeper to understand root causes and connections. This thorough approach often uncovers important details others might miss, leading to better understanding and more effective solutions. Planning benefits from careful consideration too. When considering future possibilities, you naturally consider various outcomes and their effects. This thoughtful approach helps make better choices in the long run, avoiding problems that quick decisions might miss. Understanding this natural depth as a strength changes how you approach tasks. Instead of rushing through things like others might, you can trust that your careful processing leads to valuable insights. This creates more confidence in using your natural abilities to contribute effectively.

Connection Capabilities

Natural talents for understanding people and ideas run deep in sensitive minds. When talking with others, you easily pick up on feelings and needs that aren't said out loud. A slight change in someone's voice or expression tells you they might need support or space. This natural understanding helps build trust and closer relationships. Your mind naturally sees how things connect to each other. In group settings, you might notice how one person's comment affects everyone else's mood, or how past events influence current team dynamics. This awareness helps create better teamwork and smoother collaboration. When others feel truly understood, they're more likely to share ideas openly and work together well. This skill for spotting connections goes beyond just understanding people. You might notice how a small change in one part of a project could affect many other areas. You might also see how different aspects of an organization influence each other in ways that others miss. This broad view helps solve problems more effectively since you understand how various parts work together.

Making sense of complex situations comes naturally to you. Where others might see separate pieces, you notice the threads that tie everything together. This could mean understanding how market trends connect to customer behavior, or how company culture affects work outcomes. These insights help guide better decisions that consider the full picture. Your ability to build genuine connections creates a lasting impact. People often feel more comfortable sharing their true thoughts with someone who understands them deeply. This creates opportunities for meaningful conversations that lead to better solutions and stronger working relationships. Understanding how things interconnect helps in unexpected ways. You might see how a solution from one field could solve a problem in another area, or how bringing certain people together might create new opportunities. This natural talent for spotting useful connections often leads to creative solutions that others might miss.

These connection skills make you particularly valuable in roles requiring deep understanding of people or systems. Whether helping teams work better together, seeing patterns in complex data, or building bridges between different groups, your natural ability to grasp subtle connections creates positive change.

Innovation Through Insight

Sensitive minds bring a unique talent for discovering new solutions and fresh approaches. By naturally processing information deeply and spotting subtle patterns, you often uncover possibilities that conventional thinking misses. When exploring a problem, your mind automatically examines it from multiple angles, leading to more complete and innovative answers. Consider how this works in practice: While others might focus only on apparent symptoms of a problem, your natural tendency to look deeper often reveals underlying causes and connections. You might notice that what seems like a communication issue actually stems from how the workspace is arranged or that customer complaints trace back to an earlier policy change that created unexpected ripple effects.

This thorough understanding creates a stronger foundation for innovation. Rather than jumping to quick fixes, you naturally explore how different situation aspects influence each other. This comprehensive view helps develop solutions that address root causes and consider long-term impacts. When you propose a new approach, it typically comes from understanding both obvious and subtle factors affecting the situation. Your ability to connect seemingly unrelated ideas often sparks creative breakthroughs. You might notice how a natural pattern could inspire a more efficient workflow or how concepts from one field might solve problems in another. These insights emerge from your mind's natural way of processing information deeply and noticing subtle similarities between different situations. In collaborative settings, your innovative thinking becomes particularly valuable. While others might focus on traditional approaches, you often perceive alternative possibilities that others overlook. Your capacity to sense underlying dynamics and unspoken needs frequently leads to solutions that address practical requirements and human factors.

This combination of deep processing and pattern recognition helps create more sustainable innovations. By considering multiple problem dimensions and their interactions, you develop solutions that are more likely to work well over time. Your natural thoroughness means you often spot potential issues early, allowing adjustments before problems develop. Understanding how your mind naturally approaches innovation helps you use these abilities more effectively. Rather than rushing to solutions, you can trust that your thorough processing will reveal valuable insights. This confidence in your natural approach leads to more reliable and creative problem-solving.

The Value of Thoroughness

Careful attention to detail and deep consideration of situations often lead to better results, even if it takes more time. Some dismiss unnecessary analysis as a valuable way of processing information that catches important details others miss. Think about how this works in practice. When making decisions, sensitive people naturally consider various angles, not just the obvious factors but also subtle implications and long-term effects. For example, when evaluating a job opportunity, you might notice not only the salary and responsibilities but also the office environment's impact on productivity, the effect of team dynamics on well-being, and how the role aligns with long-term goals. This natural thoroughness proves especially valuable in complex projects. Unlike quick surface-level reviews, deep consideration often reveals hidden connections and potential issues early. This might mean spotting how a seemingly small design choice could affect user experience months later in software development. Research could involve noticing patterns in data that point to essential but easily overlooked factors.

The thorough processing characteristic of sensitive minds creates particular advantages in analytical work. When examining problems, you naturally explore multiple layers of cause and effect. This comprehensive approach often leads to solutions that address root causes rather than just symptoms. While others might implement quick fixes, your careful consideration typically produces more sustainable results. Professional environments especially benefit from this meticulous attention. In quality control, thoroughness helps catch subtle defects that could cause problems later. Strategic planning enables better risk assessment by considering various scenarios and their implications. Careful attention to detail often produces more refined and impactful results even in creative work. Understanding this tendency toward thoroughness as a strength changes how you approach tasks. Instead of rushing through analysis like others might, you can trust that your careful processing serves an important purpose. This shift in perspective transforms what might feel like a limitation into a valuable asset for creating better outcomes.

The value of thoroughness extends beyond individual tasks to shape entire approaches to work and life. By embracing this natural tendency toward careful consideration, you develop more effective handling of complex situations. This thoughtful approach often prevents problems that quick decisions might create, leading to more reliable and satisfying results.

Leadership Through Understanding

Leading with sensitivity brings unique advantages that transform how teams and organizations function. The natural ability to notice subtle shifts in group dynamics and understand unspoken needs creates opportunities for more effective guidance. Consider how this plays out in team settings. While traditional leadership might focus mainly on goals and deadlines, sensitive leaders naturally tune into the human elements that shape success. They notice when team members seem hesitant about a project direction, sense growing tension before it creates problems, and recognize when people need different kinds of support to do their best work. This deep understanding enables a more nuanced approach to challenges. Rather than pushing harder when projects face obstacles, sensitive leaders often perceive underlying causes that others might miss. They might realize that what looks like resistance to change actually stems from unclear communication or that missed deadlines signal a need to adjust how work flows through the team.

Building trust becomes natural through this leadership style. Because sensitive leaders genuinely understand others' perspectives and concerns, they create environments where people feel truly heard. Team members often share ideas more openly and engage more fully when they know their leader grasps both spoken and unspoken aspects of situations. Strategic planning benefits particularly from sensitive processing strengths. The ability to see complex patterns and consider multiple factors leads to more comprehensive strategies. Sensitive leaders often anticipate potential issues before they develop and recognize opportunities that conventional analysis might overlook. This foresight helps teams navigate challenges more effectively while staying focused on long-term success.

Creating sustainable work environments comes naturally to sensitive leaders. Their thorough understanding of how different elements affect team well-being enables building systems supporting productivity and personal growth. They might notice how office layout influences collaboration, how meeting structures affect energy levels, or how communication patterns impact team morale. This leadership approach transforms how organizations handle change and growth. Instead of focusing solely on measurable metrics, sensitive leaders consider the human factors determining lasting success. They guide teams through transitions, focusing on both practical needs and emotional impacts, creating more sustainable progress. Understanding these leadership strengths helps sensitive individuals guide others more effectively while staying true to their natural processing and responding. Rather than trying to match traditional leadership styles, they can leverage their unique abilities to create positive change and foster environments where everyone thrives.

Embracing Sensitive Power

Understanding sensitivity as a source of strength changes how we view ourselves and engage with the world. When we recognize our natural abilities as valuable tools rather than burdens, we unlock new ways of contributing and connecting. Sensitive minds bring remarkable capabilities to many situations. We process information deeply, noticing subtle patterns and connections others might miss. This thorough understanding helps solve complex problems and build meaningful relationships. Our ability to sense unspoken dynamics and anticipate needs creates opportunities for more effective collaboration. Real confidence grows from recognizing these natural strengths. Instead of trying to suppress our sensitivity or match others' styles, we learn to trust our unique way of processing experiences. This self-trust allows us to engage more authentically while maintaining our natural depth of understanding.

Our capacity for deep processing serves vital purposes. When examining situations carefully, we often spot important details and implications that quick analysis overlooks. This thoroughness leads to better decisions and more sustainable solutions. Though it may take more time, our comprehensive approach frequently prevents problems that hasty choices might create. Intuitive understanding flows naturally from our sensitive awareness. Years of noticing subtle signals create a deep well of knowledge we can draw from quickly. Those gut feelings about situations often represent sophisticated pattern recognition at work. Learning to trust these insights while balancing them with careful analysis creates more reliable guidance. Building stronger relationships comes naturally through sensitive perception. We notice slight shifts in others' emotions and needs, enabling more meaningful support and connection. This deep understanding helps create environments where people feel truly heard and valued. Whether in personal or professional settings, our ability to grasp underlying dynamics strengthens collaboration.

Moving forward means continuing to develop these natural capabilities. Each new situation provides opportunities to refine our understanding and build confidence in our sensitive strengths. As we learn to work with rather than against our sensitivity, we discover increasingly effective ways to contribute our unique gifts while maintaining personal well-being. This shift in perspective transforms daily life. Instead of seeing sensitivity as something to manage or overcome, we recognize it as a sophisticated set of tools for understanding and navigating the world. This recognition enables more authentic engagement while honoring our natural way of processing experiences.

Habit 2: The Empowerment Mindset

The Hidden Power of Narrative

Think about the voice in your head, the one that's always talking to you. It's telling you stories about who you are and what you can do. Maybe you got these stories from your parents, your friends, or even TV shows. They're like invisible glasses you wear that change how you see everything around you. When you're the kind of person who feels things deeply, these stories become super important. They're like a movie playing in your mind all day long. Some of these stories help you grow stronger, while others might hold you back without you even knowing it. You can change these stories. Just like picking up a book you've read before and finding new meaning in it, you can look at your life in fresh ways. The stories you tell yourself about being sensitive aren't set in stone, they're more like clay that you can reshape.

Think about how different your day feels when you wake up thinking, "I care deeply about things, and that's a strength," versus "I'm too sensitive, and that's a problem." Same person, same feelings, but totally different story, and that changes everything about how you face your day. When you understand this, something amazing happens. You start to see that being sensitive isn't just about feeling more than others, it's about having a superpower that lets you understand the world in rich, deep ways. But like any power, it works better when you believe in it.

Breaking Free from Old Tales

Have you ever had a voice in your head telling you that you feel too much, think too deeply, or care too strongly? Many people who feel things deeply carry around these old stories in their minds. These stories often say things like "You're too emotional" or "You think about everything too much." But here's the thing, these stories aren't facts. They're more like old hand-me-down clothes that don't fit anymore. Maybe your family passed them down to you, or maybe you picked them up from friends or TV shows when you were younger. You might have started believing these stories when you were trying to protect yourself during tough times.

If someone told you the sky was purple your whole life, you might believe it until you looked up and really saw it for yourself. In the same way, many of the things we believe about being sensitive aren't true, they're just ideas we've heard so many times that we started believing them.

The first step to changing these old stories is seeing them for what they are, just stories, not facts about who you are. It's like waking up and realizing you can choose different beliefs, ones that help you grow instead of holding you back. When you start to question these old stories, you begin to see that being sensitive isn't a weakness at all, it's just a different way of experiencing the world. Just because these stories have been with you for a long time doesn't mean they have to stay with you forever. You can start writing new stories about your sensitivity, ones that show how your deep feelings and careful thinking make you stronger, not weaker.

The Voice Within

Think about the last time something tough happened. Maybe you had to speak in front of your class, and a little voice in your head said, "You're not good enough." Or perhaps you got really upset about something, and that same voice told you, "You shouldn't feel this way." These are examples of how we talk to ourselves in our minds. This inner voice is like a radio that's always playing in your head. Sometimes it plays songs that make you feel bad about yourself, especially when you're feeling things strongly. You might hear things like "You're too sensitive" or "Nobody else gets this upset." The tricky part is that we often believe these thoughts without questioning them, just like you might believe everything a friend tells you.

But here's something important to understand: just because this voice is in your head doesn't mean it's telling the truth. Think of it more like an old habit, like biting your nails or twirling your hair when you're nervous. These thoughts are patterns you've learned over time, not facts about who you are. The good news is that you can learn to notice when this voice starts being negative. It's like developing a new skill, at first, you might not catch it right away, but with practice, you'll get better at spotting these thoughts. Once you can notice them, you can start asking yourself, "Is this really true?" or "Would I say this to a friend?"

Understanding how your inner voice works is the first step to changing it. Instead of letting negative thoughts take over, you can learn to pause, take a breath, and choose to think about things differently. This doesn't mean you'll never have negative thoughts again, it just means you'll know how to handle them better when they show up. Being able to feel things deeply is actually a strength, even though it might not always feel that way. Your job isn't to stop feeling, it's to learn how to be kind to yourself when those big feelings come along.

Crafting New Narratives

Imagine your mind as a notebook where you can write new stories about who you are. Instead of keeping the old stories that make you feel bad about being sensitive, you can create new ones that show how special your sensitivity really is. For example, where you once thought "I'm too emotional," you can write a new story: "My strong feelings help me understand how others feel." When you used to tell yourself, "I think too much about everything," your new story might be, "I notice details others miss, and that helps me solve problems." These new stories aren't just about thinking happy thoughts, they're about seeing the truth of who you are. Think of it like finally getting glasses when you've needed them all along. Suddenly, you can see things clearly that were always there but hard to notice before.

Being sensitive gives you special abilities that many people don't have. You might pick up on small changes in how someone speaks or looks that tell you they're upset, even when others don't notice. You often understand complicated situations better because you think about them more deeply. When you connect with people or ideas, you do it in a way that really matters. Creating these new stories takes time and practice. It's like learning to play an instrument, at first, the new way of thinking might feel strange and awkward. But if you keep practicing, it starts to feel natural. Each time you catch yourself using an old, unhelpful story, you can gently replace it with a new one that better shows your true strengths.

The most important thing to remember is that these new stories aren't made-up fairy tales, they're honest descriptions of what makes sensitive people special. When you start seeing your sensitivity as a gift rather than a problem, you begin to use it in ways that make your life, and often the lives of others, better.

Markers of Growth

Think back to how you used to handle tough situations. Maybe crowded places used to make you feel really anxious, but now you have ways to deal with those feelings. Or perhaps you used to say "yes" to everything because saying "no" felt too hard, but now you can tell people when something doesn't work for you. These changes are like footprints in the sand, they show how far you've walked on your journey. When you start looking for them, you can find these signs of growth everywhere in your daily life. Remember that presentation that would have kept you awake for nights before? Now you might still feel nervous, but you know how to handle those butterflies in your stomach. Or think about how you used to apologize for being "too sensitive," but now you understand that your deep feelings help you connect better with others. Keeping track of these changes is like taking pictures of yourself as you grow taller; they help you see the progress that happens so slowly that you might miss it otherwise. Each time you face a hard situation and handle it better than you would have before, it's like adding a new brick to build your confidence. When you speak up for yourself instead of staying quiet, that's another piece of proof that you're growing stronger.

These small victories might seem tiny on their own, but they add up to big changes over time. It's like watching a garden grow, you don't see the plants getting bigger day by day, but after a while, you look back and realize how much they've changed. Your new way of thinking about sensitivity isn't just an idea anymore, it shows up in real ways in your life. The best part is that each success makes the next one easier. Every time you prove to yourself that being sensitive can be a strength, it becomes easier to believe it the next time around. It's like building a collection of memories that remind you of your true capabilities, helping you write a new story about who you are and what you can do.

The Architecture of Confidence

Your confidence is like a house you're building, brick by brick. Each time your sensitivity helps you understand something better, it's like adding a new brick. Maybe you noticed a friend was sad before anyone else did, or you thought carefully about a problem and found a solution others missed. These moments are the building blocks of believing in yourself. When you trust your sensitive side, you start to see how it helps you every day. It's like having a superpower that lets you tune into things deeply. You might understand what others are feeling without them saying a word, or see patterns in situations that help you make better choices. Every time this happens, you learn to trust yourself a little more. This isn't about trying to become a different person, it's about seeing the strength you've had all along. Imagine you've been wearing sunglasses that made everything look darker. Taking them off doesn't change what's there; it just lets you see things as they really are. In the same way, letting go of old ideas that made you doubt yourself helps you see how valuable your sensitivity truly is.

As you collect more and more proof that being sensitive makes you stronger, not weaker, something amazing happens. You start naturally trusting yourself more. You worry less about being "too much" and focus more on using your deep feelings and careful thinking to make your life better. It's like finally learning to ride a bike, at first, you might doubt yourself, but once you get it, you know you can do it. This kind of confidence grows slowly, like a tree. You might not notice it getting stronger day by day, but over time, you'll look back and see how much you've grown. Each small success adds up, creating a solid foundation of trust in yourself and your unique way of experiencing the world.

Shifting Perspectives

Change often happens bit by bit, like a sunrise slowly lighting up the sky. When you start looking at your sensitivity differently, you begin to notice how it helps rather than hurts you. That overwhelming feeling you get in busy places? It's actually your mind picking up on important details others might miss. Those deep emotions that sometimes feel too big? They're the same feelings that help you understand what others are going through. Think about learning to swim. At first, the water might feel scary and overwhelming. But as you learn to work with it instead of fighting against it, swimming becomes natural and even fun. Your sensitivity works the same way. Instead of trying to push down your feelings or make yourself less sensitive, you can learn to use these traits to help you navigate life better. For example, you might notice that your careful way of thinking helps you make good decisions. Or maybe your strong feelings help you create art that moves other people. These discoveries are like finding treasure in what you once thought was just heavy baggage.

This new way of seeing yourself changes how you handle everyday situations. Instead of dreading group projects because you might feel too much or think too deeply, you might start seeing how your sensitivity helps you be a better team member. You notice when someone's feeling left out, or you think of solutions others haven't considered. Changing how you see yourself takes time. It's like watching a garden grow, you won't see big changes day to day, but over time, new ways of thinking take root and bloom. Each time you catch yourself thinking "I'm too sensitive," you can pause and ask, "How might this sensitivity actually help me right now?"

The real magic happens when you stop seeing your sensitivity as something to fix and start seeing it as one of your greatest strengths. It's like finally using your whole toolbox instead of trying to build everything with just one tool. Your sensitivity isn't holding you back, it's giving you special abilities that can make your life, and often the lives of others, richer and more meaningful.

The Power of Choice

Every moment gives you a chance to think about your feelings and experiences in a new way. When big emotions come up, like feeling nervous before a test or upset after an argument, you get to decide what those feelings mean. Instead of thinking, "I wish I didn't feel so much," you can think, "These feelings are giving me important information." Let's look at how this works in real life. Imagine you're working on a school project, and you notice you're taking longer than your classmates because you're thinking about every detail. Instead of getting frustrated with yourself, you can choose to see how this careful thinking helps you create better work. It's like having a superpower that lets you see things others might miss. Your brain actually changes when you make these new choices over and over. Scientists call this "neuroplasticity", it means your brain is like a path in the woods. Each time you choose to think about your sensitivity in a positive way, it's like walking that path again.

The more you walk it, the clearer and easier to follow it becomes.

Think about learning to ride a bike. At first, you had to think about every little movement, pedaling, steering, and keeping your balance. But after practicing many times, these actions became natural. The same thing happens when you practice seeing your sensitivity as a strength. Over time, it becomes your natural way of thinking. This change isn't just about thinking happy thoughts, it's about seeing the truth of who you are and what you can do. When you feel things deeply, that same depth helps you understand others better. When you take time to think things through, that carefulness helps you make better decisions. Each time you remember this, you're helping your brain create stronger connections that support this new way of thinking. The really amazing part is that these small choices add up to big changes over time. Just like saving a little money each day can grow into a large amount, choosing to see your sensitivity as valuable, one moment at a time, helps build lasting confidence in your unique strengths.

Building Resilience

Your mind is like a garden that grows stronger when you tend to it with care. Just as a plant needs water and sunlight to thrive, your emotional awareness develops when you allow yourself to experience feelings fully. Each time you let yourself really feel something, the warmth of happiness, the weight of sadness, or the spark of excitement, you're nurturing your ability to understand yourself and others better. Your sensitivity works in a similar way. When you feel things strongly, like excitement, worry, or sadness, you're experiencing your own kind of waves. The key isn't trying to make these feelings smaller or less intense. Instead, it's about learning to understand and work with them, just like the surfer learns to work with the ocean. For example, when you feel deeply moved by music or art, that's your sensitivity helping you experience beauty more fully. When you notice small changes in how your friends are feeling, that's your sensitivity helping you be a better friend. These aren't weaknesses to fix, they're strengths to develop.

Getting stronger this way takes practice, just like any other skill. Each time you face a situation that feels overwhelming, you have a chance to practice riding these waves of feeling. Maybe you're giving a presentation in class, and instead of wishing you weren't so nervous, you can recognize how your careful preparation and attention to detail will help you do well. The amazing thing is that you don't have to become less sensitive to handle life's challenges better. That would be like asking a person with great hearing to become partially deaf! Instead, you can learn to trust that your sensitivity actually helps you navigate life's ups and downs. It's like having a built-in compass that gives you extra information about the world around you. As you practice this new way of thinking day by day, you'll likely notice something interesting: situations that used to throw you off balance become easier to handle. Not because you're feeling less, but because you've learned to trust your sensitive nature as a source of strength rather than seeing it as a problem to overcome.

Moving Forward With New Understanding

When you start seeing your sensitivity differently, it's like opening a door to a whole new way of living. Think about how a camera lens brings things into focus, as you clear away old thoughts that made you doubt yourself, you begin to see your sensitive nature more clearly. Those things you thought were problems, like feeling deeply or noticing small details, turn out to be valuable tools that help you understand life better. Imagine you're learning to play music. At first, having a good ear might seem overwhelming because you notice every little sound. But as you practice, this same ability helps you create beautiful music. Your sensitivity works the same way. Instead of seeing it as something that holds you back, you start to understand how it helps you move through life with greater awareness and understanding. This change happens day by day, choice by choice. Each time you face a situation, you get to decide how to think about your sensitivity. You may be in a crowded place and feel overwhelmed by all the energy around you. Instead of wishing you could turn off these feelings, you might use them to find a quiet spot where you can be at your best. Or when you notice subtle changes in a friend's mood, you can appreciate how your sensitivity helps you be a caring friend.

The best part is that every time you choose to see your sensitivity as helpful rather than harmful, you make this new way of thinking stronger. It's like watering a plant, each positive choice helps your confidence grow. Over time, you discover more and more ways that being sensitive makes your life richer and more meaningful. This journey isn't about becoming a different person, it's about understanding and appreciating who you already are. Your sensitivity isn't a weakness to overcome; it's a gift that helps you experience life more fully. As you continue practicing this new way of thinking, you'll likely find yourself handling life's challenges with greater ease and confidence, not because you've changed who you are, but because you've learned to trust your natural strengths.

Let me explain practical ways to use your sensitivity as a strength in everyday situations. I'll break this down into different parts of your daily life so you can understand exactly how to implement these ideas.

In School or Work Situations

Think about working on a group project. When you notice a teammate seems less engaged than usual, your sensitivity lets you pick this up early. Instead of ignoring it or thinking you're overthinking things, you might gently ask if everything's okay or if they need help understanding their part. This awareness often helps prevent bigger problems later and creates a better working environment for everyone.

In Social Settings

Let's say you're at a friend's house and you notice the energy in the room feels tense. Rather than worrying that you're being too sensitive, use this awareness to help improve the situation. Maybe you can shift the conversation to a lighter topic or suggest a fun activity. Your ability to "read the room" becomes a valuable social skill that helps everyone feel more comfortable.

During Problem-Solving

When facing a difficult decision, your tendency to think deeply about things is actually a superpower. While others might make quick choices, your careful consideration helps you spot potential problems or opportunities others miss. For example, if you're planning a class event, your attention to detail might help you remember important things like accounting for people with food allergies or making sure quieter students feel included.

In Creative Activities

Your deep feelings and rich inner world can make creative activities more meaningful. When you're writing a story, drawing, or making music, your sensitivity helps you express subtle emotions and ideas that others might not notice. This depth often creates more touching and authentic creative work.

In Relationships

Notice how your sensitivity helps you build stronger connections with others. When a friend shares good news, you might feel genuine excitement for them. When they're sad, you naturally understand their feelings without them having to explain everything. This emotional understanding helps create deeper, more meaningful friendships.

Handling Challenging Emotions

When you feel strong emotions, try treating them like weather patterns, they provide important information but aren't permanent. If you feel anxious before a presentation, instead of fighting the feeling, acknowledge it as your body's way of helping you prepare thoroughly. Your sensitivity to these feelings can actually help you prepare better and perform well.

Finding Your Inner Power

True strength starts with understanding yourself deeply, not by comparing yourself to others or trying to be perfect, but by recognizing what makes you uniquely you. Think of it like getting to know your own voice. Just as every person's voice has its own special sound, your sensitivity gives you your own special way of experiencing and understanding the world. When you really know your values, the things that matter most to you, you can make choices that feel right and true. It's like having an inner compass that helps guide you. For example, if you value kindness, your sensitivity helps you notice when others need support. If you value creativity, your deep feelings might help you express yourself through art or music in ways that touch others.

Understanding your sensitive nature is a lot like learning to play a complex instrument. At first, you might feel overwhelmed by all the different parts that need attention. But as you practice and learn, you start to see how each part works together to create something beautiful. Your sensitivity works the same way, what might seem like separate traits (like feeling deeply, thinking carefully, or noticing subtle details) all work together to make you who you are. This kind of self-understanding builds real confidence, not the loud, showy kind, but the quiet strength that comes from knowing who you are and trusting your natural abilities. When you make choices based on this understanding, it's like following a path that feels truly yours, not one that others have chosen for you. This journey of understanding yourself isn't about becoming someone different, it's about discovering the strength that's already within you. Just as a tree grows stronger by developing deeper roots, you grow stronger by understanding and trusting your sensitive nature more fully.

Finding What Really Matters

Think about what makes your heart feel truly alive and at peace. As someone who feels things deeply, your idea of what's important might be different from what others chase after. While some people focus on getting the highest grades or being the most popular, you might care more about being true to yourself, making real connections with others, helping people in meaningful ways, or expressing your creativity. Understanding what matters to you is like discovering your personal map for life's journey. This understanding often comes in quiet moments when you take time to listen to your inner voice. You might realize that being honest with yourself and others feels more important than trying to fit in. Or you could discover that having one or two close friends who really understand you means more than being part of the "popular" crowd. These discoveries about what truly matters to you are like finding your own North Star, they help guide you when you need to make choices. For example, if you value deep connections, you might spend time really listening to a friend who's struggling instead of going to a big party. If creative expression matters most to you, you might decide to take an art class even if your friends choose sports instead.

The beautiful thing about understanding your core values is that they help you make decisions that feel right for you. When you face tough choices, you can ask yourself, "Does this choice align with what I truly value?" It's like having an inner compass that points you toward what feels authentic and meaningful, rather than just following what others think you should do. This process of discovering your values takes time and patience. It's like slowly unwrapping a gift, layer by layer, you learn more about what truly matters to you. As you understand these deeper values, you'll likely find yourself making choices that feel more "you", choices that honor your sensitive nature and help you live in a way that feels genuine and fulfilling.

Turning Dreams into Clear Plans

When you have a dream or goal, it can sometimes feel like a fuzzy picture in your mind. But when you take time to think deeply about what you really want and why it matters to you, that fuzzy picture starts to become clearer. For sensitive people who notice and feel things deeply, this process of gaining clarity can be especially powerful. Think about how a camera lens works. At first, everything might look blurry. But as you adjust the focus, the image becomes sharp and clear. In the same way, when you take time to understand what truly matters to you, your goals become clearer. Instead of just thinking, "I want to be successful," you might realize, "I want to use my ability to understand others deeply to help people who are struggling." This kind of clear understanding comes from listening to your inner wisdom, that quiet voice inside that knows what truly matters to you. Sometimes what you discover might surprise you. Maybe you thought you wanted to be a lawyer because others suggested it, but when you really listen to yourself, you realize you're drawn to teaching because it lets you use your sensitivity to help others learn and grow.

Setting these clear intentions isn't like making a simple to-do list. It's more like planting a garden. You need to understand which plants will grow best in your soil and which goals match who you really are. When your intentions grow from this deep understanding of yourself, they have real power. They're not just things you think you "should" do; they're things you feel called to do from deep inside. The most important part is letting these intentions develop naturally, without rushing or forcing them to fit what others expect. Just as a flower can't be forced to bloom before it's ready, your understanding of what you want to do with your life needs time to unfold. When you give yourself this time and space, you often discover a clearer sense of direction than you ever expected.

The Power of Choice

Every day brings hundreds of small moments where you get to choose what's best for you. These choices might seem small, but they add up to shape your whole experience of life. Think of yourself as the captain of a ship, you can't control the weather or the waves, but you can choose which direction to steer and how to navigate through different conditions. When you feel things deeply, these choices become especially important. It's like having a highly tuned instrument, you need to take extra care to keep it in harmony. For example, you might notice that certain places or situations drain your energy more than others. A noisy cafeteria might leave you feeling tired, while a quiet library helps you feel focused and calm. Understanding this lets you make better choices about where to spend your time. Making conscious choices also means learning to say "no" when something doesn't feel right for you. This isn't being selfish, it's being wise about your energy, like making sure your phone is charged before a long day. Maybe you decide to take smaller breaks throughout the day instead of pushing through until you're overwhelmed. Or perhaps you choose to meet a friend one-on-one for coffee instead of going to a crowded party where you'll feel drained.

These choices extend to relationships too. You might choose to spend more time with friends who understand and respect your sensitivity, and less time with those who dismiss or criticize it. It's like choosing to plant your garden in good soil rather than trying to force plants to grow in rocky ground. Each time you make a choice that honors your sensitive nature, you build more confidence in your ability to create a life that works for you. It's like building a house, each good decision is another brick in the foundation of a stronger, more comfortable life. Over time, these choices help you move from feeling overwhelmed by your sensitivity to seeing it as a valuable tool that helps you navigate life more skillfully.

Learning to Trust Your Inner Voice

Your inner wisdom is like a quiet friend who always gives good advice, the more you listen and find the advice helpful, the more you trust that friend. When you're sensitive, you have a special ability to pick up on subtle feelings and insights that others might miss. Learning to trust these insights is like developing a valuable skill that gets stronger with practice. Your inner wisdom often shows up in different ways. Sometimes it's a gut feeling about a situation that doesn't feel right, even if you can't explain why. Other times, it's knowing you need extra time to think through a decision while others are rushing to choose. These feelings aren't weaknesses; they're your inner compass trying to guide you toward what's best for you.

Building trust in yourself happens slowly, like watching a garden grow. Each time you listen to your inner voice and things work out well, it's like adding another drop of water to help that garden flourish. For example, you may have felt you needed a quiet break during a busy day, took that break, and found yourself feeling much more focused afterward. Or perhaps you had a feeling about a friend needing support, reached out, and discovered they really did need someone to talk to. This kind of self-trust isn't about making quick decisions or forcing yourself to "just know" things. Instead, it grows when you give yourself permission to take the time you need. If everyone else is ready to decide something but you feel you need more time to think it through, honoring that need is a way of showing trust in your own process. It's like giving yourself permission to read a book at your own pace instead of rushing to keep up with others.

The beautiful thing about developing trust in your inner wisdom is that it creates a solid foundation for all other decisions in your life. When you know you can rely on your own insights and feelings, you become more confident in navigating life's challenges. This doesn't mean you'll always know exactly what to do, but it means you'll trust yourself to figure things out in your own way and time.

Let me share some practical ways to develop trust in your inner wisdom, explaining each step carefully so you can start using these techniques in your daily life.

Start with Body Awareness

Your body often gives you necessary signals before your mind fully understands a situation. Take a few quiet moments each day to notice how your body feels. Maybe your shoulders tense up around certain people, or your chest feels lighter in certain places. These physical feelings are part of your inner wisdom speaking to you. Think of it like learning a new language, at first, the signals might seem unclear, but with practice, you'll understand them better.

Practice Gentle Decision-Making

When you need to make a choice, try this approach: Instead of rushing to decide, permit yourself to sit with the question. Imagine each option and notice how your body and emotions respond. For example, if you decide whether to join an after-school activity, picture yourself doing it. Does the thought make you feel energized or drained? This isn't about right or wrong answers; it's about understanding what feels true for you.

Create Quiet Reflection Time

Your inner wisdom often speaks most clearly in quiet moments. Try setting aside even five minutes a day for quiet reflection. This could be right after waking up, during lunch break, or before bed. During this time, ask yourself simple questions like "What do I need today?" or "What felt right or wrong about today?" Write down what comes to mind without judging it. Over time, you'll start noticing patterns in what your inner wisdom tells you.

Trust Your Timeline

Remember that everyone processes things differently. If you need more time to think about something than others do, that's perfectly okay. Think of it as digesting food; some people process it quickly, others need more time, and both are normal. When someone asks for an immediate answer, try saying, "I need some time to think about this. Can I let you know tomorrow?" This honors your need for processing time.

Learn from Experience

Keep a small notebook or use your phone to record times when you followed (or didn't follow) your inner wisdom. Write down what happened and how things turned out. For instance, maybe you felt you should take a different route to school and later learned there was heavy traffic on your usual route. These experiences help build confidence in your intuition.

Build Gradually

Start with small decisions where the stakes are low. Maybe begin by choosing what to eat for lunch based on what your body tells you it needs, or decide how to spend your free time based on what feels energizing. As you practice trusting yourself in these smaller moments, you'll develop more confidence for bigger decisions.

Notice Without Judgment

Sometimes your inner wisdom might suggest something that doesn't seem logical initially. Instead of dismissing these feelings, try to stay curious about them. For example, if you feel hesitant about joining a popular activity that "everyone" loves, don't judge that feeling. Instead, ask yourself, "What might this hesitation be trying to tell me?"

Let me provide some real-life situations where you can practice trusting your inner wisdom, making each example clear and relatable.

In Social Situations

Imagine you're invited to a big weekend party. While everyone's excited about it, you feel slightly tight when thinking about going. Instead of ignoring this feeling or forcing yourself to go because "everyone else is," pause and listen to what your body is telling you. Maybe your inner wisdom is suggesting that a whole evening of loud social interaction might be too much right now.

You could practice trust by:

- Taking a moment to check in with yourself: "What's behind this hesitation?"
- Considering alternatives: "Would I feel better meeting two or three friends for coffee instead?"
- Honoring your needs: "I can say yes to parts of activities and no to others; maybe I'll go for an hour rather than the whole evening"

During School or Work Projects

Let's say your class is working on a group project, and you feel that the current approach isn't going to work well. While others rush ahead, your sensitive nature picks up on potential problems. This is a perfect time to practice trusting your inner wisdom.

You might:

- Take a moment to clarify what exactly feels off about the plan
- Share your insights respectfully: "I've been thinking about our approach, and I wonder if we might encounter some challenges with..."
- Suggest thoughtful alternatives based on your more profound understanding of the situation

In Personal Relationships

Consider a situation where a close friend has been acting differently lately. While others might not notice, your sensitivity picks up on subtle changes in their behavior or tone. Your inner wisdom might tell you something's wrong, even if everything looks fine.

Trust your insight by:

- Checking in with your friend privately
- Sharing what you've noticed: "I might be wrong, but I've noticed you seem a bit quieter lately..."
- Offering support without pressure: "I'm here if you ever want to talk"

In Daily Decision Making

Think about choosing extracurricular activities. While certain clubs or sports might be popular, your inner wisdom might guide you toward less apparent choices that better match your interests and energy levels.

Practice listening by:

- Noticing how you feel when you think about each activity
- Considering what genuinely interests you rather than what looks good on paper
- Choosing based on what energizes rather than drains you

In Creative Projects

When working on something creative, like writing, art, or music, your inner wisdom often knows what you want to express before your logical mind can put it into words.

Trust this by:

- Taking time to sit with your ideas before starting
- Following creative impulses even if they seem unusual
- Allowing your work to develop at its own pace rather than rushing to finish

Cultivating Inner Authority

Think of inner authority as a strong foundation that develops when you learn to trust your unique way of experiencing the world. As skilled wine tasters develop confidence in their ability to detect subtle flavors, sensitive individuals can learn to value their capacity to perceive nuances that others might miss.

This journey begins with recognizing that sensitivity brings valuable insights. Your ability to notice subtle changes in someone's tone of voice, pick up on underlying group dynamics, or sense when something isn't quite right in a situation aren't burdens to overcome but rather sophisticated tools for understanding the world around you. Consider how a master chef develops their expertise. They learn to trust their refined palate, understanding that their ability to detect slight variations in flavor leads to better cooking. Similarly, sensitive people can learn to trust that their deeper processing and attention to detail often lead to more nuanced understanding and better decisions.

One of the most crucial skills in developing inner authority is learning to differentiate between your genuine inner wisdom and external pressures. Your true inner wisdom often feels calm and centered, even when it's telling you something challenging. External pressures, on the other hand, usually feel rushed, anxious, or laden with "shoulds" and "musts." For example, imagine you're in a group discussion. Everyone seems ready to move forward with a plan, but something feels off to you. External pressure might say, "Just go along with it, don't make waves." Your inner wisdom, however, might calmly suggest, "This needs more consideration." Learning to recognize and trust that quiet, knowing voice takes practice but becomes more natural over time.

Developing inner authority happens gradually through consistent practice in real-life situations. Each time you notice something subtle and take it seriously rather than dismiss it, you strengthen this muscle. When your careful observation helps prevent a problem or your thoughtful approach leads to a better outcome, your trust in your perspective grows naturally.

Regular reflection plays a vital part in this development. Reflecting on situations where you either followed or ignored your inner wisdom helps you recognize patterns. What did it feel like in your body when you knew something was right? How did it feel different from when you were just reacting to external pressure? These observations help you tune in more accurately to your inner guidance.

The Strength of Boundaries

Personal boundaries are like the walls of your home; they protect your personal space and energy while letting you choose what and who to welcome in. For sensitive people, these boundaries are crucial because they process experiences more deeply than others, much like having a highly sophisticated sound system that picks up every note in a piece of music.

Boundaries aren't rigid barriers that cut you off from the world. Instead, they're more like flexible membranes that help you regulate your engagement with your environment. Just as your skin protects your internal organs while still allowing you to feel and interact with the world, good boundaries protect your emotional and mental well-being while allowing meaningful connections. Setting boundaries involves understanding what affects you and how. You might notice that long conversations in noisy places leave you feeling drained or that you need quiet time after social events to process your experiences. These aren't signs of weakness; they're valuable information about what you need to function at your best.

Setting boundaries becomes more natural when you understand that boundaries are a form of self-care rather than selfishness. Consider how a professional athlete must carefully manage their training and rest to perform well. Similarly, sensitive individuals must manage their exposure to stimulating environments and interactions to maintain their well-being and effectiveness.

Learning to set boundaries often starts with small steps. You might begin by recognizing when you need a break during social gatherings or by setting aside quiet time in your daily schedule. As you practice honoring these needs, you likely have more energy and clarity for the activities and relationships that matter most to you. The key is to set these limits confidently, knowing they serve you and others. When you maintain healthy boundaries, you bring your best self to your interactions and responsibilities. This benefits everyone involved, even if they don't immediately understand your needs.

Let me explain how to communicate your boundaries effectively while keeping your relationships strong and positive. I'll build this explanation step by step to help you master this important skill.

Communicating with Clarity and Care

Think of communicating boundaries like explaining the rules of a game you enjoy; you want others to understand so everyone can have a better experience together. When you frame boundaries this way, they become invitations to better relationships rather than walls that push people away.

The Art of Clear Communication

Start by being clear about what you need without apologizing for having needs. Instead of saying, "I'm sorry, but I get overwhelmed easily," you might say, "I've learned that I do my best when I have quiet time to recharge after social events." This helps others understand that your boundaries aren't about them; they're about taking care of yourself so you can be more present in your relationships. Using "I" statements helps keep conversations positive. For example: "I find I can listen better and be more engaged when we meet in quieter places" works better than "You always want to meet in noisy restaurants that are too overwhelming." This approach focuses on your experience rather than making others feel criticized.

Timing and Tone

Choose calm moments to discuss your boundaries when neither you nor the other person feels stressed or defensive. Think of it like planting seeds in good soil; the right conditions help understanding grow naturally. Share your needs as part of regular conversations about what helps each person thrive in the relationship. For example, you might tell a friend: "I really value our time together, and I've noticed I can be more present and engaged when we meet earlier in the day rather than late at night. Would you be open to meeting for coffee instead of dinner sometimes?"

Building Understanding Over Time

Remember that others might need time to understand and adjust to your boundaries, especially if they process experiences differently than you do. You can help them understand by sharing how honoring these boundaries helps you be a better friend, family member, or colleague. For instance, explain how taking short breaks during busy events helps you stay energized and engaged: "When I take a few minutes of quiet time during parties, I come back feeling refreshed and ready to connect more deeply with everyone."

Maintaining Connection While Setting Limits

Show appreciation when others respect your boundaries, and be sure to nurture relationships within the parameters that work for you. If you need to decline a large gathering, you might suggest an alternative: "While big parties are challenging for me, I'd love to have coffee with you next week to hear all about it."

Finding Balance

Remember that healthy boundaries create space for genuine connection. When you care for your needs, you have more energy and attention to give to relationships. Share this perspective with others: "When I honor my need for quiet time, I can be much more present and engaged when we're together."

Authentic Expression

Think of authentic expression as finding your true voice, not just in words but in all the ways you share yourself with the world. Just as a musician must first learn to hear the music within before playing it beautifully, sensitive individuals need to develop a clear connection with their inner truth before they can express it effectively.

When you build strong inner authority, expressing yourself becomes more natural, like water flowing from a clear spring. You begin to trust that your perceptions and feelings are valid and worthy of being shared. This trust allows you to speak your truth without either downplaying your insights or forcing them on others. Consider how a skilled photographer learns to trust their unique way of seeing the world. At first, they might doubt their perspective or try to copy others' styles. However, as they develop confidence in their vision, they naturally begin creating images that authentically reflect their way of seeing. Similarly, sensitive people can learn to trust and share their unique perception and understanding of the world.

When you express yourself authentically, something remarkable happens in your relationships. People often respond to genuine expression with their own authenticity. It's like opening a door that invites others to be more real and present too. This creates opportunities for deeper, more meaningful connections. For example, when you honestly share your need for processing time before making decisions, others might feel encouraged to acknowledge their own needs. Expressing your genuine appreciation for someone's kindness often inspires more authentic emotional sharing from them.

Each time you express yourself authentically, you strengthen both your inner authority and your ability to communicate effectively. Think of it as building a bridge between your inner and outer worlds. With each authentic expression, this bridge becomes stronger and more reliable.

Navigation Through Complexity

Your tendency to think carefully about situations is like having a powerful computer that can analyze many factors simultaneously. While others might make quick decisions based on limited information, your natural inclination to consider multiple angles helps you spot potential challenges and opportunities that aren't immediately obvious. For example, in a work project, you might notice how different team members' styles could affect collaboration or how timing might impact the project's success in ways others haven't considered.

Effective navigation requires combining your inner wisdom with practical external information, much like a pilot who uses both instruments and visual cues to fly safely. Your inner wisdom might tell you something doesn't feel right about a situation, while external information provides concrete facts to consider. Together, these create a more complete picture for decision-making. For instance, when considering a career change, your sensitivity might help you recognize that your current environment doesn't align with your values (inner wisdom). At the same time, research provides essential information about alternatives (external information). Using both sources helps you make personally fulfilling and practically sound decisions.

Your need for thorough processing isn't a weakness, it's a strength that leads to better decisions. Just as a master chef takes time to develop complex flavors, your careful consideration of situations often results in more nuanced and effective solutions. While sometimes slower than others prefer, this patient approach typically leads to more sustainable outcomes.

The Path to Sovereignty

Developing personal sovereignty happens through daily practices and choices. You strengthen this foundation each time you pause to check in with your inner wisdom before deciding. When you honor your need for quiet time despite external pressure to always be social, you build trust in your own judgment. These moments might seem small, but they accumulate like drops of water filling a pond, gradually creating a deep reservoir of self-trust. This process doesn't mean cutting yourself off from others' insights or wisdom. Instead, it's about developing the ability to thoughtfully consider external input while maintaining a clear connection to your own truth. Imagine having a conversation with a trusted friend; you listen carefully to their perspective, but you also know that, ultimately, you must make choices that align with your own values and needs.

Building personal sovereignty requires patience and consistent practice. Each day brings opportunities to strengthen this muscle. When you feel overwhelmed in a busy environment, practicing self-trust might mean giving yourself permission to step away for a quiet moment. When making important decisions, it might mean taking the time you need to process, even if others push for quick answers.

Consider how musicians develop mastery; they practice scales and basic techniques daily, gradually building the foundation for more complex performances. Similarly, developing personal sovereignty involves regular practice in basic skills: recognizing your true feelings, honoring your needs, maintaining healthy boundaries, and making choices aligned with your values.

Personal sovereignty has a unique quality for sensitive individuals. When you learn to trust and work with your sensitivity, it becomes a source of strength. The same deep processing that might once have felt overwhelming becomes a valuable tool for understanding situations and making wise choices. Your ability to perceive subtle nuances helps you navigate relationships and environments with greater awareness and skill.

Embracing Personal Truth

Think of your personal truth as the authentic core of who you are, your natural way of perceiving, feeling, and understanding the world. For sensitive individuals, this truth often runs deeper than what's visible on the surface, like an underground spring that feeds a river. Your sensitivity allows you to notice subtle patterns and connections that others might miss, creating a rich and nuanced understanding of life.

When you begin truly trusting your sensitivity as a strength, new possibilities open up. Your careful processing of situations becomes recognized as valuable insight rather than overthinking. Your emotional depth becomes understood as a source of wisdom rather than an overwhelming feeling. Your need for quiet reflection time becomes honored as essential self-care rather than social withdrawal. This self-trust creates a solid foundation for engaging with the world. Instead of forcing yourself to function like less sensitive individuals, you learn to work with your natural traits. This might mean structuring your day to include necessary quiet time, choosing work that allows you to use your deep processing abilities, or building relationships that honor your need for meaningful connection.

When grounded in personal truth, daily decisions become clearer. Rather than struggling with what you "should" do based on others' expectations, you can make choices aligned with your authentic nature. This might mean choosing work environments that support your sensitivity, creating relationships that value deep connection, or engaging in activities that allow for meaningful contributions in ways that honor your natural strengths.

Seeds of Transformation

Real growth often happens in gentle waves, like the steady rhythm of tides shaping a shoreline. For sensitive individuals, this natural ebb and flow holds particular importance. Your profound processing nature means you absorb and integrate experiences more thoroughly than others might, requiring time to understand and embody each step of change fully. Think of how a garden develops through the seasons. While you might wish for overnight transformation, lasting growth follows nature's patient timeline. Some days bring visible progress, new leaves unfurling, buds opening into flowers. On other days, focus on strengthening roots and building resilience, which are invisible but essential changes. Your sensitivity allows you to appreciate these subtle shifts, recognizing how minor adjustments create meaningful transformation over time.

Creating sustainable change means working with your natural rhythms rather than against them. You might notice certain times when you process experiences more clearly, perhaps in the quiet of early morning or during solitary walks. These become your cultivation times, moments when you can reflect on recent growth and gently nurture new possibilities. Rather than seeing your need for processing time as a limitation, recognize it as the fertile soil from which lasting change grows. Meaningful progress often emerges through consistent small choices rather than dramatic gestures. Each time you honor your sensitivity instead of pushing it aside, you strengthen the foundation for growth. When you permit yourself to process experiences entirely rather than rushing to keep pace with others, you create space for genuine transformation. These moments might seem insignificant individually, but like drops of water shaping stone, they gradually create profound change.

Supporting this growth requires creating environments and practices that honor your sensitive nature. This might mean establishing quiet spaces for reflection, setting aside time for thorough processing, or developing relationships that respect your natural rhythm. Rather than forcing yourself to grow according to external timelines, you learn to trust your inner wisdom about the pace and direction of change.

The Architecture of Goals

When you're sensitive, setting goals requires deeper listening, not just to what the world says you should want, but to what truly resonates within you. Think of this process like an architect designing a home. While others might focus solely on curb appeal or resale value, you understand that a truly successful design must consider how the space feels to live in, how light moves through rooms, and how the overall flow supports daily life. This careful attention to deeper factors shapes how sensitive individuals naturally approach goal-setting. Rather than simply chasing conventional markers of success, like promotions or material achievements, your goals often encompass the quality of your daily experience. You might seek to create work environments that honor your need for quiet focus or to develop relationships that allow for meaningful connection without depleting your energy.

Each goal you set creates ripples of possibility in your life, like dropping a stone in still water. For instance, a goal of establishing clearer boundaries at work isn't just about saying "no" more often. It might involve developing a deeper understanding of your energy patterns, learning to communicate your needs effectively, and creating systems that protect your sensitivity while allowing you to contribute your unique insights. The power of these goals lies in their alignment with your authentic nature. When you set objectives that honor your sensitivity rather than trying to override it, you tap into a natural source of motivation. Instead of constantly pushing against your nature, you work with it. This might mean setting goals that allow for thorough processing time, that respect your need for meaningful connection, or that utilize your ability to perceive subtle patterns and dynamics.

Consider how your sensitivity influences what success looks like for you. While others might thrive on rapid-fire decisions and constant interaction, you might define success as maintaining clear thinking amidst complexity or creating spaces where genuine connection can flourish. These goals emerge from understanding and valuing your natural way of being in the world. The most effective goals often combine practical steps with a deeper purpose. For example, creating a morning routine isn't just about being more productive; it's about honoring your need for quiet reflection time and setting an intentional tone for your day. Each goal becomes a framework for living more authentically while contributing your unique gifts to the world.

Let me explain how to create goals that work with your sensitivity rather than against it, building this understanding step by step.

When developing goals that support your sensitive nature, start by taking time to understand your natural patterns and rhythms. Observe how your energy flows throughout the day. Notice when you feel most clear and focused, and when you need more quiet or rest. These observations become the foundation for goals aligning with your natural being. For instance, if you notice you think most clearly in the morning quiet, you might create goals that take advantage of these optimal hours rather than fighting against your natural rhythm.

Your sensitivity gives you access to subtle information that others might miss. Use this depth of perception when setting goals by paying attention to how different activities and environments affect you. If certain situations consistently drain your energy while others help you feel more alive and engaged, let this wisdom guide your goal-setting. Your body and emotions often know what directions will genuinely support your growth before your logical mind catches up.

Consider creating goals that specifically nurture and protect your sensitivity. This might involve developing stronger boundaries, creating regular renewal practices, or designing environments that support your sensory needs. For example, instead of pushing yourself to maintain a pace that others consider "normal," you might set goals around creating sustainable rhythms that allow for the processing time you need.

When defining success metrics for your goals, look beyond conventional measures to include qualitative factors that matter to sensitive individuals. Instead of focusing solely on external achievements, consider how you want to feel, what kind of energy you want to maintain, or what quality of relationships you want to cultivate. This might mean measuring success by how well you maintain your inner calm during challenges, or by your ability to stay true to your values under pressure.

Goals that support sensitivity often involve creating supportive systems and structures. Think about what you need to function at your best and build goals around establishing these conditions. This could mean creating a peaceful home environment, developing routines that provide predictability, or building relationships with people who understand and respect your sensitive nature. These foundational elements become the infrastructure that supports all other achievements.

The most effective goals often combine tangible actions with deeper intentions. For instance, a goal of "improving professional boundaries" might include specific practices like taking regular breaks, communicating needs clearly, and creating quiet spaces for focused work. But beneath these concrete steps lies the deeper intention of honoring your sensitivity while sharing your gifts effectively with the world.

Let me now explain how to structure goals that support and work with your sensitivity, building this approach step by step to create a clear understanding.

Begin by setting aside quiet time for deep reflection about what truly matters to you. This initial step is crucial for sensitive individuals because your ability to perceive subtle nuances helps you understand what you genuinely want beyond surface-level desires. During this reflection time, consider what makes you feel most alive, what drains your energy, and what kinds of achievements would feel meaningful rather than just impressive to others.

Structure your goals in layers, starting with a foundation that honors your sensitive nature. Think of it like building a house, before adding any decorative elements, you need solid ground to build upon. Your foundation might include creating reliable daily rhythms, establishing essential boundaries, or developing basic self-care practices that help you maintain your energy and clarity.

Once you have this foundation, develop what I call "nested goals", smaller objectives that fit naturally within larger ones. For instance, if your larger goal is to share your creative work more widely, your nested goals might include creating quiet time for creative practice, developing comfortable ways to receive feedback, and identifying sharing platforms that feel aligned with your values. Each smaller goal supports the larger one while respecting your need for gradual, thorough processing.

Create clear timelines that account for your processing needs. Sensitive individuals often need more time to integrate experiences and changes than others might. When structuring your goals, deliberately build in this integration time. Rather than setting aggressive deadlines that create pressure, establish gentle rhythms of progress that allow for reflection and adjustment along the way.

Include what I call "sensitivity checkpoints" in your goal structure. These are regular moments to assess how your goals are affecting your energy, emotional well-being, and overall balance. Pay attention to subtle signs that might indicate a need to adjust your approach. Your sensitivity gives you early warning signals that can help you stay on a sustainable path toward your objectives.

Develop concrete ways to measure progress that honor both tangible and intangible growth. While some goals might have clear external metrics, others might be measured by how you feel, the quality of your relationships, or your ability to maintain inner peace while pursuing your objectives. Create personal indicators that help you recognize progress in ways that matter to you.

Remember to build flexibility into your goal structure. Your sensitivity allows you to notice when adjustments are needed, often before obvious signs appear. Honor this awareness by creating goals that can evolve as you gain new insights about what works best for you.

Designing Forward Motion

Creating effective forward motion involves designing steps that match your natural rhythm. Instead of pushing for rapid change, consider how you can break down larger goals into smaller pieces that feel manageable and allow for complete integration. For example, if you're working on establishing better boundaries, you might start with simply noticing situations where boundaries feel needed, then gradually progress to practicing boundary-setting in low-stakes situations before moving to more challenging contexts.

This measured approach creates what I call "sustainable momentum", steady forward progress that doesn't deplete your energy or create overwhelm. Each small success builds confidence and capability, much like a river gradually carving its path through the rock. The progress might seem slower than more aggressive approaches, but it creates lasting change that becomes deeply embedded in your way of being. The beauty of this approach lies in its respect for your sensitive nature while ensuring consistent progress. Rather than fighting against your need for processing time, you work with it, allowing each step to fully integrate before moving forward. This creates a natural flow of growth that feels authentic and sustainable rather than forced or artificial.

Nurturing Support Networks

The foundation of an effective support system starts with recognizing that not all supportive relationships look the same. Some people might offer practical guidance, while others provide emotional understanding or simply hold space for you to process experiences. Consider how different plants in a garden serve various purposes, some provide shade, others enrich the soil, and others attract beneficial insects. Similarly, different relationships in your support network can serve distinct but equally valuable purposes. When building these connections, pay particular attention to the subtle energy dynamics in each relationship. Your sensitivity gives you valuable insight into how different interactions affect you. Some people naturally help you feel more energized and understood, while others might leave you feeling drained even if they have good intentions. These feelings provide important information about which relationships will best support your growth over time.

Creating sustainable support networks also involves understanding your needs for connection and space. Sensitive individuals often require a balance between meaningful interaction and time for processing and renewal. Think about how you structure relationships to honor this rhythm, having regular but spaced-out meetings with mentors, or creating clear boundaries around when and how you engage with different support people. The most effective support networks often include people who understand or respect sensitivity, even if they aren't highly sensitive themselves. These might be friends who honor your need for processing time, family members who respect your boundaries, or professionals who understand how to work with sensitive individuals. Building these connections takes time and discernment, but the investment creates invaluable support for your ongoing growth.

Markers of Progress

Growth for sensitive individuals often appears first in quiet, almost imperceptible ways, like the gradual changing of seasons. These small shifts might show up in daily moments; perhaps you notice yourself pausing to check in with your needs before agreeing to plans or finding it easier to maintain your energy during busy days. While these changes might seem minor individually, they represent important steps in your development, like early spring flowers that signal deeper changes taking place beneath the surface. Understanding progress requires developing awareness of these subtle indicators. Think about how an experienced gardener notices small signs of plant health, slight changes in leaf color, new growth patterns, or stronger stems. Similarly, sensitive individuals can learn to recognize their own markers of growth. You might notice that situations that once felt overwhelming now feel more manageable, or that setting boundaries feels more natural and less anxiety-producing than before.

Creating a practice of tracking these changes provides valuable information about your growth journey. This doesn't mean maintaining rigid measurements, but rather developing a gentle awareness of shifting patterns. You might notice that your energy stays more stable throughout the week, or that you recover more quickly from challenging situations. These observations help you understand which strategies support your growth most effectively and where you might need to adjust your approach. The beauty of this kind of progress tracking lies in its respect for the sensitive person's natural thoroughness. Rather than focusing solely on external achievements, it honors the internal shifts that often precede visible changes. For instance, before others might notice any difference, you might recognize that you feel more centered in difficult conversations, or more confident in expressing your needs, even if you're still working on doing so consistently. These subtle improvements gradually accumulate into more significant transformations, like small streams joining to form a river. Over time, you might find yourself handling situations with greater ease that once seemed impossible or maintaining boundaries that previously felt too challenging. Each small success builds upon the others, creating lasting change that becomes deeply integrated into your way of being.

The Art of Adjustment

The key to successful adjustment lies in maintaining regular awareness of how your current approaches are serving you. This involves creating quiet moments for reflection where you can assess your progress and challenges with the same sensitivity you bring to understanding others. During these reviews, you might notice subtle signs that a strategy needs updating, perhaps it no longer feels energizing, or you sense yourself outgrowing certain protective measures.

Developing this flexibility requires building trust in your ability to read subtle signals about what you need. Your sensitivity becomes a valuable tool for recognizing when adjustments are necessary, often before obvious signs appear. You might sense an internal shift suggesting you're ready for more challenge in certain areas, or notice that previously helpful practices now feel constraining rather than supportive.

Making these adjustments doesn't mean abandoning everything that worked before, but rather refining and evolving your approach based on accumulated wisdom. Think of it as updating a map based on actual experience of the terrain. Each adjustment incorporates your growing understanding of yourself and your sensitivity, creating increasingly sophisticated strategies that support your continued development. The beauty of this approach lies in its respect for the natural evolution of growth. Rather than forcing yourself to maintain strategies that no longer serve you, or rushing to adopt new approaches before you're ready, you learn to make thoughtful adjustments that honor both your current capabilities and your potential for further development.

Building Momentum

Think of building momentum like starting a large wheel turning. At first, it requires consistent small pushes and the movement might seem barely noticeable. But gradually, as the wheel gains speed, it becomes easier to maintain its motion. This same principle applies to personal growth for sensitive individuals, small, consistent actions create a natural momentum that supports ongoing development. The key lies in understanding that lasting progress often emerges from these modest but regular steps rather than dramatic leaps. Consider how a river shapes stone, not through sudden force, but through a persistent, gentle flow. Your sensitivity actually supports this approach because it allows you to notice and appreciate subtle changes that others might miss. When you recognize these small signs of progress, each one becomes a motivation for continued growth. Using your natural sensitive strengths accelerates this momentum-building process. Your deep processing abilities serve as a powerful tool for understanding patterns in your growth journey. You might notice, for instance, that certain approaches consistently lead to sustainable progress while others, though perhaps faster initially, tend to create overwhelm. This pattern recognition helps you refine your strategies over time, making each step more effective than the last.

Your emotional intelligence plays a crucial role in maintaining momentum. Rather than pushing through resistance, which often leads to setbacks for sensitive individuals, you can use your emotional awareness to navigate challenges more skillfully. You might sense when you need to adjust your pace, when to press forward, or when to allow time for integration. This emotional wisdom helps you maintain steady progress without burning out. The beauty of building momentum this way lies in its sustainability. Instead of depleting your energy with aggressive pushes for change, you create a natural flow of growth that builds upon itself. Each small success strengthens your confidence, making the next step feel more manageable. Your pattern recognition abilities help you identify what works best for you, allowing you to focus your energy on the most effective approaches. Consider how this momentum takes shape in practical terms. You may begin with tiny steps toward better boundary-setting, first just noticing when boundaries feel needed, then practicing with safe people, and gradually building to more challenging situations. Each successful experience, however small, creates confidence and understanding that carries forward into future situations. Your sensitivity allows you to fully process and integrate these experiences, turning them into lasting capabilities rather than temporary changes.

The Power of Process

When we shift our focus from reaching specific endpoints to appreciating the journey itself, something remarkable happens. Each step of growth becomes meaningful in its own right, much like how a musician finds joy not just in perfecting a piece, but in discovering new subtleties during practice. This perspective particularly suits sensitive people because it honors their natural inclination to engage deeply with experiences rather than rushing toward outcomes. The process-oriented approach creates space for the kind of thorough exploration that sensitive individuals often need. Instead of feeling pressured to quickly achieve certain milestones, you can fully absorb and integrate each stage of growth. Consider how a master chef develops their craft, they don't just memorize recipes but develop a deep understanding of how ingredients interact, how flavors develop, and how subtle adjustments affect the final dish. Similarly, sensitive individuals can use their natural depth of processing to understand the nuances of their growth journey.

This way of thinking transforms potential obstacles into opportunities for deeper learning. When challenges arise, rather than seeing them as setbacks from a destination, they become valuable parts of the growth process. Your sensitivity becomes an asset here, allowing you to perceive subtle lessons and insights that might be missed with a more goal-focused approach. The beauty of process-oriented thinking lies in how it maintains clear direction while removing the pressure of immediate transformation. Like a river finding its way to the ocean, you can maintain a sense of where you're heading while allowing the journey to unfold naturally. This approach creates space for the deep processing and integration that sensitive individuals often need while still ensuring meaningful progress over time.

Creating Sustainable Change

Understanding your sensitive traits becomes essential in designing sustainable change. Consider how your need for thorough processing, though sometimes seen as slow, enables deeper integration of new patterns. Rather than fighting against this natural tendency, you can structure your growth approach to take advantage of it. This might mean allowing more time between significant changes, creating detailed reflection practices, or breaking more enormous transformations into smaller, more manageable steps. The foundation of sustainable change lies in finding the right balance between different elements of growth. Like an ecosystem maintaining harmony between various species, you must balance forward movement with integration time, individual effort with community support, and challenge with rest. This balance looks different for sensitive individuals because they often need more substantial integration time and more carefully managed energy levels to maintain steady progress.

Creating strong support systems plays a crucial role in sustainable transformation. Think of how climbing plants use sturdy structures to reach new heights; similarly, sensitive individuals often need well-designed support systems to maintain growth without becoming overwhelmed. This might involve developing relationships with understanding mentors, creating regular check-in practices, or establishing consistent renewal routines that maintain energy for continued growth. The key to lasting change lies in developing approaches that work with your sensitivity rather than trying to override it. Consider how your more profound processing abilities can help you understand patterns more thoroughly or how your emotional intelligence can guide you in maintaining healthy boundaries. When you align your growth strategies with these natural strengths, change becomes more sustainable because it flows from your authentic way of being rather than fighting against it.

The Journey Continues

As you develop stronger foundations in understanding and working with your sensitivity, what once seemed overwhelming often becomes manageable. Consider how an experienced dancer moves with natural grace through complex sequences that once required careful attention to each step. Similarly, practices like setting boundaries or managing energy levels gradually become more intuitive as you build confidence in honoring your sensitive nature. New possibilities naturally emerge as your capabilities expand. Just as a musician who masters basic techniques discover more complex and nuanced ways of expressing themselves, sensitive individuals often find fresh ways to engage with life as they develop stronger foundations. What might have seemed impossible during earlier stages of growth, like maintaining energy in stimulating environments or sharing sensitive insights in professional settings, becomes increasingly accessible.

The beauty of this continuing journey lies in how each accomplishment creates the foundation for further growth. Your sensitivity becomes an increasingly valuable asset as you learn to work with it more effectively. The deep processing that might once have felt like a limitation transforms into a source of wisdom, helping you navigate new challenges and opportunities with more extraordinary skill and confidence. This ongoing evolution maintains natural engagement with personal growth because each step reveals new horizons to explore. Rather than reaching a fixed destination, you discover ever-expanding possibilities for expressing your sensitive strengths and contributing your unique gifts to the world. The journey continues not from external pressure but from a genuine curiosity about what might be possible as you continue developing.

The Inner Conversation

Inner dialogue is the background music playing throughout your daily life. Just as music can transform how we experience a scene in a movie, the tone and content of our inner conversation color everything we encounter. This internal soundtrack holds particular power for sensitive individuals, who naturally process experiences more deeply.

Your inner voice acts like a continuous interpreter of your experiences. When you walk into a crowded room, that voice might whisper messages of overwhelm and anxiety or remind you of your capability to navigate such situations with care for your needs. These internal messages shape not just how you feel about the situation, but how you respond to it.

Consider how your sensitivity amplifies this inner conversation. Because you process experiences more thoroughly than others might, each thought carries more weight, creating deeper ripples through your emotional landscape. When your inner voice speaks of limitation, "I'm too sensitive," or "I can't handle this," these messages sink deeply into your experience. Conversely, when that voice speaks with understanding and encouragement, it creates a powerful foundation for confident engagement with life.

The beauty of understanding this internal dialogue lies in recognizing its malleability. Just as you might adjust the volume or change the station on a radio, you can learn to modify your inner conversation. This doesn't mean forcing artificial positivity but rather developing an internal voice that honors your sensitive nature and capabilities.

The Language of Thoughts

Your thoughts are like a river flowing through your mind, carving channels in how you see yourself and the world. For sensitive individuals who experience life more intensely, these thought patterns cut especially deep paths. A single challenging moment might set off a cascade of thoughts questioning your worth or capabilities. When someone seems distant, your mind might weave elaborate stories about what you did wrong; each thought deepening well-worn paths of self-doubt. These thought patterns often develop gradually, like trails formed by walking the same route many times through a forest. Perhaps early experiences taught you to see your sensitivity as a flaw rather than a strength. Or maybe you learned to set impossibly high standards for yourself, believing perfection would protect you from criticism or rejection. These deeper beliefs flow beneath your daily thoughts like underground streams, influencing everything above without being clearly visible.

What makes these thought patterns particularly powerful for sensitive individuals is how thoroughly they process each experience. Your natural depth of processing means that each self-critical thought or harsh judgment doesn't just pass through, it resonates deeply, creating lasting impressions in how you understand yourself. A fleeting moment of feeling overwhelmed might trigger an entire narrative about being "too sensitive" or "not strong enough." Understanding these patterns reveals something important: thoughts that feel utterly natural and true often simply reflect habits of thinking developed over time. Just as a river can be redirected with conscious effort, these thought patterns can shift when recognized and gently questioned. The same sensitivity that makes negative thoughts cut deeper also allows for profound positive transformation when you begin interpreting your experiences differently.

Transforming Internal Speech

Transforming your inner dialogue is like tending a garden where certain plants have grown wild over time. Rather than trying to forcefully uproot established thought patterns, which often create more tension, you can gently cultivate new ways of thinking while allowing old patterns to fade naturally. When harsh self-talk emerges, instead of fighting it, you can learn to pause and observe it with curiosity, much like noticing an interesting but unwelcome plant in your garden. This process isn't about forcing yourself to think positively when you feel negative. Instead, it's about developing more accurate ways of seeing yourself and your experiences. Consider how you might view a friend who shares your sensitive traits; you likely see both their challenges and their unique gifts with more balance than you apply to yourself. This same balanced perspective can be developed in your self-talk through patient practice.

The key lies in learning to question thoughts that have long been accepted as truth. When your inner voice suggests you're "too sensitive" to handle a situation, you might gently ask yourself: Is this really true? Have there been times when your sensitivity helped you navigate similar challenges? What would you say to someone else with your capabilities facing this situation? These questions help create space between automatic thoughts and your conscious response to them. Each time you pause to question a habitual thought pattern, you create an opportunity for new understanding to emerge. Like water gradually wearing a new channel through rock, each tiny choice to view yourself and your experiences differently helps establish new neural pathways. Over time, these new patterns of thinking become more natural, requiring less conscious effort to maintain.

The beauty of this approach lies in its respect for the sensitive person's need for gentle, thorough processing. Rather than forcing rapid change, it allows for gradual transformation that can be fully integrated into your way of being. Your sensitivity actually becomes an asset in this process, as your natural depth of processing helps you notice subtle shifts in your thinking and appreciate small signs of progress.

The Heart of Compassion

Self-compassion is like cultivating a wise and caring inner friend who understands your sensitive nature and genuine efforts to grow. Just as you might naturally notice subtle signs of struggle in others and respond with understanding, you can learn to extend this same perceptive kindness to yourself. This shift often proves particularly powerful for sensitive individuals who readily offer compassion to others while maintaining harsh internal standards for themselves. The foundation of self-compassion builds upon recognizing a simple truth, being sensitive means you experience life more intensely, which brings both gifts and challenges. When encountering difficulties, rather than immediately turning to self-criticism, you can acknowledge the inherent complexity of navigating the world with deep sensitivity. Just as you wouldn't expect someone with acute hearing to feel comfortable in a noisy environment, you can learn to honor your natural needs without harsh judgment.

This gentler approach doesn't mean avoiding growth or excusing yourself from responsibility. Instead, it creates a safer internal space for honest self-reflection. When you know that acknowledging a mistake won't lead to harsh self-punishment, you become more able to look clearly at areas needing development. Like a skilled teacher who knows that students learn best in an atmosphere of support rather than criticism, your inner voice can guide growth while maintaining fundamental kindness. Consider how you might respond to a dear friend sharing their struggles with sensitivity, you would likely listen with understanding, acknowledge their challenges, and gently explore possibilities for positive change. This same balanced perspective can be developed in your relationship with yourself. Each time you catch yourself in harsh self-judgment, you can practice pausing and asking what words of wisdom you would offer a friend in your situation.

Building Supportive Dialogue

When you talk to yourself, think of it like having an ongoing conversation with someone who truly understands your sensitive nature. Each thought shapes how you see yourself and influences your next steps forward. The way you speak to yourself in quiet moments affects everything from how you handle daily challenges to how deeply you believe in your own abilities. Strong inner support starts with catching those automatic thoughts that pop up throughout your day. Notice the tone, does it lift you up or weigh you down? Instead of telling yourself, "I'm making too many mistakes," try, "I see what happened here, and next time, I can approach it differently." Each time you shift a harsh thought into a helpful one, you strengthen your foundation for growth.

Looking at the full picture matters, too. Rather than focusing only on what needs work, notice the small wins and steady progress you're making. When you handle a situation better than you would have months ago, acknowledge that growth. If something doesn't go as planned, remember that each experience teaches you something valuable about yourself. Building a supportive inner voice takes practice and patience. Start by listening to your thoughts without judgment. Then, gradually begin choosing words that guide rather than criticize, encouraging rather than demanding. As you develop this kinder way of talking to yourself, you'll likely find more emotional space to explore, grow, and try new things.

The beauty of developing supportive self-talk lies in how it creates room for both acceptance and growth. You can acknowledge where you are right now while gently encouraging yourself toward where you want to be. This balanced approach helps you stay grounded in reality while maintaining hope and direction for your journey forward.

The Power of Perspective

Viewing your experiences from a distance changes everything, like watching waves from a hilltop instead of being tossed around in them. When you're dealing with something hard, taking a moment to remember how far you've come helps put the current challenge in context. Think about times you've handled similar situations before or how past difficulties led to unexpected growth. Your sensitivity lets you notice subtle patterns in your life. You might realize certain situations always spark specific thoughts, or particular places affect your energy in predictable ways. This awareness becomes valuable information, helping you understand yourself better and make choices that support your well-being.

Over time, you see how your inner world shapes your outer experiences. The thoughts you carry into a situation often influence how it unfolds. When you approach something expecting it to drain you, it usually does. But when you remember your strengths and past successes, you often find new ways to handle challenges.

Life's difficulties begin to look different through this wider lens. Instead of seeing a setback as proof of failure, you might view it as information about what works for you and what doesn't. Each experience becomes a chance to learn more about your unique way of moving through the world. This broader view brings freedom too. When you're not caught up in seeing each moment as a final judgment of your worth or abilities, you can explore life with more openness and curiosity. Your sensitivity becomes a tool for understanding rather than a source of struggle.

Dancing with Doubt

When questions and uncertainty bubble up during growth, you can greet them with openness rather than resistance. Your sensitivity often brings a deeper awareness of potential challenges or areas needing attention. This natural caution, when approached thoughtfully, can actually strengthen your path forward. Sometimes, doubt whispers important messages worth hearing. It might point out places where you need more support or highlight aspects of a situation you haven't fully considered. Rather than pushing these thoughts aside, you can listen for their wisdom while staying grounded in your capabilities.

Learning to dance with doubt means balancing careful consideration and forward motion. You might pause to reflect on what your uncertainty tells you, gather information that helps you feel more prepared, or adjust your approach based on valid concerns. Yet you also recognize when doubt has served its purpose and it's time to move ahead.

Your sensitivity allows you to engage with doubt in nuanced ways. Instead of seeing it as simply negative or positive, you can understand its specific flavor in each situation. Does this doubt stem from needing more information? From past experiences? From genuine wisdom about timing? Each answer guides your next steps differently. This transformed relationship with doubt creates space for both careful consideration and confident action. Instead of getting stuck in cycles of questioning or rushing past necessary signals, you develop skills in working with doubt as a natural part of growth.

The Art of Balance

Finding a middle ground in your inner voice starts with accepting that both strength and struggle can exist at the same time. When facing a challenge, you might feel overwhelmed while also having the wisdom to handle it. Your sensitivity might make certain situations difficult while giving you unique insights others miss. Building this balanced perspective requires regular attention to your inner talk. When you catch yourself being overly critical, pause and ask what a more complete view might include. Notice the actual facts of a situation rather than letting assumptions or old stories take over your thoughts. This way of thinking develops naturally through steady practice. Each time you shift from harsh judgment to fair assessment, you strengthen new patterns in your mind. Small moments add up, acknowledging what worked and what didn't in a situation, seeing both your natural gifts and areas where you're still learning.

Your sensitive nature brings depth to this practice. You likely notice subtle shifts in how you talk to yourself, picking up on underlying tones and hidden assumptions. This awareness helps you catch unbalanced thoughts earlier and adjust them more skillfully. Rather than swinging between extremes of criticism or denial, you learn to hold multiple truths at once. Over time, this balanced dialogue creates a strong foundation for growth. You can look honestly at areas needing development while maintaining confidence in your core capabilities. This clear-eyed yet compassionate view supports lasting positive change.

Creating Inner Harmony

Inside your mind, various perspectives naturally arise as you navigate life. One voice might point out potential problems, while another highlights opportunities. The critical part notices what needs work, while the hopeful part sees possibilities for growth. Learning to work with all these voices, rather than letting anyone overshadow the others, creates a richer inner world. When these different viewpoints come together harmoniously, they offer more profound insight than any single voice could provide alone. The careful questioner ensures you've thought things through, while the visionary keeps you moving toward meaningful goals. The critic helps you spot areas needing attention, while the encourager reminds you of your strengths and progress.

Your sensitivity allows you to notice subtle differences between these inner voices. Instead of seeing them as conflicting forces, you can recognize how each contributes to your understanding. When faced with a decision, let each perspective share its wisdom: the practical voice considering logistics, the intuitive voice sensing underlying patterns, and the protective voice noting potential challenges. This balanced inner dialogue supports better choices and steadier growth. Rather than bouncing between harsh self-judgment and unrealistic expectations, you develop the ability to see situations clearly while maintaining compassion for yourself. Each voice adds its unique insight to create a more complete picture.

Seeds of Change

Small moments carry hidden power. You plant a seed when you catch yourself in self-criticism and choose a gentler thought instead. When you notice yourself feeling overwhelmed and respond with understanding rather than judgment, another seed takes root. These brief shifts might seem minor at the moment, but they gradually reshape your entire inner landscape. Your sensitivity makes you especially attuned to these subtle inner shifts. You might notice how speaking to yourself more patiently affects your energy throughout the day or how acknowledging your efforts rather than focusing on flaws helps you approach challenges differently. Each small change ripples outward, touching many areas of your life. Over time, these new patterns of thinking become more natural. The voice that once defaulted to harsh judgment learns to lead with understanding. The part that used to expect perfection begins to appreciate progress. What started as conscious choices becomes your natural way of relating to yourself and your experiences.

This transformation unfolds through steady attention to your inner world. Each time you choose more supportive self-talk, you strengthen these new patterns. Every instance of catching and adjusting an old habit builds momentum toward lasting change. The process requires patience and consistent practice, but each small shift contributes to meaningful growth. The beauty of this approach lies in its sustainability. Instead of trying to force dramatic changes, you allow transformation to emerge naturally from many small adjustments. Your sensitivity becomes an ally in this process, helping you notice subtle opportunities for positive change and appreciate the gradual unfolding of new patterns.

The Architecture of Strength

When you embrace your sensitivity instead of seeing it as something to overcome, a different kind of power emerges. This strength comes from understanding the value of your deep processing, emotional awareness, and ability to notice subtle patterns. Instead of trying to push through situations with force, you learn to move through life with wisdom and skill. Your natural way of experiencing the world deeply gives you unique insights and capabilities. Perhaps you notice early signs of tension in a group that others miss or sense essential aspects of a situation that aren't immediately obvious. When trusted and developed, these perceptions become valuable tools for navigating life effectively.

Building authentic strength means creating ways of living and working that honor your sensitive nature. Rather than exhausting yourself by trying to match others' pace or style, you develop approaches that use your natural traits effectively. You can process information thoroughly before making decisions or create spaces in your schedule for quiet reflection. True power grows as you learn to trust these natural inclinations rather than doubting them. Each time you honor your need for processing time instead of rushing, each instance of paying attention to subtle feelings rather than dismissing them, you strengthen this foundation. Your sensitivity becomes a source of clarity and insight rather than something that holds you back.

Rooted in Truth

Real power emerges when you fully recognize what makes you unique. Your ability to notice subtle details others miss, think deeply about situations and understand complex emotional dynamics aren't weaknesses to overcome but valuable gifts. When you truly accept these aspects of yourself, confidence grows naturally from this understanding rather than requiring constant outside approval. This inner knowing shows up in your whole being. Your shoulders relax instead of tensing against judgment. Your breath flows easier rather than catching with anxiety. Your movements become more fluid and natural rather than guarded. These physical changes reflect a more profound shift from trying to protect yourself to trusting your natural way of being.

Standing in your truth means honoring your natural rhythms and needs. Instead of forcing yourself to match others' pace, you trust your need for thorough processing. Rather than dismissing subtle feelings as oversensitive, you recognize them as valuable information. Each time you honor these aspects of yourself, your foundation grows stronger. This kind of power carries a different quality than many think of as strength. It doesn't come from pushing harder or being tougher. Instead, it flows from deep alignment with who you really are. Like a tree with deep roots, you can overcome life's challenges while maintaining your essential nature. The confidence that grows from this self-recognition has a quiet steadiness to it. You don't need to prove anything to anyone because you trust your own experience and wisdom. This creates freedom to share your gifts authentically rather than trying to fit someone else's idea of strength.

The Voice of Conviction

When you perceive things deeply, you often notice important aspects of situations that others might miss. These insights deserve to be shared, not hidden away, because they seem too subtle or complex. Finding your voice means learning to trust and share these perceptions in ways that feel natural to you. Speaking your truth doesn't require becoming more forceful or changing your thoughtful nature. Instead, it flows from recognizing the value of your perspective. Whether you notice early signs of conflict in a group, since important factors others haven't considered, or understand emotional dynamics at play, these insights matter.

Your natural tendency to process things thoroughly actually strengthens what you have to say. Instead of rushing to speak first or loudest, you can share deep and substance thoughts. This measured approach often carries more impact than quick reactions or aggressive statements. Clear expression grows stronger as you practice trusting your inner knowing. You might start by sharing observations in situations where you feel safe, gradually building confidence in your ability to communicate what you perceive. Each time you speak from this genuine place, your voice becomes more natural and assured. The power of your words comes from their alignment with truth, not from volume or force. Like clear water reflecting what lies beneath, your communication can reveal deeper understanding while maintaining its essential quietness and clarity.

Decisive Action

Your thorough way of thinking brings valuable insight into choices. Instead of seeing careful consideration as indecision, recognize how it helps you understand situations more completely. This depth of processing, when used effectively, leads to decisions grounded in genuine understanding rather than rushed judgment. Making choices becomes clearer when you trust your natural wisdom. You might notice subtle factors others overlook or sense essential aspects of timing that aren't immediately obvious. These perceptions add richness to your decision-making process rather than complicating it.

Learning to recognize when you have enough information marks an important shift. Instead of endless analysis, you develop skills in knowing when further consideration won't add meaningful insight. This doesn't mean rushing, it means trusting when your thorough processing has given you what you need to move forward. Each time you make a clear choice based on your deeper understanding, your trust in your judgment grows stronger. You begin recognizing patterns in how your insight serves you, building confidence in your ability to navigate decisions effectively. This confidence comes from experience rather than forcing yourself to be more decisive. The ability to adjust course if needed creates freedom in decision-making. When you trust that you can make changes based on new information or circumstances, you feel less pressure to make perfect choices. This flexibility, combined with your natural thoroughness, creates a powerful foundation for effective decisions.

Moving with Purpose

Movement becomes more powerful when it matches your authentic rhythm. Understanding that you process deeply lets you create approaches that work with this trait rather than fighting it. You might break larger goals into smaller pieces that feel manageable, or develop detailed plans that honor your need to think things through. Progress flows more smoothly when you align your actions with what truly matters to you. Instead of pushing yourself to match others' pace or style, you learn to trust your natural timing. This might mean taking time to fully understand each step before moving forward or creating space between activities to process and integrate experiences. Your sensitivity helps you notice what kinds of movement feel genuine and sustainable. You might sense when pushing harder would lead to burnout, or when taking a slower, more thorough approach would actually serve you better. This awareness becomes a valuable guide for pacing your progress.

Each step forward carries more impact when it comes from full understanding and commitment. Rather than scattered action or forced movement, your choices become more focused and intentional. This creates natural momentum, like a river finding its path, each aligned action makes the next one clearer and more natural. True progress often looks different for sensitive people. Success comes not from overriding your nature but from working skillfully with it. When you honor both your goals and your natural way of being, you create a sustainable movement toward what matters most.

The Strength of Limits

Setting boundaries flows naturally from understanding what you truly need. Your deep sensitivity helps you notice when situations drain your energy or when interactions feel overwhelming. Instead of pushing through these signals, you can use them as valuable information about where to draw lines that protect your well-being. Limits work best when they come from genuine self-knowledge rather than fear or defensiveness. You might recognize that you need quiet time between social events, space to process important decisions or environments that don't overwhelm your senses. These aren't signs of weakness, they're ways of honoring your natural way of experiencing the world.

Your ability to sense subtle shifts in your energy and mood helps you maintain healthy boundaries. You might notice early signs of overwhelm before they become severe, or recognize when certain situations consistently affect your wellbeing. This awareness lets you adjust your limits before reaching the point of exhaustion. Each time you honor your boundaries, you build trust in your right to maintain them. Whether declining an invitation that would drain you, creating space for processing time, or designing your environment to support your sensitivity, these choices strengthen your sense of personal authority. Setting clear limits actually expands your capacity for meaningful engagement. Like the banks of a river that channel its flow, good boundaries direct your energy toward what matters most. They create space for you to share your gifts effectively while maintaining your essential well-being.

Let me explain practical ways to create and uphold boundaries that protect your sensitivity while allowing meaningful connection.

Start by noticing your energy levels throughout each day. Pay attention to which situations leave you feeling depleted and which help you feel renewed. You might discover that long conversations in noisy places drain you quickly, while one-on-one talks in quiet settings energize you. This awareness helps you design interactions that work better for your sensitive nature.

Learn to recognize early warning signs in your body. Perhaps your shoulders tense when you need space, or your breathing becomes shallow when overwhelmed. These physical signals often appear before mental awareness catches up. When you notice these signs, take them seriously, they're your internal wisdom telling you that a boundary needs attention.

Practice saying no to things that don't serve you well. Begin with smaller situations where declining feels safer. Instead of agreeing to after-work events that leave you exhausted, you might say "I need my evenings for recharging, but I'd love to meet for lunch instead." Each time you honor these needs, saying no becomes more natural.

Create space between activities rather than scheduling things back-to-back. Your sensitivity means you need time to process experiences fully. Build in regular breaks during your day, even short ones help. This might mean taking a quiet lunch alone between meetings or spending a few minutes in nature between errands.

Develop responses for when others push against your limits. Instead of defending or explaining, try simple, clear statements: "This doesn't work for me" or "I'll need to think about that and get back to you." Remember that you don't need to justify your needs or convince others they're valid.

Living Truth

True power grows when you shape your life around what genuinely works for you rather than what others expect. This might mean creating a morning routine that starts with quiet reflection, designing your workspace to minimize sensory overload, or choosing projects that use your deep processing abilities effectively. Each choice that honors your nature adds to your foundation of strength. Living truthfully changes how you move through your days. Instead of pushing yourself to match others' social energy, you might schedule interactions in ways that feel sustainable. Rather than forcing quick decisions, you give yourself time to process thoroughly. Your schedule begins reflecting your actual needs instead of arbitrary standards.

This authenticity naturally extends into your work and relationships. You might discover ways to use your sensitivity professionally, perhaps noticing subtle patterns others miss or understanding complex situations more deeply. In relationships, you learn to share your perceptions honestly while maintaining boundaries that protect your energy. When you consistently honor your truth, something remarkable happens. The energy once spent trying to fit in or meet others' expectations becomes available for meaningful pursuits. You find yourself moving through life with more ease and confidence, not because you've become less sensitive, but because you've learned to work with this central part of who you are. Making choices that align with your nature creates a sense of coherence in your life. Your outer world begins matching your inner reality, reducing the strain of trying to be someone you're not. This alignment builds genuine confidence that comes from living authentically rather than meeting external standards.

Let me explain practical ways to live authentically in different areas while staying true to yourself under pressure.

Begin by examining how you spend your mornings. Instead of rushing into the day, create space for natural rhythms. If you think it best in early quiet, wake before others to have uninterrupted reflection time. If you need gradual transitions, build in time between waking and engaging with others. Let your genuine needs shape these important first hours.

Look at your work environment with fresh eyes. Notice what drains you and what supports your natural way of functioning. You might need a quieter workspace, better lighting, or regular breaks for processing. Instead of accepting standard office setups, find ways to adjust your space that honor your sensitivity. When others question these changes, remember they stem from a genuine understanding of what helps you work effectively.

Consider how you handle social connections. Rather than forcing yourself into draining social patterns, create authentic ways of connecting. This might mean deeper conversations with fewer people, choosing quieter meeting places, or being honest about your need for recovery time between gatherings. When friends pressure you to socialize more, explain that meaningful connection requires honoring your natural limits.

Examine your decision-making approach at work. Instead of trying to match others' quick responses, acknowledge your need for thorough processing. You might say, "I'll need time to think this through," or "Let me process this and get back to you." Frame your careful consideration as a strength that leads to better outcomes.

Look at how you recharge. Your sensitivity might mean you need more recovery time than others. Create regular rituals that truly restore you, perhaps time in nature, creative activities, or quiet reflection. When others suggest this is excessive, remind yourself that honoring these needs enables you to bring your best to everything you do.

Your sensitivity shapes how you handle challenging situations. Rather than pushing through overwhelm, develop strategies that work with your nature. This might mean stepping away briefly to process, writing out your thoughts before difficult conversations, or creating a structure that helps you navigate uncertainty. When others push for different approaches, stay anchored in what you know works for you.

The Dance of Adaptation

Your deep awareness helps you understand different situations clearly. Like water finding its natural path, you can sense when to hold steady and when to adjust your approach. This ability to read circumstances and respond thoughtfully comes from your natural sensitivity rather than trying to force change. Making skillful adjustments doesn't mean losing yourself. Instead, think of it as choosing how much of your inner world to share in each situation. Sometimes you might express your thoughts more directly, other times more carefully. The key lies in maintaining your core truth while varying how you present it. Your sensitivity gives you valuable information about when and how to adapt. You might notice slight changes in group dynamics that signal a need to shift your communication style, or sense when an environment requires you to protect your energy differently. These subtle readings help you navigate situations more effectively.

This flexible strength shows up in daily life. Perhaps you maintain your need for processing time while finding creative ways to meet work deadlines. Or you might honor your need for quiet while developing comfortable ways to participate in group activities. Each successful adaptation builds confidence in your ability to stay true to yourself while meeting life's varying demands. Learning to trust these adaptive abilities strengthens your foundation. Rather than seeing the need to adjust as a weakness, you recognize how your sensitivity helps you navigate life's complexities with greater skill and authenticity.

I want to share how you can remain authentic while adapting to various environments and expectations.

In professional settings, maintain your thorough processing style while finding ways to communicate effectively. Rather than forcing quick responses, you might say "I've noticed some important details I'd like to think through. Can I share my complete thoughts in tomorrow's meeting?" This honors your natural depth while meeting workplace needs.

During social situations, adapt the level of interaction while protecting your energy. You might fully engage in meaningful conversations for a while, then step away briefly to recharge. Instead of pushing through overwhelm, excuse yourself for short breaks: "I'm going to get some fresh air and will be back soon." This lets you participate while honoring your needs.

When handling family dynamics, acknowledge others' styles while maintaining your boundaries. If relatives push for more frequent contact than feel comfortable, suggest quality time on your terms: "I'd love to have a real conversation with you over tea next week instead of quick daily calls." This preserves connection while respecting your natural rhythm.

In busy environments, find ways to create small spaces of calm. This might mean wearing noise-canceling headphones during commutes, finding quiet corners in open offices, or taking brief walks between meetings. These adaptations let you function in stimulating settings while protecting your sensitivity.

When faced with pressure to make quick decisions, explain your needs clearly: "I make better choices when I have time to process fully. Can we discuss this after I've had a chance to think it through?" This maintains your thorough approach while acknowledging others' timelines.

Trust your subtle reading of situations to guide these adaptations. Your sensitivity helps you notice what adjustments each environment needs while staying connected to your authentic self. This creates flexibility without compromising your essential nature.

Creating Impact

When you trust your natural way of perceiving and engaging with the world, your presence itself begins shifting situations in meaningful ways. Your ability to notice subtle dynamics might help a tense meeting find better direction, or your deep understanding of others' feelings could transform a difficult conversation into a moment of real connection. Your careful observations often reveal important patterns others miss. In work settings, you might notice early signs that a project needs adjusting, or sense when team members need different kinds of support. These insights, shared thoughtfully, can help groups make better decisions and work together more effectively.

The depth you bring to relationships creates space for authentic connection. Your natural ability to sense what others feel, combined with your thoughtful way of responding, helps create conversations that matter. People often find themselves sharing more openly with you, knowing you'll understand nuances others might miss. Your impact grows stronger as you trust your natural gifts more fully. Instead of trying to be louder or more forceful, you learn that your quiet depth carries its own kind of power. A carefully considered observation, offered at the right moment, can shift an entire discussion. Your ability to hold space for complexity helps others see situations more clearly. This influence flows naturally from living authentically rather than trying to create specific effects. Each time you engage fully from your genuine nature, you create opportunities for meaningful change, often in ways you might not even notice at first.

The Path of Integration

As you develop trust in your sensitivity, various elements begin flowing together smoothly. The way you speak your truth, make decisions, and protect your energy starts feeling more natural and connected. Instead of thinking consciously about each aspect, you find yourself responding to situations with integrated wisdom that draws on all these strengths at once. This coming together happens gradually through real experience. Each time you navigate a challenging situation successfully, your confidence in your natural abilities grows stronger. When you speak up about something you've noticed and others benefit from your insight, trust in your perceptions deepens. As you maintain boundaries that serve you well, doing so becomes more automatic.

Your sensitivity actually helps this integration process. You notice subtle shifts in how different aspects of your strength work together, picking up on what combinations serve you best in various situations. This awareness helps you refine your approach naturally, without forcing change. Living in this integrated place changes how you handle daily life. Instead of questioning whether to speak up or hold back, you find yourself naturally choosing the right moment. Rather than analyzing whether to maintain a boundary, you respond smoothly to protect your energy when needed. These responses emerge from deep understanding rather than conscious calculation. The beauty of this integration lies in how it makes everything easier. You spend less energy thinking about how to handle situations because your various strengths work together naturally. This creates more space for engaging meaningfully with life instead of managing yourself.

Seeds of Transformation

Living authentically changes everything, not just how you feel inside, but how you connect with life itself. When you stop trying to be less sensitive and start recognizing this trait as a source of strength, your whole relationship with the world shifts. Like a plant finally getting the right conditions to thrive, you begin growing in natural and powerful ways. Each choice to honor your true nature adds to this transformation. When you trust your deep perceptions instead of doubting them, you might notice solutions others miss. Your careful way of processing situations often leads to more thoughtful decisions. The emotional understanding that once felt overwhelming becomes a gift that helps you connect meaningfully with others.

Your sensitivity gives you unique ways to contribute. You may notice early signs of conflict and help prevent problems before they grow. Perhaps your thorough understanding of complex situations helps groups find better solutions. Your ability to sense what others feel might create space for authentic connections that make work and relationships richer. This way of living builds on itself. Each time you successfully navigate a situation by working with your sensitivity rather than against it, your trust in this approach grows stronger. Every instance of sharing your insights effectively or maintaining healthy boundaries adds to your foundation of authentic strength. Moving through life from this genuine place creates a natural positive impact. Instead of trying to force change or prove your worth, you find yourself naturally contributing in ways that matter. Your presence itself, when fully authentic, often helps situations and relationships develop in healthier directions.

Habit 3: Energy Management System

The Energy Architecture

The concept of personal energy architecture stands as a profound truth about human nature. You see, each of us moves through life with distinct patterns of vitality and depletion that are uniquely our own. These aren't just simple cycles of being tired or awake, they represent a complex tapestry of mental, emotional, and physical states that shift throughout our days and weeks. Think about it deeply, some individuals burst with creative energy in the early morning hours, while their minds grow quiet as evening approaches. Others find their intellectual clarity emerging as the sun sets. These aren't random fluctuations, but rather manifestations of our internal energy signatures. It's fascinating, and more importantly, it's fundamentally meaningful.

When you begin to recognize and honor these personal rhythms, something remarkable happens. The daily challenges that once felt like wrestling with chaos start to feel more like flowing with a natural current. It's about understanding when your mind is primed for deep work, when your emotional resilience is at its peak, and when your body needs to retreat into restoration. This isn't just about productivity or self-improvement, it's about aligning yourself with your own natural order. By mapping and respecting these internal patterns, you transform your relationship with time and energy. The periods of fatigue become not failures to push through, but essential parts of your personal cycle that deserve respect. The moments of heightened capability become opportunities to engage fully with life's demands.

Consider how profoundly this understanding could reshape your existence. Instead of fighting against your nature, you learn to move with it. This isn't mere adaptation, it's the discovery of your own unique rhythm in the grand symphony of human experience.

Natural Rhythms Revealed

It's fascinating how our inner rhythms aren't just random fluctuations, but rather form a predictable pattern, like a fingerprint of vitality that's uniquely our own. Think about those mornings when you wake up feeling sharp and focused, your mind ready to tackle complex challenges. These aren't just good days, they're expressions of your natural energy signature. Then there are the quieter mornings when your system needs a gentler approach to engage with the world. Neither state is better or worse, they're both essential parts of your personal rhythm.

As the day unfolds, you might notice how your energy shifts and transforms. That afternoon lull isn't a failure of willpower, it's a natural part of your daily cycle, perhaps signaling a need for brief renewal. And those evening hours, when creative insights seem to flow effortlessly? That's your system operating in one of its peak states. Understanding these patterns transforms how you approach your day. Instead of fighting against your natural tendencies, you can align your most demanding work with your periods of peak capacity. When you know that your analytical abilities shine brightest in the morning, you can schedule your most complex problem-solving then. If creative work flows better in the afternoon light, that becomes your time for innovation. This isn't just about maximizing productivity, it's about living in harmony with your natural rhythms. By honoring these patterns, you turn the challenge of energy management into an intuitive flow, where each part of your day has its own purpose and power. It's about creating a sustainable relationship with your energy that supports both peak performance and essential recovery.

The Landscape of Depletion

Let me unpack this crucial insight into how different activities impact our inner resources. When you look closely at your daily experiences, you'll notice that certain situations affect your vital energy in profound and predictable ways. Consider the raw experience of navigating a bustling shopping mall versus sitting quietly in your backyard. For many people, especially those with sensitive systems, that crowded environment acts like a steady drain on their internal battery, while time spent in nature serves as a gentle recharge. This isn't merely about preference, it's about recognizing how different environments fundamentally shape our capacity to engage with the world.

The same principle applies to our mental exertion. Working on a complex project that requires deep focus might deplete your cognitive resources far more rapidly than handling routine emails or familiar tasks. Some social interactions, perhaps those requiring careful navigation of challenging dynamics, might demand a longer recovery period than casual conversations with old friends. But here's what's truly fascinating, your body and mind offer early warning signals long before you hit empty. That slight edge in your voice when responding to a simple question, or that barely noticeable tension creeping into your shoulders, these aren't random occurrences. They're sophisticated alert systems, telling you it's time to adjust course before reaching complete exhaustion.

By developing this heightened awareness of your system's signals, you move from constantly reacting to energy crises to skillfully managing your resources. It's like having an early warning system that lets you make small adjustments before major depletion occurs. This isn't about limiting your engagement with life, it's about sustaining your capacity to engage fully and authentically over the long term. Think of it as learning to read the weather patterns of your inner landscape. Just as a skilled sailor reads the clouds to navigate safely, you can learn to interpret these subtle cues to maintain steady engagement while avoiding the storms of complete exhaustion.

The Recovery Equation

Let me illuminate this fascinating relationship between energy output and restoration. Consider how each type of daily drain on your system calls for its own unique form of replenishment, much like different soils require specific nutrients to remain fertile. When your mind feels foggy after hours of intense problem-solving, you might discover that sitting quietly with your thoughts provides the perfect reset. Yet when you're emotionally drained from supporting others through difficult times, that same solitude might not be enough, perhaps you need the gentle presence of a trusted friend or the comfort of familiar routines to restore your emotional reserves.

Your body speaks its own language of recovery too. The tension that builds from long hours at a desk might dissolve through mindful movement, while the overwhelm from a day of sensory intensity, bright lights, loud sounds, and constant movement might require you to retreat into a cocoon of stillness and quiet. What's particularly crucial to understand is how the duration of recovery varies dramatically based on both the intensity of the drain and your personal capacity at that moment. Sometimes a ten-minute break between tasks might be sufficient to reset your system. Other times, especially after prolonged periods of intense engagement or when dealing with particularly challenging situations, you might need several days to fully restore your reserves.

This isn't about being weak or strong, it's about recognizing and honoring your system's sophisticated restoration needs. By mapping out these patterns, you can begin to structure your commitments in a way that allows for appropriate recovery time. Instead of pushing through until you crash, you learn to weave periods of restoration into your daily rhythm, creating a sustainable flow that maintains your vital energy over the long term. Think of it as conducting an orchestra where each instrument needs different care and attention. Some need frequent tuning, others require longer periods of rest, but all must be maintained thoughtfully to create harmonious performance over time.

Mapping Energy Cycles

Just as waves in the ocean follow patterns beyond individual swells, our energy moves through extended cycles that span weeks and even seasons. Think deeply about how your capacity for engagement ebbs and flows throughout the month. You might notice periods when ideas flow effortlessly and challenges feel manageable, followed by times when your system naturally calls for more gentleness and restoration. These aren't random fluctuations; they're part of your unique, energetic signature playing out across a broader timeline.

Your body's internal chemistry orchestrates some of these patterns. Hormonal cycles can profoundly influence energy levels, mental clarity, and emotional resilience. These biological rhythms interweave with external factors like changing daylight hours, shifting temperatures, and varying environmental demands. During winter months, you might find your system requiring more rest and internal focus, while spring could bring a natural surge in outward energy and creativity. Understanding these extended patterns transforms how you approach planning and commitments. Instead of maintaining the same intensity year-round, you can learn to flow with these natural variations. Perhaps you schedule major projects during your historically high-energy periods while protecting space for deeper rest when you know your system typically needs more recovery.

This isn't about limiting your potential, it's about aligning your ambitions with your natural rhythms. By recognizing and honoring these broader cycles, you create a sustainable approach to energy management that supports both periods of intense engagement and essential restoration. It's like understanding the seasons of your own inner landscape, knowing when to plant, when to harvest, and when to let the fields lie fallow. Consider this wisdom as a pathway to deeper self-understanding and more effective life planning. When you align your expectations and commitments with these natural cycles, you transform the struggle against time into a dance with your own natural rhythms.

Strategic Energy Investment

Picture each day as a sequence of waves, with distinct peaks and troughs in your mental clarity and physical vigor. During those brilliant moments when you feel most alert and capable, tackle your essential projects and meaningful work. These might be the early hours when creativity surges, or peaceful afternoons when your analytical abilities shine brightest. Notice these natural high points and align your crucial tasks accordingly.

The quieter periods, those times when your sharpness naturally dims, become perfect opportunities for simpler activities. Handle routine paperwork, organize your space, or complete familiar tasks that don't demand intense concentration. This natural ebb and flow creates a sustainable rhythm that honors your body's cycles. Life occasionally presents situations that demand exceptional effort, perhaps a vital deadline, crucial presentation, or family emergency. These moments require conscious choices about expending your reserves. By acknowledging these intense periods will need substantial replenishment afterward, you can plan accordingly. Clear upcoming commitments, arrange support systems, and establish specific practices to help your mind and body recuperate.

This approach isn't about avoiding challenges or limiting your impact. Instead, it's about making informed choices regarding when to push forward and when to preserve your resources. Understanding both your capabilities and restoration needs allows you to fully commit to important moments while maintaining long-term well-being. Think of it as conducting an orchestra of personal vitality; sometimes, certain sections need to play fortissimo, but you always maintain awareness of the overall harmony and balance. This mindful strategy transforms daily energy management from constant struggle into an artful dance of engagement and renewal.

The Restoration Arts

Sometimes, when physical tension has built up from stillness, a gentle walk or flowing yoga sequence awakens fresh energy in ways that lying down cannot achieve. These mindful movements send ripples of renewal through tired muscles and foggy minds, creating space for vitality to return naturally. The mind often seeks its own peculiar forms of refreshment. Engaging in playful creativity, perhaps sketching, writing, or crafting, can mysteriously restore mental clarity after hours of analytical work. These activities aren't mere distractions but rather act as bridges to renewed cognitive vigor.

Time spent among trees, beside water, or under open skies works remarkable transformations on our emotional landscape. Nature's rhythms have a way of resetting our internal patterns, washing away accumulated stress and restoring our capacity for resilience and connection. Understanding these nuanced pathways to renewal transforms how we approach self-care. Rather than viewing rest as an indulgence stolen from productivity, it becomes essential maintenance, as crucial as regular oil changes for a car or careful tuning for a fine instrument. This shift in perspective allows us to weave restoration into the fabric of daily life without guilt or hesitation.

By developing a personal palette of renewal practices that resonate deeply with your individual needs, you create sustainable patterns that support both intense engagement and thorough recovery. Think of it as crafting your own restoration garden, with different areas designed to nurture specific aspects of your well-being. Some spaces might invite physical renewal, others mental clarity, and still others emotional replenishment.

Building Energy Resilience

When you develop an intimate understanding of your personal thresholds, you begin to recognize the subtle signals your system sends long before exhaustion sets in. Perhaps you notice how your voice changes slightly when approaching your limits, or how your thought patterns shift when nearing cognitive fatigue. These early indicators become trusted guides, allowing you to adjust course before depletion takes hold. This deepening awareness naturally leads to establishing clear boundaries, not from a place of limitation, but from wisdom about what truly sustains you. You learn which commitments align with your capacity and which might require additional support or preparation. It's like developing an internal compass that reliably points toward choices supporting your well-being.

The beauty of this approach lies in its focus on skillful navigation rather than attempting to override natural sensitivities. Instead of trying to become less responsive to your environment, you learn to dance more gracefully with its challenges. Each experience, whether navigating a demanding project or managing an emotionally charged situation, adds to your repertoire of effective responses.

As this understanding deepens, recovery becomes more efficient. You develop a precise knowledge of which restoration practices serve different types of fatigue. Like a master craftsperson with a refined set of tools, you learn exactly which approaches best address physical exhaustion, mental fatigue, or emotional depletion. This growing resilience manifests not as toughness or immunity to stress, but as increased flexibility and wisdom in managing life's ebbs and flows. Every challenge successfully navigated adds another layer of understanding to your personal energy mastery, making future situations easier to read and respond to effectively.

The Balance Point

Maintaining vital force isn't about pushing forward relentlessly until collapse forces you to stop. Instead, it's about developing an exquisite awareness of your system's natural cadence. By noticing the subtle signals your body and mind provide, you can adjust your activities before reaching complete depletion. Perhaps you sense when to take a brief pause during intense work, or when to shift to gentler tasks as your energy begins to wane. Life's demands shift constantly, like changing weather patterns affecting that river's flow. What worked perfectly during summer's abundance might need adjustment during winter's slower pace. Career intensity, family needs, and personal projects each create their own unique patterns of demand and replenishment. Even your own internal landscape evolves, requiring different approaches to energy management during various life phases.

True sustainability emerges not from rigid adherence to fixed rules, but from cultivating adaptability while honoring core principles of balance. Some weeks might call for intense focus followed by significant recovery time. Other periods might thrive on a gentler, more consistent rhythm. The key lies in maintaining awareness of these changing needs while staying committed to the fundamental practice of energy balance. Consider it like sailing, you don't control the wind, but you can learn to adjust your sails skillfully as conditions change. This flexible responsiveness, combined with unwavering attention to maintaining equilibrium, creates a sustainable approach that can weather life's various seasons and challenges while preserving your essential vitality.

Forward Motion

When we truly understand our innate rhythms, we unlock a more graceful way of moving through the world, one that embraces our authentic nature rather than battling against it. Instead of viewing sensitivity as a limitation, we can recognize it as a sophisticated guidance system. Like a finely tuned instrument, our heightened awareness offers valuable feedback about which activities nurture our vitality and which situations require careful management. This insight allows us to craft days that flow with our natural tendencies rather than constantly swimming upstream.

Every time we successfully navigate a challenging period while honoring our needs, we add another layer of practical wisdom. Perhaps we discover that breaking intense projects into smaller segments maintains our momentum, or that certain types of rest rejuvenate us more effectively than others. These lessons accumulate into a personal playbook for sustainable living. The beauty of this approach lies in its compounding nature. As our understanding deepens, we become more skillful at reading our internal signals and responding appropriately. What once felt like limitations transform into useful information guiding us toward more effective choices. Gradually, we develop an intuitive sense of how to structure our lives to support both achievement and well-being.

This growing mastery opens up expanded possibilities for meaningful participation in life. Rather than exhausting ourselves through a constant override of natural rhythms, we learn to channel our energy strategically. Like a skilled sailor working with the wind rather than against it, we discover how to make progress while honoring our fundamental nature. Each refined understanding becomes another stepping stone toward a more sustainable and fulfilling way of being in the world.

The Daily Energy Blueprint

Picture creating a framework for your day that's both strong enough to hold you steady and flexible enough to bend with life's inevitable surprises. Think about how a thoughtfully designed schedule acts like a riverbank, it guides the flow of your energy without forcing it into rigid channels. You might discover that beginning your day with quiet reflection helps steady your system for later engagement. Perhaps you find that alternating focused work with brief renewal breaks maintains your stamina more effectively than pushing through long stretches.

The key lies in crafting routines that respect your natural patterns while providing reliable touchstones throughout the day. These aren't constraining boxes but rather supportive rhythms that help you maintain equilibrium. Like a skilled choreographer, you learn to sequence activities in ways that honor both your peak periods and natural lulls. Yet within this structure lives an essential flexibility, space for unexpected opportunities, challenging situations, or simply days when your energy moves differently. Some mornings might call for a gentler start, while others find you ready for immediate engagement. Your framework becomes a living thing, adapting to serve both your consistent needs and changing circumstances.

Over time, this balanced approach creates a sustainable way of moving through your days. Rather than exhausting yourself through rigid adherence to fixed schedules or becoming scattered without any supporting structure, you develop an artful blend of routine and responsiveness. This dynamic equilibrium allows you to engage fully with life while maintaining the delicate ecology of your sensitive system. Think of it as creating a personal energy blueprint that's both robust and adaptable, one that provides reliable support while remaining responsive to the natural ebb and flow of your vitality. Through this thoughtful design, you build a foundation for sustainable living that honors both your need for structure and your inherent sensitivity to life's varying demands.

Dawn's Gentle Opening

Rather than forcing our systems into sudden alertness, we can create a graceful transition from sleep to wakefulness that honors our natural rhythms. Picture emerging from rest like a flower gradually opening to the morning light. Instead of shocking your system with blaring alarms, you might allow natural light to filter through curtains, gently signaling your body that it's time to stir. This soft awakening preserves the delicate balance of your nervous system, allowing it to shift naturally from rest to activity.

The way we inhabit these early moments matters deeply. Perhaps you begin with a few conscious breaths while still lying in bed, letting awareness slowly return to your body. Gentle stretches might follow, like a cat awakening from a nap, allowing your muscles to release night's stillness without demand or force. Simple movements, rolling shoulders, flexing fingers, pointing and circling feet invite circulation to flow while respecting your body's need for a gradual transition. Creating the right sensory environment proves crucial during this delicate time. Soft, warm lighting helps eyes adjust without strain while maintaining relative quiet protects sensitive hearing from jarring input. You might choose to sit quietly for a few moments, allowing your mind to naturally orient to the day ahead rather than immediately reaching for phones or diving into tasks.

This thoughtful approach to morning transitions isn't about following rigid rules but rather about discovering what allows your system to wake most harmoniously. By honoring these subtle needs in the day's first moments, you establish a foundation of stability that supports whatever challenges lie ahead. Each gentle choice in these early minutes compounds into greater resilience as the day unfolds. Think of it as crafting a personal sunrise, one that allows your mind, body, and spirit to awaken at their own perfect pace, setting the stage for sustained vitality rather than depleted energy. Through this mindful attention to morning's opening moments, you create a launching pad for steady engagement with life's demands.

Midday Restoration Points

During the day's middle stretch, our natural rhythms often signal a need for recalibration. Instead of pushing through these dips with caffeine or willpower, consider how brief, intentional breaks can reset your entire system. Perhaps you notice your focus beginning to drift around 11 a.m. This becomes your cue to step away for a few minutes of conscious renewal.

These restoration points needn't be lengthy to prove effective. A five-minute walk outside can shift your entire perspective, allowing fresh air and natural light to revive tired senses. Even simply closing your eyes and taking ten deep breaths at your desk can create surprising clarity. Some find that gentle stretching or mindful movement helps release accumulated tension before it builds into discomfort. The art lies in timing these moments skillfully and learning to recognize the subtle signs that precede significant energy drops. Maybe you notice your shoulders tensing, your breathing becoming shallow, or your thoughts starting to scatter. These early warnings become valuable guides, telling you it's time for a brief reset before depletion sets in.

By scattering these small oases of renewal throughout your day, you maintain a steadier energy flow rather than riding the extremes of surge and crash. Think of it as regular tune-ups for your system rather than waiting for a complete breakdown to force rest. This preemptive approach allows you to maintain engagement with your work while honoring your body's natural need for periodic restoration. Consider these pause points as strategic investments in your day's productivity rather than interruptions to it. Each mindful break becomes a bridge carrying you smoothly through the hours, enabling sustained focus without the cost of complete exhaustion.

The Evening Descent

Like the sun setting gradually rather than plunging instantly to darkness, our minds and bodies benefit from a measured descent into night's quieter rhythms. Think of how these final hours hold special significance for sensitive systems. After navigating the day's stimulation, your body and mind need clear signals that it's time to begin powering down. You should start by dimming lights throughout your space, letting the softer illumination cue your system that activity is waning. Gentle stretching or slow walking might help release the physical tension gathered during desk work or concentrated tasks.

The key lies in discovering which practices most effectively guide your particular system toward calm. Spending time with quiet hobbies, perhaps reading, knitting, or listening to gentle music, helps create distance from the day's mental chatter. Others might need more active forms of release like writing in a journal to download lingering thoughts or practicing simple yoga poses to unwind from physical tension. Understanding your personal timing proves crucial in this transition. Your system requires a full hour of gradual deceleration to prepare for sleep, or you thrive with a shorter but more focused wind-down ritual. These aren't universal formulas but rather personal discoveries about what allows your unique nervous system to shift from engagement to rest most harmoniously.

Creating clear boundaries between daytime activity and evening restoration helps reinforce these transitions. Setting gentle but firm limits around work hours, screen time, or stimulating conversations signals to your system that it's safe to begin releasing the day's accumulated energy. Like drawing curtains at sunset, these boundaries help create the conditions for natural rest to emerge. Think of these evening practices as creating a graceful bridge between day and night, allowing your sensitive system to make this important transition without jarring shifts or resistance. Through this mindful attention to the day's end, you lay the foundation for deep restoration that will support tomorrow's fresh beginning.

Weekend Recovery Architecture

Instead of viewing weekends as simply "free time" filled with endless activities, consider how these precious hours can serve your deeper recovery needs. Your system might benefit from designating certain periods for complete stillness, perhaps a quiet Sunday morning where you allow yourself to simply be, without demands or expectations. These moments of genuine rest enable your nervous system to fully release accumulated tension from the week. The art lies in crafting a natural flow between gentle engagement and true restoration. Early hours might welcome invigorating activities that awaken your body mindfully, a leisurely walk in nature, unhurried yoga, or peaceful gardening. As the day progresses, you might transition to quieter pursuits that nourish without depleting, reading in a sunny corner, sketching, or simply watching birds visit your window.

Later hours can open space for meaningful connection but with careful attention to energy boundaries. Perhaps you enjoy an early dinner with close friends, knowing that evening hours need to remain protected for winding down. Understanding your capacity for social engagement while honoring your need for solitude creates sustainable patterns that prevent Monday morning exhaustion. These weekend rhythms work best when they flow naturally rather than following rigid schedules. Some mornings might call for extended meditation or journaling, while others find you drawn to gentle movement or creative projects. The key lies in maintaining awareness of what truly restores your energy rather than defaulting to busy activity or complete collapse. These weekend hours are a time for skillful resource management, not just recovering from the past week but actively building reserves for the one ahead. Through this mindful approach to larger blocks of free time, you create the conditions for deeper renewal that sustains your sensitive system through life's ongoing demands.

Emergency Reset Protocols

Let me explore the vital importance of having well-practiced recovery techniques ready for those intense moments when life suddenly demands more than we anticipated. Like a pilot's emergency checklist, these protocols provide reliable guidance when our energy systems face unexpected stress. These reset practices are your personal restoration toolkit, techniques you've refined through regular use during quieter times. Perhaps you've discovered that five minutes of specific breathing patterns can rapidly settle an overwhelmed nervous system, or that certain gentle stretches quickly release tension from your shoulders and neck. These aren't complex routines but rather simple, effective methods you can call upon instantly.

The power of these protocols lies in their familiarity. When you've practiced brief meditation during calmer moments, your system recognizes and responds more readily to these same techniques during stress. It's like having a well-worn path through challenging terrain, your body and mind know the route because you've walked it many times before. Creating these reset points doesn't require lengthy time investments. Maybe you find that stepping outside for three minutes of conscious breathing helps clear mental fog, or that a specific sequence of hand movements helps ground scattered energy. Some discover that humming quietly shifts their nervous system from fight-or-flight to calm, while others might use simple tapping techniques to restore balance.

The key lies in developing these practices before you desperately need them. Regular integration of these tools during ordinary days builds neural pathways that remain accessible even under pressure. It's similar to athletes who practice basic moves repeatedly; when a challenge arrives, these foundations provide stability and support. These protocols are your energy management insurance policy, not something you hope to need, but invaluable when circumstances push beyond your usual capacity. Through consistent practice and refinement, you build reliable methods for navigating life's unexpected demands while maintaining your system's fundamental balance.

The Flow State Framework

Picture your energy like a river finding its natural course, sometimes flowing swiftly, other times moving more gently, but always maintaining its essential momentum. The secret lies in developing routines that honor your unique rhythms while supporting sustained activity. Instead of pushing relentlessly forward or collapsing into exhaustion, you learn to recognize the subtle signals that indicate when to shift gears. Perhaps you notice how morning hours naturally support analytical work, while afternoon periods favor creative tasks or collaborative projects.

These transitions become most graceful when they align with your body's innate patterns. Like a skilled dancer moving between different sequences, you develop an intuitive sense of when to lean into focused work and when to ease into gentler activities. Some moments might call for intense concentration, while others benefit from lighter engagement or brief renewal breaks. The beauty of this approach emerges as these routines become second nature. Each day of successfully navigating between different energy states strengthens your understanding of what works best for your system. You might discover that alternating focused work with short movement breaks maintains stamina better than long stretches of uninterrupted effort, or that certain types of tasks naturally flow better at specific times.

Think of it as crafting a personal energy symphony, one where periods of intensity and quieter moments complement each other naturally. Rather than fighting against your sensitive nature, you learn to work with it skillfully. Every successfully managed day adds another layer of wisdom to your approach, refining your ability to maintain steady energy while meeting life's varied demands. This framework isn't about perfect execution but rather about creating sustainable patterns that support both productivity and well-being. Through consistent attention to these natural rhythms, you develop a flowing dance between activity and rest that enables lasting engagement with life's essential tasks.

Seasonal Adjustments

Winter's shorter days and longer darkness often signal our bodies to slow down, requiring more gentle restoration and quiet reflection. During these months, you might find yourself naturally drawn toward earlier bedtimes and slower mornings. Rather than fighting this tendency, consider how your daily routines could shift to honor this need for additional rest and internal focus.

As spring emerges, many experience a natural surge in creative energy and outward drive. Your system might welcome more dynamic movement and increased engagement during this season of renewal. This could be the perfect time to initiate new projects or expand social connections, working with rather than against your body's natural rhythms.

Summer's abundant light often supports peak energy and activity. Your capacity for engagement might expand, allowing for fuller schedules and more vibrant participation in life's offerings. Yet even in this season of expansion, maintaining awareness of your sensitive system's needs remains crucial for preventing depletion.

Autumn has a unique energy signature, often calling for a more measured approach as nature begins its transition toward rest. You might notice a natural pull toward completing projects and creating space for reflection, honoring your system's intuitive preparation for winter's quieter period.

The key is not rigid adherence to fixed schedules but developing routines flexible enough to adapt to seasonal shifts. Think of this as creating a living framework that breathes with nature's cycles while maintaining essential support for your sensitive system. Through this balanced approach, you develop sustainable patterns that serve you through all of life's seasons.

Building Sustainable Patterns

Understanding your energy patterns requires becoming a skilled observer of your own system. You might notice that certain morning practices set you up beautifully for focused work one season, yet need refinement as daylight hours shift. Perhaps meditation supports your energy best when done at dawn during summer months, while winter calls for this practice to move later as your body naturally desires more rest. The power lies in maintaining flexibility while staying committed to the core principles of energy management. Rather than clinging to methods that once served you perfectly, develop the wisdom to recognize when subtle adjustments might better support your current needs. Maybe a previously energizing exercise routine now feels depleting, signaling time for a gentler approach.

Each successfully navigated day adds another layer of practical knowledge to your understanding. You learn how different types of rest serve various forms of fatigue, how to read your body's early warning signals, and which practices most reliably restore your equilibrium. These insights compound over time, building a sophisticated toolkit for managing your sensitive system. Think of it as developing your personal energy mastery, not through rigid control but through deepening awareness and skillful response. Every challenge you navigate successfully and every recovery period you manage effectively strengthens your capacity to engage fully with life while honoring your natural sensitivity. This growing wisdom transforms what once felt like limitations into valuable guidance for creating a sustainable and meaningful life.

Through this thoughtful attention to your patterns and needs, you discover expanded possibilities for participation in life's offerings. Like a master musician who knows exactly how to care for their instrument, you develop an intuitive understanding of how to maintain your energy while fully expressing your gifts in the world.

The Path Forward

When you deeply understand your unique energy patterns, entirely new living approaches become possible. Instead of pushing through fatigue until you crash or withdraw completely to avoid being overwhelmed, you discover the artful middle path. Perhaps you learn that alternating focused work with brief renewal breaks maintains your stamina far longer than forcing constant productivity. You may notice how certain types of engagement actually energize you when timed appropriately, while the same activities drain you at other moments. This growing wisdom about your personal patterns creates a foundation for sustainable engagement. Like a skilled navigator reading subtle changes in wind and water, you develop an intuitive sense of when to lean in and when to ease back. Each successfully managed day adds another layer of understanding to your approach, refining your ability to participate fully in life while honoring your sensitive nature.

The beauty of this path lies in its continuous evolution. As your awareness deepens, you uncover increasingly nuanced ways to support your system's needs. What begins as basic energy management grows into a sophisticated practice of self-awareness and skilled response. Through this ongoing attention to your patterns, you build a greater capacity for meaningful engagement while maintaining essential balance. Think of it as cultivating a garden of vitality, one that requires consistent care and attention but yields increasingly abundant harvests over time. Each refined practice, each moment of successful navigation through challenge, strengthens your ability to live fully while honoring your fundamental nature. This isn't about reaching a final destination but rather about continuing to grow in your understanding of how to move through life with grace and effectiveness.

The Balance of Connection

Understanding how different types of interaction affect your energy creates the foundation for sustainable engagement. Some connections might naturally energize you, perhaps quiet conversations with close friends or collaborative work with like-minded colleagues. Other situations, though valuable, might require more careful energy management, like large group settings or emotionally intense encounters. Learning to recognize these distinctions helps you engage meaningfully while maintaining your internal balance. The skill lies in developing clear yet flexible boundaries that protect your essential vitality. Rather than automatically saying yes to every request or withdrawing completely to avoid depletion, you learn to assess each situation thoughtfully. Maybe you discover that scheduling demanding interactions during your peak energy times allows for fuller participation. Perhaps you find that building in recovery periods after intense engagements helps maintain your capacity for connection.

Creating sustainable patterns of engagement often means reimagining traditional social expectations. Instead of lengthy group gatherings, you might prefer shorter, more focused interactions. Rather than constant availability, you could establish specific times for deep connection while protecting your needs for solitude and renewal. Imagine it as conducting a beautiful orchestra of relationships, where each connection gets the care it deserves while keeping the harmony of your energy system intact. By embracing this balanced approach, you cultivate the ability to engage wholeheartedly in meaningful relationships, all while respecting your sensitive nature's need for thoughtful energy management.

This thoughtful attention to connection and energy enables the creation of rich, sustainable relationships that enhance rather than deplete your life force. The goal isn't isolation but rather finding ways to engage that support both genuine connection and personal well-being.

The Workplace Energy Matrix

The modern workplace often presents persistent sensory challenges, the hum of fluorescent lights, conversations floating across open spaces, and constant movement in your peripheral vision. Rather than merely enduring these inputs, you might craft strategic adjustments that create protective bubbles within challenging spaces. Perhaps you discover that positioning your desk near a wall reduces visual overwhelm, or that noise-canceling headphones provide crucial audio sanctuary during focused work.

Timing becomes a powerful ally in managing professional energy effectively. By mapping your natural peaks and valleys against your workday, you can align demanding tasks with your periods of highest capacity. Complex analysis might flow more smoothly during your morning clarity, while routine administrative work could fill those natural afternoon lulls. Understanding these patterns enables you to structure your calendar in ways that support rather than strain your system.

Team dynamics require particularly thoughtful energy management. Important meetings might benefit from brief centering practices beforehand and designated recovery time afterward. Rather than scheduling back-to-back interactions, you might build in small buffer zones that allow your system to reset between engagements. These aren't indulgences but rather essential practices that maintain your professional effectiveness.

Think of it as creating a personal energy infrastructure within your workplace. Just as buildings need proper ventilation and lighting systems, your sensitive nature requires thoughtful support structures to function optimally. Through careful attention to these needs, you develop sustainable ways to contribute your best work while maintaining your essential well-being. Building these workplace strategies isn't about limiting your professional impact but rather about maximizing it through skilled energy management. Each refined approach adds to your capacity for meaningful contribution while honoring your natural sensitivity.

The Social Energy Economy

Different social contexts create distinct energy patterns in your system. A quiet coffee with a close friend might actually replenish your spirits, while a crowded party could quickly drain your reserves. Some conversations flow naturally, requiring little conscious energy management, while others, perhaps those involving conflict or complex emotions, demand more careful attention to your internal state. The art lies in crafting social engagement that aligns with your natural rhythms. Instead of defaulting to extended group gatherings, you might discover that shorter, more intimate connections better serve both your relationships and your well-being. Perhaps you find that meeting friends for morning walks provides an energizing connection, while evening events require more recovery time.

Strategic planning transforms social life from a potential drain to sustainable joy. This might mean scheduling meaningful conversations during your peak energy periods or ensuring quiet recovery time after family gatherings. Rather than maintaining constant availability, you could establish clear windows for connection while protecting essential restoration periods. Consider it as nurturing a thoughtful approach to building relationships that fosters authentic connections and helps you preserve your valuable energy. Through this balanced engagement, you create space for meaningful bonds without sacrificing your sensitive system's need for careful management. Each thoughtfully planned interaction builds your capacity for sustainable social connection while honoring your fundamental nature. These aren't selfish boundaries but rather essential practices that enable you to show up fully present for the relationships that matter most. Understanding and respecting your social energy patterns can nurture deep connections while maintaining your internal balance.

Family System Dynamics

Deep familial bonds often carry their unique energy signature. The comfort of being with those who know you best can provide natural restoration, like settling into a familiar sanctuary. Yet these close connections might also intensify emotional currents, requiring skillful navigation of boundaries and needs. Perhaps you notice how shared meals nourish body and spirit, while extended family gatherings demand more careful energy management.

Creating sustainable family patterns requires open dialogue about personal needs. Instead of forcing yourself to match others' energy levels, you might establish a gentle understanding of your requirements for quiet time or solitary restoration. Morning hours could become a sacred space for individual reflection, while evening routines might center around calm connection, perhaps reading together or sharing peaceful activities that support everyone's well-being.

Weekend rhythms benefit from a thoughtful structure that balances togetherness with personal space. Maybe Saturday mornings feature active family time when energy naturally runs higher, while Sunday afternoons preserve space for individual restoration. These aren't rigid rules but rather flexible frameworks that honor family bonds and personal needs. Imagine it as creating a warm family ecosystem where everyone's unique rhythms are cherished and nurtured. Through this mindful attention to both connection and individual needs, you create patterns that strengthen bonds while maintaining essential energy boundaries. Each successfully navigated family situation adds to your understanding of how to blend meaningful togetherness with necessary personal care.

This balanced approach transforms family life from a potential drain to sustainable joy. By developing clear yet loving ways to express your needs, you enable deeper connection while honoring your sensitive nature's requirements for careful energy management.

Community Engagement Rhythms

Contributing to your community creates rich opportunities for impact and connection but requires thoughtful selection of how and where to invest your energy. Instead of dispersing your resources across many initiatives, you might discover deeper fulfillment through focused involvement in projects that deeply align with your values and natural abilities. Organizing small group discussions draws on your gift for creating intimate connections, while large public events quickly deplete your reserves.

Strategic timing transforms community participation from potential overwhelm to sustainable engagement. Morning volunteer sessions align with your natural energy peaks, while evening commitments require more careful management. Some roles allow you to set clear boundaries around your involvement, like project-based work with a defined scope rather than open-ended commitments that risk constant energy drain.

Think of developing specific niches where your sensitive nature becomes an asset rather than a limitation. Your heightened awareness might make you particularly effective at one-on-one mentoring or behind-the-scenes planning that requires careful attention to detail. By choosing roles that harness your natural strengths, you create sustainable ways to contribute meaningfully while honoring your energy needs. The key lies in maintaining clear boundaries around your involvement. Rather than feeling obligated to attend every event or respond to every request, you develop the wisdom to choose engagements that allow you to show up fully while preserving your essential vitality. This focused approach teaches you how to make a meaningful impact while maintaining personal balance.

This thoughtful participation enables lasting contribution to your community's well-being. By understanding and honoring your energy patterns, you create sustainable ways to share your gifts while protecting your sensitive system's need for careful management.

Digital Domain Management

Digital technology often generates an unrelenting stream of demands on our attention. Each notification, email, or social media update sends ripples through our nervous system, requiring energy to process and respond. Rather than remaining constantly available to these inputs, you might establish deliberate rhythms for engagement. Perhaps morning hours remain protected for deep work before opening digital channels, or you discover that batching email responses during natural energy peaks allow more effective communication while preserving internal balance. The art is creating clear structures supporting necessary connections without inviting constant drains. Instead of checking messages throughout the day, you could designate specific windows for digital communication while maintaining sacred spaces free from technological demands. Some find that using "airplane mode" during focused work provides essential sanctuary, while others benefit from removing social media apps from their phones to prevent unconscious checking.

Managing digital boundaries often requires reimagining expectations around availability. Rather than feeling obligated to respond instantly to every message, you might establish reasonable response windows that honor both professional needs and personal energy limits. Perhaps you communicate clearly that emails receive attention during designated periods, while urgent matters have specific alternate channels. Think of it as developing a sophisticated digital input filtering system that allows essential connections to flow while screening out unnecessary drains. Through this mindful approach to technology use, you create sustainable patterns that support genuine connection while protecting your sensitive system from constant stimulation. These aren't arbitrary restrictions but rather essential practices that enable you to engage effectively with digital tools while maintaining your vital energy. Each refined boundary strengthens your ability to use technology purposefully while preserving your fundamental well-being.

Professional Boundary Architecture

The modern workplace often operates with an assumption of constant availability. Instead of accepting this default, you might craft deliberate structures that better serve both your work quality and energy needs. Perhaps you block out specific "deep work" periods where notifications remain off and colleagues know to expect delayed responses. These protected windows enable the focused attention that complex tasks require while honoring your need for uninterrupted concentration. Communication about boundaries requires particular finesse. Rather than appearing unavailable, you might frame your approach in terms of enhanced productivity and quality. For example, explaining that you batch email responses at specific times allows you to provide more thoughtful replies while maintaining focus during project work. Setting clear expectations about response timing, noting that non-urgent matters receive attention within 24 hours, creates realistic parameters for interaction.

Meeting participation benefits from strategic planning. Instead of accepting every invitation, you could evaluate each gathering's essential purpose and your required contribution. When meetings prove necessary, you might request agendas in advance to prepare effectively or suggest time limits that maintain everyone's energy and focus. Building brief breaks between meetings provides crucial reset time for your system. Imagine these boundaries as a helpful framework that allows you to showcase your best contributions! Through careful attention to both workplace needs and personal energy requirements, you develop sustainable patterns that support long-term effectiveness. Each thoughtfully established boundary strengthens your ability to engage fully with work while maintaining essential well-being. These aren't limitations but rather vital practices that enable consistent, high-quality performance. By understanding and honoring your professional energy needs, you create conditions supporting meaningful contribution and personal sustainability.

Relationship Energy Investment

Each relationship carries its own unique energy signature. Time spent with longtime friends who truly understand your nature might feel effortless, even restorative, like settling into a comfortable conversation where no performance is required. These connections often provide natural renewal, allowing you to relax fully into being yourself. Yet building new relationships, while potentially enriching, typically demands more conscious energy as you navigate unfamiliar dynamics and establish mutual understanding. The art lies in creating sustainable connection patterns that honor relationships and personal needs. Instead of forcing yourself to maintain the same level of engagement with everyone, you might develop different rhythms for different bonds. You may schedule regular brief check-ins with certain friends, while others naturally flow into deeper but less frequent conversations. Some connections thrive through shared activities that energize both parties, like quiet walks or creative projects.

Understanding your personal capacity for engagement enables setting clear, kind boundaries. Rather than pushing yourself to attend every social gathering or remain in draining situations, you learn to recognize when you need to step back for renewal. This might mean choosing intimate coffee dates over large group events or being honest about needing to leave gatherings when your energy wanes. Think of it as developing a skilled approach to relational investment that allows genuine connection while maintaining your vital energy. Through this balanced engagement, you create space for deep bonds without sacrificing your sensitive system's need for careful management. Each thoughtfully planned interaction builds your capacity for sustainable connection while honoring your fundamental nature. These boundaries aren't selfish restrictions but rather essential practices that enable you to be fully present for the relationships that matter most. By understanding and respecting your social energy patterns, you can nurture meaningful connections while maintaining your internal balance.

Digital Detox Design

The constant ping of notifications and endless scroll of information creates a subtle but persistent drain on our nervous systems. Instead of remaining tethered to these digital demands, you might establish regular periods of conscious disconnection. Perhaps you begin each morning with an hour of offline presence, reading, journaling, or simply being still before engaging with the digital world. This morning sanctuary enables your system to find its natural center before facing external input.

Structuring your day with deliberate offline windows transforms digital use from a constant companion to a conscious tool. You could designate specific periods for email and social media engagement while maintaining other times as digital-free zones. Some find that afternoon breaks from screens help reset mental clarity, while others benefit from transitioning to offline activities several hours before sleep.

Clear communication about these boundaries prevents misunderstanding while supporting consistent practice. Rather than disappearing without explanation, you might inform colleagues and friends about your digital rhythm, perhaps noting that you check messages at specific times or maintain offline evenings. Setting realistic expectations about response timing enables others to adjust their patterns accordingly.

The Integration Dance

Life rarely presents demands in neat, isolated packages. Work projects overlap with family needs; social commitments interweave with personal obligations, and digital connections thread through everything. Rather than maintaining rigid separations, you might develop fluid approaches that adapt to changing circumstances. Perhaps you discover that some weeks support higher engagement in certain areas while others require pulling back to maintain balance.

The skill lies in reading these shifting patterns and adjusting your engagement accordingly. Instead of maintaining fixed responses, you learn to recognize when different aspects of life require more or less attention. Some periods allow for increased professional focus, while others demand a more significant emphasis on family connection or personal restoration.

Creating sustainable patterns requires ongoing attention to subtle signals. Your system might indicate through small signs, perhaps increased tension or scattered thoughts, when current arrangements need adjustment. These aren't failures but rather valuable feedback guiding you toward a more effective balance.

Sustainable Engagement Patterns

Understanding your unique engagement patterns creates a foundation for sustainable participation. Instead of swinging between overcommitment and complete withdrawal, you discover the artful middle path. Perhaps you learn that alternating periods of connection with intentional solitude maintain your capacity for meaningful involvement. You may notice how certain types of engagement energize you when adequately timed, while similar activities might drain you in different contexts.

The wisdom lies in creating flexible structures that support both connection and preservation. Like a skilled navigator reading weather patterns, you develop an intuitive sense of when to lean into engagement and when to protect your energy. Each successfully managed interaction adds another layer of understanding, refining your ability to participate fully while honoring your sensitive nature.

Building these patterns requires ongoing attention and adjustment. Rather than seeking permanent solutions, you recognize that different periods of life might demand different approaches. Some seasons might support greater external engagement, while others call for more intentional boundaries and increased restoration time.

The Energy Reservoir

The shift happens when we move beyond merely surviving daily to thoughtfully cultivating our well-being. Rather than pushing until collapse forces stillness, you might discover practices that continuously refresh your spirit. You may notice how brief meditation breaks throughout the day sustain your clarity or that particular gentle movement increases vitality rather than diminishes it. Developing this inner abundance requires understanding how your system generates and preserves strength. Like nurturing a thriving garden, you learn which activities replenish you and which subtle patterns might create unnecessary strain. Maybe you find that dawn's quiet moments fill your reserves more effectively than extended rest or that specific creative pursuits energize rather than exhaust when approached mindfully.

The skill lies in maintaining harmony between giving and receiving. Instead of waiting until complete depletion sets in, you develop an instinctive awareness of when to engage in restorative practices. This could mean taking short renewal pauses before fatigue emerges or ensuring regular periods of deeper nourishment that sustain your foundation.

Consistent attention to generating and preserving vitality allows you to meet challenges from a place of fullness rather than lack. Each refined approach deepens your understanding of maintaining this essential wellspring while engaging meaningfully with daily activities. This perspective transforms sensitive living from constant defense against exhaustion into an artful practice of energy stewardship. You create conditions supporting vibrant engagement and lasting resilience by honoring your need for regular renewal.

Daily Energy Conservation

Dawn hours present unique opportunities for establishing nourishing rhythms. Rather than plunging into tasks, you might begin with practices that replenish your spirit. Perhaps welcoming morning light while sipping tea allows natural awakening or fluid movement invigorates without demanding intensity. Selecting breakfast mindfully and foods that provide steady strength rather than temporary stimulation builds a foundation for balanced living.

Throughout the day, seemingly insignificant choices accumulate meaningful impact. Quiet pauses between activities, even moments of conscious breathing, enable natural restoration. Choosing spaces that support your sensitivity transforms the experience when feasible, such as finding a peaceful corner for focused work or selecting less stimulating venues for meetings.

Crafting thoughtful boundaries around challenging tasks shifts potential exhaustion into sustainable participation. Instead of pushing through demanding projects until depletion, you might divide them into manageable segments with renewal breaks. Recognizing which situations require extra preparation allows proper planning, perhaps scheduling quiet time after intensive interactions.

Weekly Resource Building

Larger blocks of unscheduled time allow your system to settle into genuine restoration. Instead of filling these precious hours with busy activity, you might designate specific periods for complete stillness. Perhaps early Saturday brings extended meditation or quiet reading that allows your nervous system to fully release accumulated tension. Time spent among trees or beside water can wash away the week's residual stress, restoring your natural rhythms.

Strategic planning prevents falling into deceptively draining patterns. Activities that seem relaxing, like endless social media scrolling or catching up on emails, might actually deplete your reserves further. Instead, you could structure weekends thoughtfully, maybe dedicating Saturday mornings to true renewal through nature walks or creative pursuits that energize rather than exhaust.

The afternoon hours might transition to gentle productivity, tasks that need attention but don't demand intense focus. Sunday could involve mindful preparation for the week ahead, perhaps organizing spaces or preparing nourishing meals, while maintaining the calm energy you've cultivated.

Monthly Strategic Planning

Observing your patterns across weeks reveals deeper rhythms in your capacity and needs. Perhaps you notice certain times when focus naturally sharpens, making those periods ideal for complex projects. Other phases might bring heightened sensitivity, suggesting the need for additional protective measures. Understanding these cycles enables proactive rather than reactive approaches to preserving well-being.

Strategic allocation transforms how you approach significant commitments. Instead of tackling major initiatives whenever they arise, you might align them with periods of natural strength. Routine responsibilities could fill times when your system prefers steadier, less demanding engagement. Building deliberate space between intensive projects allows proper restoration before the next challenge.

Creating buffer zones proves essential for maintaining stability. Rather than scheduling every available hour, you might reserve specific periods for unexpected demands or necessary recovery. This flexibility enables responding to sudden requirements without sacrificing your fundamental balance.

Seasonal Rhythm Recognition

Winter's shortened days and heightened darkness often signal our bodies to slow down naturally. During these months, your system might require additional quiet moments and deeper restoration. Rather than fighting this tendency, you could adjust schedules to include more gentle practices, perhaps emphasizing restorative movement instead of intensive exercise or creating cozy spaces for reflection and renewal.

Spring awakens different patterns in our systems. Like plants pushing through the soil toward sunlight, you might notice fresh energy arising naturally. This surge could support starting new projects or expanding activities, yet still requires thoughtful management to prevent overextension. Maybe morning hours become perfect for creative work while afternoons balance activity with gentle grounding practices.

Summer's abundant light often enables peak engagement with life. Your capacity for activity might naturally expand, allowing fuller schedules and more vibrant participation. Yet even in this expansive season, maintaining awareness of your sensitive system's needs remains crucial. Perhaps you structure demanding tasks during cooler morning hours while reserving afternoons for lighter engagement.

Autumn brings its own unique cadence, often calling for measured scaling back as nature prepares for winter's rest. You might feel drawn to completing projects and creating space for reflection, honoring your system's intuitive preparation for the quieter season ahead. This natural winding down supports building reserves that will sustain you through winter's darkness.

These seasonal shifts aren't limitations but rather opportunities to align more deeply with natural rhythms. Through conscious attention to these larger patterns, you develop increasingly sophisticated ways to preserve and direct your vital energy throughout the year.

Yearly Energy Architecture

Observing patterns throughout the year uncovers valuable insights about your system's natural flow. You might discover that February consistently challenges your vitality, suggesting the need for additional protective practices during winter's depth. Perhaps September will bring renewed clarity and focus, making it ideal for launching significant initiatives. July could emerge as a time when your system naturally thrives in more social settings, while November calls for increased solitude and reflection.

Understanding these broader cycles transforms how you approach significant commitments. Rather than distributing demanding projects evenly across months, you might cluster them during periods when your system historically demonstrates greater resilience. Gentler months could focus on building reserves and completing routine tasks that require less intensive energy investment.

Creating this yearly map involves noting both external demands and internal patterns. Professional cycles, perhaps busy seasons or regular project deadlines, weave together with personal rhythms and natural energy fluctuations. Family patterns, like school schedules or holiday gatherings, add another layer to consider when planning energy allocation.

The Preservation Practice

Building sustainable reserves requires skillful weaving of multiple approaches. Rather than relying solely on protective boundaries or restorative activities, you might discover how combining both creates more robust energy maintenance. Morning meditation helps generate inner quiet while carefully structured workdays prevent unnecessary drain. Weekly walks in nature could restore depleted reserves while thoughtful limits on commitments preserve existing energy.

The art lies in developing consistency with these practices before exhaustion forces rest. Like tending a garden, regular attention prevents problems rather than trying to rescue wilting plants. You might establish daily moments of complete stillness that allow your system to reset naturally. Weekly immersion in natural settings could wash away accumulated tension, while monthly periods of more profound retreat enable full restoration.

Creating this preservation practice involves understanding which activities truly regenerate your spirit.

Some might find that creative pursuits actually build energy when engaged mindfully, while others discover that certain forms of movement generate rather than consume vitality. Regular periods of solitude could serve as essential restoration points between social engagements.

Cultivating Abundance

The transformation begins when we move beyond merely defending against depletion to actively nurturing our inner resources. Instead of rationing energy through rigid boundaries, you might discover practices that generate natural abundance. You may notice that certain creative activities increase your vitality when approached with presence. Time spent in nature could multiply rather than deplete your reserves, while meaningful connections might energize rather than exhaust.

Recognizing your distinctive patterns allows you to foster environments where energy can thrive naturally. Like a skilled gardener who knows precisely what each plant needs to thrive, you learn which environments and activities support your system's natural vitality. Maybe early morning solitude creates an overflow of clarity that sustains you through busy days, or regular moments of stillness generate unexpected reserves of strength.

The wisdom lies in recognizing that abundance emerges through balanced attention to giving and receiving. Rather than constantly monitoring your energy levels with anxiety, you develop trust in your ability to maintain steady vitality. Each well-managed challenge adds to your confidence, while every effective restoration period deepens your capacity for generous engagement.

The Investment Strategy

Think of your vital energy as something precious that needs thoughtful care and attention. When you understand which activities drain you and which restore you, you can create better patterns for engaging with life. Instead of pushing until exhaustion forces you to stop, you learn to balance activity with renewal in ways that feel natural. Taking time to notice how different situations affect your energy reveals essential patterns. You might discover that morning sunshine helps you feel naturally energized, while artificial lighting leaves you feeling drained. Or perhaps you notice that creative activities increase your vitality when you engage with them mindfully.

Regular attention to these patterns helps you refine your approach over time. Some quiet moments restore you deeply, while others pass the time without real renewal. Certain kinds of engagement might energize you when timed well, even if they would feel draining at other moments. Understanding these subtle differences enables you to make choices that maintain your vitality.

The key lies in finding ways to participate fully in life while honoring your need for restoration. This might mean taking brief renewal breaks between activities, creating quiet spaces in your schedule, or choosing environments that naturally support your energy. These aren't restrictions but rather intelligent choices that help you bring your best to what matters most. As you develop this balanced approach, you discover an increased capacity for meaningful engagement. Rather than constantly struggling against depletion, you learn to move through life with steady energy that supports both active participation and essential rest. Each refined choice builds a greater understanding of maintaining this vital balance.

Sustainable Abundance Creation

Building steady vitality starts with understanding your natural rhythms. You notice what times of day you feel most energized when you need quiet moments, and how different activities affect your energy flow. Instead of pushing through fatigue, you learn to work with these natural patterns, creating space for both meaningful activity and essential rest. Developing strong energy reserves happens through daily choices that honor your needs. Like establishing a peaceful morning routine that sets a calm tone for your day or taking quiet breaks before reaching exhaustion. These aren't indulgences but vital practices that maintain your capacity to engage fully with life.

Think about designing your days with intentional space for renewal. When you recognize early signs of energy depletion, you can respond with restorative practices that work best for you. Spending time in nature refreshes you deeply, or creative activities help restore your spirit. Understanding these personal patterns helps you maintain steady vitality. The beauty of this approach lies in how it builds upon itself. Each time you honor your need for restoration before reaching complete depletion, you strengthen your energy foundation. Every successfully managed demanding period adds to your understanding of how to maintain balance. This growing wisdom enables you to engage more fully with life while maintaining essential well-being.

The River of Vitality

Your vitality moves in natural patterns throughout each day. Sometimes energy flows strongly, bringing moments of clarity and capability. Other times, it grows quieter, signaling the need for gentler engagement or rest. Learning to notice these shifts helps you move through life more effectively. Managing your energy well means developing awareness of what affects its flow. Certain situations might naturally energize you, while others require more careful attention to maintain balance. Understanding these patterns enables you to structure your days to support steady vitality rather than swinging between extremes.

When you align your activities with these natural rhythms, you discover smoother ways of moving through life. Instead of forcing yourself to maintain constant high energy, you learn to engage more fully when vitality flows strongly and step back for renewal when it naturally ebbs. This creates sustainable patterns that support meaningful participation while maintaining essential well-being. Your sensitivity actually helps you notice subtle shifts in energy that others might miss. These early signals become valuable guides, helping you adjust before reaching depletion. As you develop trust in this natural wisdom, you move through life with greater ease and effectiveness.

The Pulse of Energy

Think of checking your energy levels, like taking regular readings of an essential inner gauge. You might start each morning by noticing how restored you feel, check in during busy periods to sense your remaining capacity, and end your day by understanding what kind of renewal you need most. Your energy shows up in different forms that don't always align. Maybe your mind feels sharp and ready for complex thinking, but your body signals a need for rest. Or perhaps you feel emotionally strong and connected while your creative spark needs rekindling. Understanding these distinct aspects helps you make better choices about using your resources.

Developing awareness of these subtle variations brings valuable insights. You begin noticing patterns in how different activities affect your energy, which ones restore specific types of vitality, and which create particular kinds of drain. This understanding helps you structure your days more effectively. These regular energy checks become natural touchstones throughout your day. Instead of waiting until you feel completely depleted, you learn to notice early signals that suggest a need to shift activities or take time for renewal. This ongoing awareness helps you maintain steady vitality rather than swinging between extremes. Your sensitivity gives you access to nuanced information about your energy state. Paying attention to these subtle signals allows you to adjust your engagement before reaching exhaustion. This creates smoother transitions between activity and rest, helping you maintain sustainable energy levels daily.

The Art of Adjustment

Regular attention to your energy levels enables small adjustments that prevent larger problems. When you notice your morning energy emerging more slowly than usual, you might shift important tasks slightly later rather than forcing yourself to match your typical schedule. These gentle modifications help maintain your natural rhythm while still accomplishing what matters.

Responding to changing conditions requires ongoing awareness. Some days might need more space between activities than others, or certain tasks might demand additional recovery time. By noticing these subtle needs early, you can adjust your approach before getting overwhelmed. This helps maintain steady energy even when circumstances shift unexpectedly.

Building extra space into your plans allows room for natural variation. Instead of scheduling things back-to-back, you might create buffer zones that can expand or contract based on your daily needs. This flexibility helps you maintain stability even when energy patterns fluctuate.

Recovery's Sacred Space

Recovery spaces serve a vital purpose in maintaining your well-being. Instead of pushing through until exhaustion stops you, you learn to create regular pauses that allow natural restoration. Think of these moments not as breaks from life but as essential parts of living effectively. Understanding different kinds of tiredness helps you choose the right way to restore yourself. When your mind feels foggy from complex thinking, you might need quiet reflection time or gentle movement to clear your thoughts. If your emotions feel drained from intense connections, seeking solitude in nature might restore your spirit. Physical tiredness could call for rest, while sensory overload might require finding calm and quiet spaces.

Your sensitivity gives you clear signals about what kind of recovery you need. You might notice when mental effort affects your clarity or emotional engagement begins depleting your reserves. These subtle signs help you choose recovery practices that match your current needs. Creating reliable ways to restore yourself transforms how you handle daily challenges. Instead of reaching complete exhaustion before resting, you develop regular practices that maintain your energy. This might mean taking brief renewal breaks between activities, finding quiet moments during busy days, or setting aside longer periods for deeper restoration.

The Balance Dance

Keeping your energy balanced requires ongoing attention to subtle shifts. You might notice early signs that your reserves are dipping; perhaps your thoughts become less clear, or your emotions feel more intense than usual. These quiet signals help you adjust before reaching complete depletion. Creating balance means paying attention to what drains and restores you. When you know an important presentation lies ahead, you might schedule quiet time afterward for recovery. During intensive projects, you could build in regular moments for renewal rather than waiting until the work finishes. These thoughtful choices help maintain steady energy through demanding periods.

Your sensitivity helps you notice small changes that signal the need for adjustment. Before obvious fatigue sets in, you might sense a slight shift in your focus or a subtle change in how you respond to others. These early warnings enable you to make minor changes that prevent larger energy drops. Maintaining balance transforms how you move through your days. Instead of swinging between intense activity and complete exhaustion, you learn to navigate with smaller, more frequent adjustments. This creates smoother energy flow and more sustainable engagement with life's demands.

Foundations of Sustainability

Developing sustainable vitality starts with noticing how different parts of your life affect your energy. Depending on its lighting, noise levels, and overall feeling, your living space might either restore or drain you. Work patterns could support or strain your natural rhythms based on how they align with your peak energy times and needed rest periods. Understanding these deeper patterns helps you create structures that work with your nature. You might arrange your workspace to protect you from overwhelming sensory input or schedule essential tasks during times when you naturally feel most clear and focused. When you notice certain activities consistently restoring your energy, you can build them into your routine.

Your relationships play a crucial role in maintaining steady vitality. Some connections might naturally energize you, while others require more careful attention to boundaries. Learning which interactions support your well-being helps you create sustainable patterns of engagement that maintain rather than deplete your energy. Personal practices become essential foundations for lasting vitality. Regular renewal activities, whether quiet reflection time or gentle movement, help maintain your natural energy flow. Creating consistent ways to process experiences and restore yourself prevents depletion from building up over time. Your physical environment greatly influences your energy levels. Consider how your home supports or hinders natural restoration. Simple adjustments to lighting, sound, or organization can create spaces that help maintain your vitality rather than drain it.

The Monitoring Matrix

Watching your energy flow reveals important patterns in your daily life. You might notice that certain regular activities consistently refresh you while others quietly drain your reserves. Some environments naturally support your vitality, while others require extra energy to navigate. These observations help you make more informed choices about structuring your days. Checking in with yourself throughout the day uncovers valuable information. Morning reviews help you assess your starting energy and plan accordingly. Midday pauses let you notice if adjustments are needed. Evening reflections reveal what worked well and what might need changing tomorrow. Each check adds to your understanding of your personal patterns.

Your sensitivity helps you pick up early signals before problems develop. You might sense a slight shift in your focus, a subtle change in your emotional state, or a quiet feeling that something needs attention. These early warnings enable you to adjust course before reaching depletion.

Understanding your patterns deeply transforms how you handle daily life. Instead of pushing through until exhaustion forces you to stop, you learn to recognize and respond to early signs that you need to shift activities or take time for renewal. This creates a smoother energy flow and prevents the buildup of excessive fatigue.

Calibration's Gentle Touch

Regular attention to how your system responds to different situations helps refine your understanding over time. Certain morning practices set a steadier tone for your day, or specific kinds of breaks restore you more effectively than others. These insights enable increasingly skillful adjustments to maintain your vitality. Making small refinements often works better than large changes. When your energy starts to dip, slight modifications to your schedule or environment might be enough to restore balance. These gentle adjustments help maintain a steady flow without creating additional strain from dramatic shifts.

Your sensitivity serves as a sophisticated guidance system for these refinements. Before apparent signs of fatigue appear, you might sense subtle changes in your clarity or emotional state that suggest a need for adjustment. These early signals help you maintain balance through small, timely changes rather than waiting for major problems to develop. Understanding both patterns and exceptions strengthens your ability to maintain steady energy. While regular reviews help you see broader trends, staying attuned to daily variations enables flexible responses to changing needs. This combination of structured awareness and intuitive adjustment creates more sustainable patterns over time.

The Sustainability Cycle

Understanding your energy moves through natural cycles of learning and growth. Each time you notice how different activities affect you, adjust your approach and see the results, you build more profound wisdom about what helps you thrive. These cycles of discovery strengthen your ability to maintain steady vitality. Your sensitivity helps you recognize subtle patterns in how your energy flows throughout days and weeks. You might notice seasonal changes in what restores you or how different types of engagement affect your need for renewal. This awareness grows richer over time, enabling more skillful choices about structuring your life.

Moving with these natural cycles changes how you approach daily living. Instead of pushing through exhaustion or withdrawing completely, you learn to navigate between engagement and rest sustainably. Each successful adjustment adds to your understanding of maintaining steady energy while participating fully in life. This approach's beauty lies in transforming energy management from a constant battle into a natural rhythm. Maintaining balanced energy becomes more intuitive as you develop a greater understanding of your patterns. What once required careful monitoring gradually shifts into fluid movement between activity and restoration.

Vision of Vitality

Working with your natural rhythms transforms daily living. When you stop fighting against your sensitivity and start using it as a guide, you discover more effective ways to participate in life's activities. Your deep awareness becomes a valuable tool for knowing when to engage fully and when to step back for renewal. Managing your energy skillfully opens up fresh possibilities. Instead of exhausting yourself by pushing through fatigue, you learn to maintain steady vitality that supports meaningful involvement in what matters most. This might mean structuring your days around your natural energy peaks, creating regular renewal practices that truly restore you, or designing your environment to support rather than drain your resources.

Your sensitivity actually helps you develop more sophisticated energy patterns. You notice subtle shifts that others might miss, helping you adjust before reaching depletion. These early signals guide you in maintaining balance while staying actively engaged in life. This approach builds upon itself naturally. Each time you successfully navigate a demanding period while maintaining your energy, you strengthen your understanding of what works for you. Every refined practice adds to your ability to participate fully in life while honoring your restoration needs. The journey toward sustainable vitality continues evolving as you develop a deeper awareness of your patterns. Rather than reaching a fixed destination, you keep discovering new ways to align your energy management with both your sensitive nature and your meaningful goals.

The Path Forward

Creating sustainable patterns requires ongoing attention and practice but leads to profound shifts in how you move through each day. Instead of fighting constant exhaustion or withdrawing to avoid overwhelm, you learn to navigate between activity and rest in ways that maintain your vitality while allowing meaningful participation. Your sensitivity becomes a valuable guide in this process. The same deep awareness that can make you tire more easily also helps you notice subtle signals about what restores or depletes your energy. When you learn to trust these early signs, they guide you in making choices that support steady vitality.

Each successful experience strengthens your understanding. You may discover that taking brief renewal breaks helps you maintain focus longer than pushing through fatigue. Or you might notice that certain kinds of activities actually energize you when timed well, even if they would feel draining at other moments. Over time, managing your energy becomes more natural and intuitive. What starts as careful monitoring gradually shifts into fluid movement between engagement and restoration. You develop increasing trust in your ability to participate fully in life while maintaining essential balance. This approach's beauty lies in transforming sensitivity from a limitation into a strength. Rather than seeing your need for careful energy management as a weakness, you recognize how it enables you to engage more deeply and sustainably with what matters most.

Habit 4: Emotional Intelligence Development

The Emotional Landscape

Within the depths of emotionally attuned people lies a profound capacity for experiencing life's full spectrum. These individuals don't merely observe the world; they feel it coursing through their very being, creating a rich tapestry of sensations and insights illuminating their internal and external landscapes. While sometimes overwhelming, this heightened awareness serves as an extraordinary compass for understanding oneself and others. When we learn to decode these emotional signals, what might initially feel like an unbearable flood of feelings becomes a sophisticated guidance system. It's rather like developing a new sense, one that reveals layers of meaning in everyday experiences that others might miss entirely. The sensitive soul perceives subtle shifts in atmosphere, unspoken tensions, and moments of genuine connection that together form a more complete picture of reality.

When properly understood and channeled, this emotional intelligence transforms from what might seem like a burden into a remarkable gift. By embracing rather than resisting these deep feelings, sensitive individuals can access profound wisdom about human nature and the underlying currents that shape our collective experience. Their natural ability to process complex emotional information becomes a source of strength rather than vulnerability. The key lies in recognizing that this sensitivity isn't a flaw to be corrected but rather a finely tuned instrument for understanding life's deeper dimensions. By accepting and working with this heightened awareness, these individuals can develop an extraordinary capacity for empathy, creativity, and insight that enriches their lives and those of everyone around them.

Trigger Territory

Beneath our everyday experiences lies a complex network of emotional tripwires connected to past experiences, core beliefs, and unresolved tensions. These triggers often catch us off guard, like underwater currents suddenly pulling us into emotional depths we didn't expect to encounter. A simple phrase, a particular tone of voice, or even the quality of light in a room can activate powerful emotional responses that seem disproportionate to the present moment. Yet these triggers aren't arbitrary; they're more like signposts pointing toward essential parts of our psychological landscape that need attention. They become valuable teachers when we approach them with curiosity rather than judgment. Each emotional surge carries information about what matters to us, what we fear, and what remains unresolved in our inner world.

The process of mapping these trigger points is like creating an emotional atlas. By carefully noting when and how these reactions arise, we begin to see patterns emerge. Some people might consistently react to perceived criticism, while others might be particularly sensitive to feeling excluded or overlooked. These patterns often trace back to formative experiences that shaped our way of interpreting the world. The real power comes when we shift from being unconsciously ruled by these triggers to consciously working with them. This doesn't mean suppressing our emotional responses; it involves developing the capacity to recognize when we've been triggered and respond thoughtfully instead of reactively. This transformation turns our triggers from sources of distress into opportunities for deeper self-understanding and personal growth. We can gradually rewire our automatic responses by engaging with our triggers mindfully. What once sent us into an emotional tailspin might become a moment of pause and reflection. In this way, our emotional triggers become not just challenges to overcome but gateways to greater emotional freedom and authenticity.

The Response Matrix

Our emotional response systems operate like intricate neural networks, where a single input can create a chain reaction of interconnected responses. Picture a stone dropped into still water; the initial impact creates not just one ripple but concentric circles that spread outward with varying intensity and speed. Similarly, when we encounter an emotional trigger, it often initiates a sequence of responses that unfold over time. These emotional cascades follow distinct patterns unique to each individual. For some, an emotional trigger might first manifest as a subtle physical sensation, perhaps a tightening in the chest or a slight change in breathing. This initial response then ripples outward, potentially intensifying into more pronounced emotional states; anxiety might bloom into fear, or irritation might deepen into anger. Finally, the experience often requires a period of reflection and integration, like waves gradually returning to stillness. Understanding these personal response patterns gives us invaluable insight into our emotional landscape. Some situations might act like emotional accelerants, rapidly intensifying our reactions and requiring immediate attention. Others might create slower, more subtle shifts that build gradually over time, demanding different management approaches. By recognizing these patterns, we can develop tailored strategies for each type of response.

This self-knowledge becomes particularly powerful in challenging situations. When we understand our typical response sequences, we can better anticipate and prepare for emotional challenges. We might recognize early warning signs that have previously gone unnoticed or identify specific points in our response pattern where intervention is most effective. This deeper understanding transforms our relationship with emotional responses from one of reactivity to one of informed navigation. Rather than being caught off guard by our emotional cascades, we become skilled observers and guides of our inner experience, able to work with rather than against our natural response patterns.

Intensity's Hidden Language

Our emotional intensity functions as a sophisticated internal communication system, speaking to us through varying levels of feeling and sensation. As pain tells us about physical boundaries, emotional intensity delivers crucial messages about our psychological and spiritual well-being. These aren't random outbursts to be suppressed but rather intelligent signals carrying specific information about our relationship with ourselves and our environment. Think of emotional intensity as having its own vocabulary, where the strength of feeling corresponds to the urgency or importance of the message. A gentle unease might whisper about small misalignments in our daily choices, like when something doesn't quite fit with our values. Moderate emotional responses often point to areas that need attention but aren't critical, perhaps relationships that require maintenance or personal boundaries that need slight adjustments.

When we experience intense emotional reactions, these are like emergency broadcasts from our deeper selves. Such powerful responses often indicate significant boundary violations, unmet core needs, or compromised essential values. The intensity itself serves as an exclamation point, highlighting issues that demand immediate attention and shouldn't be ignored. The real skill lies in learning to calibrate our emotional reading system. By paying attention to the nuances of our emotional responses over time, we develop a more sophisticated understanding of what different intensity levels mean for us personally. This isn't about judging some emotions as "too much" or "too little," but rather about understanding what each level of intensity is trying to communicate. By treating emotional intensity as a language rather than a problem, sensitive individuals can transform what might seem like overwhelming feelings into valuable guidance. This shift in perspective allows us to work with our emotional nature rather than against it, using the full spectrum of our feelings as a sophisticated navigation system for life's complexities.

The Cycle of Feeling

Our emotional lives move with a natural ebb and flow, much like tides responding to unseen forces. When we study these patterns closely, we find that feelings don't simply strike at random; they follow distinct cycles of emergence, intensification, expression, and release. A wave of sadness might rise gradually, reach its peak, and slowly recede. Joy might spark suddenly, burn brightly, and gently fade into contentment. Understanding these emotional rhythms transforms our relationship with intense feelings. Instead of seeing strong emotions as endless states that might overwhelm us, we begin to recognize them as temporary visitors moving through our emotional landscape. This knowledge brings comfort; even the most powerful feelings will eventually shift and change, making space for new experiences.

Each person's emotional cycles have their unique timing and character. Some might process anger quickly, letting it flash hot and fade fast, while grief might need longer to work its way through their system. Excitement might build in predictable stages, while anxiety might follow more complex intensity patterns. We develop a more nuanced understanding of our emotional nature by mapping these personal patterns.

This deeper awareness of our emotional cycles becomes particularly valuable during intense experiences. When we know that feelings move in predictable patterns, we can better gauge where we are in the cycle and what might come next. This knowledge helps us respond more effectively, perhaps creating space for processing when we recognize the beginning of an emotional wave or seeking support when we know we're entering a challenging part of the cycle. Recognizing these patterns also helps us develop more self-compassion. Instead of fighting against our emotional rhythms or forcing feelings to move faster than they naturally do, we can work with these cycles, giving each emotion the time and space it needs to complete its natural course through our experience.

Recovery's Gentle Time

Small emotional bumps might only need a few quiet minutes to settle. We're back on track after a brief walk and some deep breaths. But the bigger waves? They demand their own timeline. Major emotional events carve deeper channels through our inner landscape. These experiences, whether a heated conflict, a profound disappointment, or an unexpected joy, often need days to process fully. Trying to rush this natural integration period is like trying to force a flower to bloom faster. It simply doesn't work.

Our bodies and minds have their own wisdom about healing rhythms. Sometimes, we need solitude, curled up with our thoughts, or lost in gentle activities that don't demand much from us. Other times, we might process better through movement, walking, dancing, or working with our hands. The key is learning to trust these instincts. Each person's recovery pattern tells a unique story. Some might bounce back quickly from social stress but need extended time after emotional confrontations. Others might weather criticism well but require longer to process praise or success. Understanding these personal patterns helps us protect the time we need without judgment or guilt.

This knowledge becomes practical wisdom when planning our lives. If we know certain situations typically need longer recovery times, we can build buffer zones around them. We may not schedule important meetings right after emotionally charged events. Perhaps we leave extra space on our weekends after socially demanding weeks. It's not about limitation, it's about honoring our emotional needs with the same respect we give to physical ones. The beauty lies in accepting that different experiences leave different emotional footprints, each deserving their own path to resolution. When we permit ourselves to take the time we need, we often find we actually need less of it. There's a paradox there, the more we accept our natural recovery rhythms, the more efficiently our emotional system processes experiences.

The Pattern Recognition Dance

It starts with tiny revelations. A slight tension in the jaw becomes a familiar messenger, whispering of stress before we consciously register feeling overwhelmed. The subtle quickening of breath might signal approaching anxiety, while a familiar restlessness in our hands could herald rising frustration. Once invisible to us, these bodily whispers transform into clear early warning systems. Our emotional patterns weave through time in predictable ways, though we rarely notice initially. That mid-afternoon irritability might have less to do with our colleagues and more to do with blood sugar patterns. The heightened sensitivity during certain lunar phases or seasons isn't mystical; it's our body's natural rhythm playing out in emotional responses.

Sometimes, the patterns surprise us with their precision. We might discover that rainy Mondays combined with looming deadlines consistently trigger a specific type of anxiety. Or that family gatherings followed by social obligations create unique emotional exhaustion requiring specific recovery strategies. These insights arrive like pieces of a puzzle, gradually revealing a larger picture of our emotional landscape. The real magic happens when we start anticipating these patterns. A challenging meeting scheduled for 4 PM? We may need that protein-rich snack at 3:30. Holiday season is approaching. Time to strengthen our emotional support systems and adjust our expectations. It's not about control, it's about dancing with our patterns rather than being blindsided by them. Each new pattern we recognize becomes part of our emotional toolbox. The more we understand these intricate dances of feeling and circumstance, the more gracefully we can move through our emotional world. We become like skilled sailors, reading the weather of our inner seas with increasing accuracy and responding with hard-won wisdom.

This growing awareness transforms our relationship with our emotional nature. Instead of viewing ourselves as being at the mercy of unpredictable feelings, we become skilled interpreters of our inner world's complex language.

Integration's Sacred Space

Some feelings slip through us like summer rain, barely leaving a trace. Others sink deep into our bones, demanding we stop and listen. These more profound experiences can't be rushed away or filed for later; they need their own sacred time for processing and understanding. Think of emotional integration like digestion. Just as our bodies need time to break down and absorb food, our psyche needs space to process significant emotional experiences. Pushing too hard or moving too fast means we miss a vital understanding of nutrients. Sometimes this means saying no to external demands. Sometimes it means sitting quietly with our feelings while the world rushes by outside.

Movement often speaks when words fail. A slow walk might untangle complex emotions better than hours of thinking. Drawing, dancing, or working with clay can shape feelings that defy verbal expression. Each person's integration tools are as unique as their fingerprints; what soothes one soul might agitate another. The wisdom lies in matching the method to the moment. A minor disappointment might dissolve during a morning shower while processing grief could require weeks of gentle attention. Learning these differences helps us respond appropriately to each emotional experience.

Regular integration practices into daily life create a container for this essential work. It could be ten minutes of morning journaling or an evening walk under the stars. These aren't indulgences; they're necessary maintenance for emotional well-being, as vital as sleep or food. When we honor our need for emotional integration time, something remarkable happens. Our capacity for handling life's intensities actually grows. Like a well-tended garden, our emotional world becomes more resilient and productive when given the care it needs.

The Wisdom Within

Our emotions carry messages as precise as any scientific instrument. A flash of unease in a seemingly pleasant conversation might alert us to subtle manipulation we haven't consciously noticed yet. The sudden lift in our spirits when entering a particular space could signal an environment that profoundly aligns with our needs. These aren't random reactions; they're sophisticated readings of reality that our emotional system processes faster than our conscious mind. Learning this emotional language transforms our relationship with sensitivity. What once felt like a burden, being moved by everything, feeling things so deeply becomes a finely tuned guidance system. That knot in your stomach during a job interview might not be anxiety after all, but your emotional wisdom detects a misalignment between the role and your authentic path.

As this understanding deepens, we begin to map the territory of our inner world with increasing precision. Each trigger becomes a signpost, and each emotional response is a message to be decoded. The overwhelm that strikes during certain social situations might reveal important boundaries we need to set. The persistent sadness when engaging in seemingly successful work could point toward necessary life changes we've been avoiding. The real power emerges when we learn to pair this emotional wisdom with conscious awareness. Instead of being hijacked by our reactions, we develop the capacity to pause, feel full, and respond from a place of integrated understanding. This isn't about suppressing our sensitivity; it's about harnessing its intelligence. Through this process, we discover that our emotional nature isn't a weakness to be overcome but rather a sophisticated internal compass. Each understood pattern adds another layer of discernment to our navigation system, allowing us to move through life with increasing grace and authenticity. What begins as overwhelming sensitivity gradually transforms into one of our greatest strengths, the ability to read and respond to life's complexities with remarkable precision.

Forward Motion

Small victories build foundations for lasting change. The first time we navigate a triggering situation without being overwhelmed marks a turning point. Something shifts when we successfully set a boundary that honors our sensitivity instead of apologizing for it. Each tiny success tells us that a different way is possible.

Living with deep sensitivity doesn't mean choosing between emotional authenticity and practical effectiveness. We learn to weave these threads together, creating a deeply felt and highly functional life. Maybe we structure our mornings to include quiet time before diving into demands. Perhaps we should schedule recovery periods between intense interactions. These aren't compromises, they're intelligent adaptations that entirely use our emotional capacity. Our emotional systems grow more sophisticated with each experience we process consciously. That overwhelming sensitivity that once felt like static noise gradually tunes itself into clear signals. We begin to trust the whispers of our emotional wisdom, recognizing them as valuable data rather than inconvenient disruptions.

The transformation runs deeper than just managing feelings better. As we develop this emotional fluency, we discover that our sensitivity actually enhances our effectiveness in the world. We read situations with remarkable accuracy. We form deeper connections. We make decisions that align with both practical reality and inner truth. What once seemed like an endless struggle, trying to function in a world that felt too loud, too fast, and too much, becomes an ongoing dance of adjustment and alignment. We stop trying to be less sensitive and instead learn to be more skillful with our sensitivity. The qualities that once seemed to hold us back become our greatest strengths, offering unique insights and capabilities that less sensitive individuals might miss entirely.

This journey doesn't end; it continues to unfold with each new understanding, refined response, and integrated experience. But instead of feeling exhausted by this constant evolution, we find ourselves energized by it. We're no longer fighting against our nature but flowing with it, allowing our sensitivity to guide us toward ever more authentic and effective ways of being in the world.

The Art of Processing

The art of processing emotions demands the patience of a master potter at their wheel. Some feelings arrive like rough clay, needing gentle but persistent work to reveal their proper form. Others come like delicate glass, requiring the lightest touch to shape without shattering. Each emotion presents its own unique texture and possibilities. Time moves differently in this inner workshop. Just as an artisan knows rushing fine work only leads to flaws, seasoned emotional craftspeople understand that certain feelings need slow, careful attention. A moment of anger might need hours of gentle turning to become useful insight. Grief often arrives as a block of marble that only reveals its meaning through years of patient chiseling.

Skills develop through steady practice. At first, we might handle our emotions clumsily, either gripping them too tight or letting them slip away unexamined. But gradually, our touch grows more assured. We learn when to apply pressure and when to step back, when to engage directly with a feeling and when to let it rest and settle. The tools of this trade are subtle but essential. Meditation might serve as sandpaper, smoothing the rough edges of challenging experiences. Writing could act as a chisel, helping carve clarity from confusion. Movement, art, and music each become an instrument for shaping raw emotional material into meaningful form.

Our emotional workshop also needs proper maintenance. Regular clearing of mental space, like a craftsperson cleaning their studio, prevents emotional clutter from overwhelming the delicate work. Creating proper conditions, quiet time, safe spaces, and supportive relationships enables the finest emotional craftsmanship to emerge. The masterpiece isn't the processed emotion but the growing wisdom and skill that emerge from this patient practice. Each feeling we work with teaches us something new about our inner craft, developing an ever more refined ability to transform emotional experiences into deeper understanding and personal growth.

The Foundation of Awareness

Our emotional awareness grows increasingly refined through dedicated attention. At first, we might only recognize the loudest feelings, the crashing cymbals of anger, or the deep bass notes of sadness. But with practice, the softer harmonies emerge. That flutter in the chest might be anxiety, yes, but listen closer, there's also a bright thread of anticipation weaving through it.

Some emotional states whisper so softly we need absolute inner quiet to hear them. A faint feeling of unease might signal that something isn't entirely aligned with our values long before we consciously understand why. The barely perceptible lift in our energy when starting a new project could indicate we're moving in the right direction, even if doubts cloud our conscious minds. The body becomes our most sensitive instrument for emotional detection. Each feeling carries its own physical signature, the way excitement dances in the stomach, how contentment settles into the shoulders, and the particular way anxiety tightens the throat. These bodily sensations often register emotional shifts before our thinking mind catches up.

More complex emotional experiences create intricate compositions. Joy might sing the melody while a subtle melancholy undertone adds depth and texture. Fear could provide a driving rhythm while curiosity weaves through it like a counterpoint. Understanding these layered emotional experiences helps us respond more skillfully to life's complexities. This growing awareness transforms our relationship with emotional intensity. Instead of being overwhelmed by the full orchestra of feelings playing at once, we learn to focus on individual instruments, tracking how they contribute to the whole. This ability to distinguish and name subtle emotional states gives us more choices about how to work with them.

This deepening awareness reveals that our emotional landscape is far richer and more nuanced than we initially imagined. Each newly recognized feeling, each subtle shift we learn to detect, adds another layer of sophistication to our emotional intelligence.

Crafting Response Architecture

Think of emotional response architecture like designing a house that can weather any storm. The foundation must be solid, basic grounding practices that never fail. Maybe it's three deep breaths, a splash of cold water, or stepping outside momentarily. These simple but reliable responses become our first support line when emotions surge. Building on this foundation, we develop more sophisticated responses for varying intensities of feeling. Small emotional ripples might need just a brief pause and acknowledgment. Medium waves could call for a walk around the block or a quick journaling session. But when the big storms hit, those overwhelming waves of feeling, we might need to activate our full support system: trusted friends, professional guidance, and carefully crafted self-care routines.

Real art creates responses that serve immediate needs and provide deeper healing. During an anxiety spike, we might use breathing techniques to calm our nervous system while also noting patterns that trigger the response. This dual approach helps us manage the present moment while gathering wisdom for long-term growth. Our response architecture needs flexible spaces, too, and room to adapt when familiar strategies aren't working. Sometimes what helped yesterday might not help today. Having multiple options for each level of emotional intensity gives us the freedom to respond creatively rather than rigidly to our changing needs. As our emotional wisdom grows, these response frameworks become more nuanced and effective. We learn to read early warning signs and deploy appropriate strategies before emotions become overwhelming. This isn't about controlling our feelings but creating sustainable ways to honor and work with our emotional nature while maintaining functional lives.

With practice, these response patterns become second nature, like a well-designed home that naturally supports all aspects of living. We move from feeling at the mercy of our emotions to skillfully navigating their varying intensities, always growing in our capacity to handle life's emotional complexities.

Navigating Emotional Storms

Strong emotions surge through sensitive people like powerful ocean swells. Fighting against these waves only depletes our energy. The key lies in learning to float with their motion while keeping our heads above water. Sometimes, this means holding onto sturdy emotional anchors: a grounding meditation, a trusted friend's voice, or the simple rhythm of conscious breathing. These anchors don't stop the storm, but they keep us stable enough to weather it.

Our emotional capacity grows like a muscle, strengthening with each storm we survive. Today's overwhelming feeling might become tomorrow's manageable wave, not because the emotion grows weaker, but because we grow stronger in our ability to hold it. This growth requires patience, though; rushing emotional resilience only leads to exhaustion. The wisdom lies in knowing when to contain and when to release. Some emotional storms need immediate soothing, like anxiety that threatens to spiral out of control. Other feelings, like deep grief or justified anger, might need safe spaces for expression. Perhaps we pound clay, wail into pillows, or write furious letters we'll never send. These controlled releases act like pressure valves, preventing emotional overload while honoring the feeling's power.

Learning to read emotional weather becomes crucial. Just as sailors watch the sky for signs of approaching storms, we learn to notice our personal warning signs. Maybe our sleep grows restless before big emotional swells, or our appetite changes when intense feelings approach. This awareness helps us prepare rather than being caught off guard. Each successfully navigated emotional storm builds confidence in our ability to handle the next one. We discover that even the most intense feelings eventually pass and that we're stronger than we once believed. This growing trust in our emotional resilience transforms our relationship with intensity, from something to fear into something we know we can navigate.

The goal isn't to calm the storms but to become skilled sailors of our emotional seas. We learn to read the weather, work with the winds, and keep our course even in challenging conditions. Through this practice, what once felt like dangerous waters becomes familiar territory we know how to navigate.

The Architecture of Resilience

Small victories lay the first stones of resilience. Each time we successfully ride an emotional wave without being pulled under, we add another layer of confidence to our foundation. That moment when we catch ourselves before spiraling into anxiety, or when we maintain boundaries despite guilt, these aren't just isolated successes. They're building blocks, gradually constructing a more robust emotional architecture.

Protection and growth dance together in building true resilience. During intense emotional experiences, we could first reach for our tested grounding techniques, mindful breathing or sensory awareness. However, once the initial storm passes, these challenges become laboratories for developing new skills. That overwhelming social interaction that triggered anxiety becomes an opportunity to practice new coping strategies. The conflict that sparked intense feelings teaches us about our triggers and response patterns. Experience weaves wisdom into our emotional DNA. We discover that sensitivity isn't a weakness to be overcome but a strength to be refined. Like a master glassblower who learns to work with the delicate nature of their material rather than fighting it, we develop techniques that honor our sensitive nature while building our capacity to handle intensity.

The tools of resilience multiply with each challenge we face. Some days, we might need gentle self-care practices, quiet moments, soothing activities, and protective boundaries. Other times, we're ready to stretch our comfort zones, deliberately engaging with challenging situations to expand our emotional range. This flexibility, knowing when to protect and when to grow, becomes a cornerstone of lasting resilience. Our relationship with emotional intensity transforms through this process. Instead of bracing against strong feelings or trying to shut them down, we learn to move with them skillfully. What once felt like overwhelming vulnerability gradually reveals itself as deep emotional intelligence, capable of navigating life's complexities with increasing grace and wisdom.

This journey never really ends. We continue to encounter new emotional territories that test and strengthen our resilience. But with each experience, our foundation grows more stable, our responses more nuanced, and our capacity deeper. We become not less sensitive but more skillfully sensitive, turning what might have once seemed like a liability into one of our greatest strengths.

Maintaining Dynamic Balance

Finding equilibrium with our emotional nature resembles walking a tightrope, it requires constant micro-adjustments rather than rigid control. Some days, we might have the space to dive deep into our feelings, spending extra time with our journal or in quiet reflection. On other days, when deadlines loom and responsibilities pile up, we need to acknowledge our emotions briefly before focusing on immediate tasks.

The art lies in reading what each moment truly needs. Just as skilled sailors adjust their sails to changing winds, we learn to modify our emotional engagement based on current conditions. A challenging work project might require us to pause our emotional processing to maintain focus temporarily. Yet we don't abandon our feelings entirely, instead, we might create specific times for checking in, like emotional pit stops throughout the day. Life's seasons demand different approaches to balance. During calmer periods, we might expand our emotional practices, perhaps exploring new processing techniques or working with a therapist to understand deeper patterns. In busier seasons, we might streamline our emotional maintenance to essential practices that keep us grounded without overwhelming our schedule.

The key is developing an honest relationship with our capacity at any given time. In some weeks, we can handle intense emotional work alongside our regular responsibilities. Other times, just maintaining basic emotional hygiene takes all our available energy. Learning to honor these fluctuations without judgment helps us maintain a sustainable balance over the long term. This dynamic balance isn't about achieving perfection, it's about staying responsive to our changing needs and circumstances. We become like skilled dancers, constantly adjusting our movements to stay in harmony with both our inner rhythms and the external world's demands.

Through this practice of flexible attention, we discover that emotional awareness and practical functionality aren't opposing forces but complementary aspects of a well-lived life. When we learn to balance them with wisdom and care, each supports the other.

The Integration Process

Raw feelings arrive like uncut diamonds, their value is hidden beneath rough surfaces. An unexpected burst of anger might initially feel jagged and unwelcome, but careful processing often reveals essential truths about our boundaries or unmet needs. A wave of inexplicable sadness, given space to unfold, might carry important messages about changes we need to make in our lives.

Different emotions require different processing environments. Some feelings are like quick-growing seeds; they just need a brief period of quiet attention before their insights are yielded. Others resemble slow-ripening fruits, requiring weeks or months of gentle observation before their full meaning emerges. Rushing this natural timing only leads to incomplete integration. The tools of integration vary with the emotion's nature. The physical movement might best process stuck energy or anxiety. At the same time, writing could better serve complex grief or confusion. Creative expression through art, music, or dance often unlocks emotional understanding that defies verbal processing. Learning which approach serves different emotional states becomes part of our growing wisdom.

Time alone doesn't guarantee integration; quality of attention matters deeply. We might need periods of complete solitude, free from external demands, to fully process intense experiences. Other times, processing happens best in the presence of trusted others who can witness our journey without trying to fix or change our emotions. Each successfully integrated emotion becomes a reference point for future experiences. That overwhelming fear we worked through teaches us about our courage. The grief we honored shows us our capacity for healing. These processed experiences build an emotional library we can draw from when facing new challenges.

The real art lies in recognizing that integration isn't about reaching a final destination but rather about maintaining an ongoing relationship with our emotional world. Each processed feeling opens new doors of understanding, leading us deeper into the rich territory of emotional wisdom.

Building Processing Capacity

Regular practice creates subtle but profound shifts in our emotional capacity. Today's overwhelming feeling becomes next month's manageable challenge, not because the emotion grows weaker, but because our ability to hold and process it grows stronger.

Natural life experiences serve as our most potent training ground. A disagreement with a friend might teach us how to hold conflicting feelings simultaneously, disappointment and care, frustration and understanding. An unexpected success could help us navigate the complex waters of joy tinged with anxiety. Each experience adds another layer to our processing repertoire. The structured side of practice proves equally vital. Setting aside specific times for emotional check-ins, like a daily writing practice or weekly quiet reflection, builds our processing muscles systematically. These dedicated spaces let us explore our feelings without the immediate pressures of responding to life's demands. Our capacity grows most powerfully when we learn to match our processing approach to each emotion's unique character. Sometimes we need active practices, movement, creation, expression. Other times, still practices serve us better, meditation, journaling, quiet contemplation. This flexibility in approach helps us develop a fuller range of processing skills. Like any profound learning, this growth isn't linear. We might handle complex emotions skillfully one day and then struggle with seemingly simple feelings the next. These apparent setbacks often contain their own wisdom, teaching us about our changing needs and the dynamic nature of emotional processing.

Through this sustained practice, we discover that our capacity for holding and processing emotions expands naturally. What once overwhelmed us becomes manageable, and our tolerance for sitting with complex feelings grows. This isn't about becoming immune to emotional intensity but rather about developing the strength and wisdom to work with it more skillfully.

The Flow of Understanding

The shift in perception happens gradually, like dawn slowly illuminating a landscape. What once felt like a flood of overwhelming sensations begins to reveal distinct patterns and meanings. That pit in the stomach during important decisions isn't just anxiety to be managed, it becomes recognized as intuition speaking through physical sensation. The tears that spring up unexpectedly while creating art aren't just emotional overflow, but signals of deep resonance with authentic expression.

Understanding flows differently for each person. Some might first notice patterns in their dreams or sudden insights during quiet moments. Others might find clarity through movement or creative work. These individual pathways of understanding become more reliable with practice, like well-worn trails through once-confusing territory. Our emotional experiences start speaking in more precise voices. The initial chaos of feeling gradually sorts itself into meaningful messages. That surge of unexplained irritation might reveal itself as a warning about crossed boundaries. A persistent melancholy could unveil important truths about needed life changes. Each emotion becomes a thread in a larger tapestry of understanding.

The relationship with sensitivity itself undergoes a profound transformation. Instead of seeing it as a burden to manage, we begin recognizing it as a sophisticated guidance system. Our quick emotional responses to situations often carry accurate readings of dynamics others might take much longer to perceive. This sensitivity becomes a kind of emotional radar, offering valuable information about both ourselves and our environment. Processing emotions turns from a chore into an engaging exploration. Each feeling becomes an invitation to deeper understanding, like following an intriguing trail of clues. Even challenging emotions take on new meaning when we approach them with curiosity rather than resistance.

This evolving understanding creates a more fluid relationship with our emotional nature. Instead of battling against our sensitivity or trying to control it, we learn to move with it gracefully, allowing it to inform our choices while maintaining our center amidst emotional currents.

Creating Sustainable Patterns

Sustainable emotional patterns need daily care and long-term planning. Some days require intensive emotional work, such as processing a difficult interaction or sitting with complex feelings. Other days might focus more on maintenance practices, brief check-ins, or simple grounding exercises between tasks. This flexibility helps prevent emotional burnout while keeping us connected to our inner world.

The architecture of sustainability builds from small, consistent practices. A few minutes of quiet reflection in the morning might prevent emotional overwhelm later. Regular movement breaks could help process accumulated feelings before they become overwhelming. These aren't grand gestures but rather reliable rhythms that carry us through both calm and challenging times. Growth happens in the balance between protection and expansion. When facing intense emotions, we might first reach for familiar coping tools, trusted grounding practices or reliable self-care routines. But once stabilized, these experiences become opportunities to stretch our emotional muscles, try new processing approaches, or develop a deeper understanding.

Our patterns need to flex with life's changing demands. During high-stress periods, we might streamline our emotional practices to essential maintenance while storing more complex processing for calmer times. This isn't avoidance but rather an intelligent resource management like a farmer rotating crops to preserve soil fertility. The key lies in creating patterns that serve both immediate emotional needs and long-term development. We could pair quick calming techniques with deeper reflection practices, or combine protective boundaries with gentle exploration of triggering situations. These layered approaches help us maintain current stability while building greater emotional capacity.

Through consistent attention to sustainable practices, we discover that emotional depth and practical functioning aren't opposing forces but complementary aspects of a well-lived life. When we learn to balance them with wisdom and care, each supports the other.

The Journey Forward

Each refined processing skill, each successfully managed intensity, and each integrated Incremental growth creates profound change. Like pearls forming layer by layer, each small success in processing emotions adds to our emotional wisdom. A moment of staying present with difficult feelings instead of running away. The first time we notice a trigger before it overwhelms us. Each tiny victory lays another stone in the foundation of emotional resilience.

What begins as conscious effort gradually becomes a natural rhythm. The practices that once required careful attention, grounding ourselves during stress, setting boundaries when overwhelmed, making space for emotional processing, slowly weave themselves into the fabric of daily life. We find ourselves responding skillfully to emotional challenges that once would have derailed us completely.

The relationship with sensitivity itself undergoes a remarkable transformation. Rather than seeing it as a weakness to overcome, we discover it's actually a sophisticated guidance system. Our quick emotional responses often carry precise readings of situations that others might take much longer to understand. This sensitivity becomes one of our greatest strengths, offering unique insights into both ourselves and the world around us.

Personal patterns emerge that honor our sensitive nature and practical needs. For example, we could learn to schedule recovery time after intense social interactions or develop specific practices for processing emotional experiences before they accumulate. These aren't limitations but rather intelligent adaptations that allow us to function more effectively.

Each integrated experience adds to our emotional vocabulary. That overwhelming anxiety we learned to work with teaches us about our capacity for growth. The grief we moved through shows us our ability to heal. Even our struggles become valuable teachers, showing us where we need to develop new skills or adjust our approaches.

This journey never really ends. It continues to unfold with each new understanding, refined response, and integrated experience. But instead of feeling exhausted by this constant evolution, we find ourselves energized by it. We're no longer fighting against our nature but flowing with it, allowing our sensitivity to guide us toward ever more authentic and effective ways of being in the world.

The Sanctuary Within

Building emotional safety requires the same care as constructing a physical shelter. The foundation must be solid, basic self-trust and core practices that ground us in stormy times. Some days, we might need to retreat to our innermost rooms, those quiet spaces where we can simply be with our feelings without judgment or pressure. Other times, we inhabit the outer chambers, engaging with the world while maintaining our sense of inner security.

Windows and doors in this sanctuary serve essential purposes. They let in light, new insights, fresh perspectives, and moments of joy and connection. But they can also close when we need protection, like boundaries that shield us from overwhelming situations or relationships that drain our emotional resources. Learning when to open and when to close these passages becomes part of our growing wisdom.

The interior design matters deeply. We could create cozy corners for gentle self-reflection, open spaces for emotional expression, or sturdy workrooms where we process challenging feelings. Each room in our inner sanctuary serves different needs, some for rest, others for active emotional work, and still others for quiet contemplation. The architecture must be flexible enough to accommodate growth. As our emotional capacity expands, we might need to renovate, adding new spaces for emerging aspects of ourselves, strengthening supports that carry increasing emotional depth, or creating passages between previously separate areas of our experience.

Maintenance becomes an ongoing practice. Regular emotional check-ins act like routine repairs, preventing small issues from becoming major problems. Periodic deeper work resembles renovation projects, updating our inner space to match our evolving needs and understanding. This sanctuary isn't about hiding from life but rather creating a stable base from which to engage with it fully. When we know we have a safe space to return to, we can venture out more confidently into the world, knowing we can always come home to ourselves when we need to restore and integrate our experiences.

Architecture of Boundaries

Good boundaries aren't walls. They're more like smart filters, letting nourishing connections flow while screening out what drains us. Creating these boundaries requires careful attention to our actual needs, not just our fears or habits. Sometimes, we discover that old protective patterns no longer serve us. What once needed a fortress might now work better with a garden fence. Other times, we realize we need stronger limits than we've allowed ourselves to set.

The art lies in matching boundaries to specific situations and relationships. Close friends might access our emotional world more easily, while work relationships maintain more structured limits. Even within intimate relationships, certain topics or types of interaction might need clear boundaries to protect everyone's well-being.

These limits aren't static. They need regular adjustment as we grow and circumstances change. A boundary that felt essential last year might feel unnecessarily rigid today. Or we might suddenly need stronger protection in areas where we used to be more open.

Healthy boundaries emerge from self-respect rather than defensiveness. They say "I honor my needs" rather than "I fear your impact." This subtle shift transforms how we create and maintain our limits. Understanding boundaries as acts of self-care rather than barriers against others changes everything. We learn to set them with quiet confidence instead of apologetic hesitation. Each carefully chosen limit becomes another way we show up for ourselves while remaining open to genuine connection.

The most sustainable boundaries grow from deep self-knowledge. They reflect our actual needs rather than reactive patterns or borrowed rules. This authenticity makes them both more substantial and more flexible, able to protect us while still allowing real intimacy to flourish.

The Support Network

Trusted allies make all the difference. Someone who gets it, who understands without us having to explain every detail of our sensitivity. These rare connections become anchors in stormy times. Not everyone needs to understand everything, but having a few people who truly get us changes everything. Each supporter plays a unique role. Maybe it's that friend who knows exactly when to listen quietly and when to offer a gentle perspective. Or the family member who can tell from a single text message that we need space to process. These different types of support create a safety net beneath our emotional journey.

Professional guidance fills crucial gaps. A skilled therapist or counselor brings tools we might not discover independently. They help us see patterns we've missed and offer techniques tailored to our specific needs. Sometimes we just need presence, not solutions. Having people in our lives who can sit with us in difficult feelings without trying to fix them is invaluable. Their steady acceptance helps us learn to accept ourselves. Emergency supports require careful planning. Who can we call at 3 AM when anxiety strikes? Which professional resources are available for crisis moments? Having these protocols in place before we need them provides crucial peace of mind.

The daily check-ins matter just as much as crisis support. Regular coffee dates with understanding friends, weekly calls with supportive family, or monthly sessions with helping professionals maintain our emotional equilibrium. Like tending a garden, this regular care prevents small challenges from becoming overwhelming.

Building these networks takes time and trust. Through experience, we learn who can accommodate our sensitivity and who might need different boundaries. Not everyone needs to be part of our innermost circle, but each supportive connection adds strength to our foundation.

Creating Protected Space

Physical spaces shape our inner world. A soft blanket in a quiet corner, gentle lighting that soothes overstimulated senses, the familiar comfort of a favorite chair—these aren't just objects and arrangements—they're anchors for our emotional safety.

Time can be a sanctuary, too. Those precious morning moments before the world wakes up. A quiet lunch break away from office chaos. The peaceful hour after everyone else has gone to bed. We learn to guard these intervals jealously, knowing their value for our emotional balance. Each person's safe space looks different. Some need absolute quiet and solitude. Others find comfort in gentle background sounds, rainfall, soft music, the distant hum of city life. The key lies in discovering what genuinely supports our particular nervous system rather than following someone else's recipe for calm.

Setting up these spaces requires attention to detail. Temperature matters and textures matter. Even seemingly small things, like the weight of a blanket or the softness of lighting, can make the difference between feeling settled and on edge.

The emotional atmosphere needs just as much care as the physical setup. Clear boundaries protect these spaces from intrusion. Perhaps a "do not disturb" signal helps others respect our processing time. Certain rituals mark the transition into this protected space, helping us shift from doing mode to being mode.

Objects hold power too. A cherished photo that reminds us of love and support. A smooth stone that grounds us in the present moment. A journal ready to receive our unfiltered thoughts. These aren't just decorative elements, they're tools for emotional processing and anchors for our sense of safety. The most effective sanctuaries grow and change with us. What soothes us today might need adjustment tomorrow. Staying attuned to these changing needs helps us maintain spaces that truly serve our emotional well-being.

The Trust Journey

Small moments shape our sense of safety. When someone responds to our "no" with understanding instead of pressure, something shifts inside. A friend remembered our need for quiet processing time. A partner notices our subtle signs of overwhelm before we voice them. These seemingly minor incidents lay the groundwork for deeper trust.

Learning to trust ourselves comes first. We start recognizing our own signals more clearly, that flutter of unease warning of emotional overload, the subtle lift in energy indicating a genuine connection. Each time we honor these internal messages, our self-trust grows stronger. It takes time, sometimes lots of it. Sensitive people often need to see patterns of reliability over extended periods before fully opening up. This isn't about being difficult, it's wisdom born from deep emotional awareness.

Discernment develops through both positive and painful experiences. We learn to distinguish between those who simply claim to understand sensitivity and those who demonstrate it through consistent actions. Trust builds in layers like sediment forming solid rock. The journey involves careful testing of the waters. Let's share something small first, watching how others handle this vulnerability. Their response guides our next steps. Do they hold our sharing with care? Do they respect our boundaries? These observations inform our choices about deeper trust.

Each person earns different levels of trust. Some might be safe for sharing daily challenges but not deep emotional processing. Others become rare confidants who can handle our full sensitivity. Understanding these distinctions helps us create appropriate boundaries with different people. Self-trust and interpersonal trust weave together. As we learn to rely on our own emotional wisdom, we become better at recognizing those who can truly support our sensitive nature. This growing discernment protects us while allowing genuine connections to flourish.

Foundations of Stability

Basic rhythms create the first layer of stability. A morning meditation that centers us before the day begins. Regular meals that keep our blood sugar steady. Consistent sleep patterns that support our sensitive nervous system. These aren't rigid rules but rather gentle anchors that help us stay grounded. Our environment shapes us more than we realize. Clean, uncluttered spaces help clear mental static. Natural light affects our mood. Even the sounds around us, or blessed silence, influence our emotional baseline. Learning to craft surroundings that support rather than drain us becomes essential practice.

Tools matter too. That journal by the bedside ready to catch swirling thoughts. The playlist that helps us regulate overwhelming feelings. A weighted blanket for moments of anxiety. These aren't crutches, they're intelligent supports that help us maintain balance. Some stabilizing factors are less obvious. Perhaps it's the friend who never pushes us to socialize when we're depleted. Or the partner who understands our need for processing time after intense experiences. These relationships become part of our foundation, offering quiet support when we need it most.

Different moments require different kinds of stability. High-stress periods require more structured routines and frequent grounding practices. Calmer times allow for more flexibility while maintaining core supportive habits. The strongest foundations combine preventive practices and crisis responses. Regular emotional maintenance, like checking in with our feelings throughout the day, helps prevent overwhelm. Clear plans for handling intense moments ensure we don't lose our footing when challenges arise.

Building stability doesn't mean becoming rigid. Instead, it's about creating flexible strength, systems that can bend without breaking, routines that support rather than constrain, and practices that evolve as we do.

The Container's Strength

Think of emotional capacity like a well-crafted bowl. Its walls must be strong enough to hold intense feelings yet flexible enough to expand with experience. Too rigid, and it might crack under pressure. Too loose, and it won't provide the needed containment.

Different emotions require different kinds of holding. Some, like anger, require tight containment, like anger, which requires careful management. Others benefit from gentler boundaries, allowing them to breathe and transform naturally. Learning these distinctions becomes crucial wisdom. Our capacity grows through conscious practice. Each time we successfully hold a difficult feeling without being overwhelmed by it, our container strengthens. Sometimes, this means sitting with discomfort just a bit longer than usual. Other times, it's about knowing when we need extra support.

Edges matter deeply in this work. We learn to recognize the line between productive challenge and harmful overwhelm. That subtle signal that tells us we need to pause and ground ourselves. The internal whisper that says, "Enough for now." These boundaries aren't limitations, they're intelligence in action. Support structures reinforce our containers. Like buttresses on a cathedral, they help us hold more than we could alone. Maybe it's regular therapy sessions that help process intense experiences. Or trusted friends who understand when we need to pause and regulate. These supports don't make us weak, they make us wise. Growth happens at the edges of our capacity, but not beyond them. We learn to stretch gradually, testing new emotional depths while maintaining our foundation. This isn't about forcing ourselves to handle more than we're ready for, but rather about mindful expansion of our natural capabilities.

The strongest containers emerge from this balance of holding and growing, protecting and expanding. Through patient practice, we build the capacity to experience life's full emotional richness while maintaining our center.

Nurturing Inner Safety

Self-trust builds in tiny moments. When we pause to check our gut feeling about a situation. That quiet "no" we honor even when others push for "yes." The simple act of resting when we're tired instead of pushing through. These small choices lay the foundation for profound inner security. Different parts of us heal at their own pace. The anxious part that needs extra reassurance. Our inner critic learning to speak more gently. The wounded pieces waiting to trust again. We can't rush this process, forcing growth often sets us back.

Safety reveals itself in layers. First, maybe we learn to trust our physical needs, hunger, rest, movement. Then emotional needs might feel safer to acknowledge. Eventually, we develop trust in our deeper intuitions and wisdom. Each layer builds on the ones before. Sometimes we need to be our own best protector. Setting a boundary that others won't like. Leaving situations that don't feel right, even without a clear reason why. Taking breaks when we sense overwhelm approaching. These choices tell our inner world that we're committed to its well-being.

The practices that build safety often look simple but feel profound. Regular check-ins with our emotional state. Gentle self-talk during difficult moments. Consistent routines that honor our needs. Like tending a garden, these small, regular acts create the conditions for growth. Our nervous system learns safety through experience. Each time we respond to our own needs with care, each moment we catch ourselves before pushing too hard, we're teaching our system that it can rely on us. This isn't about perfection, it's about persistence and repair when we miss the mark. The journey to inner safety transforms our relationship with ourselves. Instead of harsh self-judgment or ignored needs, we develop a gentle, reliable presence that knows how to hold all parts of our experience with care and wisdom.

The Balance Point

Protection and growth dance a subtle tango. Some days call for strong boundaries and extra self-protection, like after an emotionally draining event. A quiet evening alone. Minimal social contact. Extra rest. Our system needs these periods of careful holding. Yet growth requires gentle stretching. Staying too safe for too long can shrink our world. Maybe we try a new social situation with a trusted friend nearby. Or process difficult feelings in small doses with support ready if needed. These calculated risks build our capacity.

The sweet spot shifts constantly. Tonight we might need absolute quiet and solitude. Next week, those same protective measures could feel stifling. Learning to read these changing needs becomes an essential skill. Our balance point varies with circumstances. High-stress periods might require more robust protection. Times of natural expansion might support more growth-oriented choices. Neither state is better, they're both vital parts of our journey.

Signs of imbalance deserve our attention. Too much protection might manifest as increasing isolation or anxiety about normal activities, while too little might manifest as frequent overwhelm or emotional exhaustion. These signals help us adjust our course. External support helps maintain balance. A therapist who understands sensitivity can help us gauge when to stretch and when to protect. Trusted friends might notice patterns we miss. Their perspective adds valuable data to our own inner wisdom.

Finding this balance isn't a destination but an ongoing practice. Each day brings new opportunities to tune our emotional boundaries, adjust our protective measures, and explore potential growth edges. Through patient attention to these subtle shifts, we develop increasing skill at maintaining our center while engaging fully with life.

Creating Lasting Safety

Small choices accumulate into lasting change. Honoring a boundary today makes setting tomorrow's limit easier. The quiet "no" we speak builds confidence for future self-advocacy. When we handle an overwhelming situation skillfully, our confidence deepens. If we stumble, the repair process teaches us even more about what we need to feel secure. These experiences aren't failures but necessary steps in building robust emotional safety.

Trust in ourselves becomes the cornerstone. We learn to recognize our early warning signs, that flutter of anxiety, the subtle tension in our shoulders, the slight narrowing of our focus. These signals become reliable guides rather than sources of worry. Eventually, emotional safety shifts from a conscious effort to a natural rhythm. The practices that once required careful attention, setting boundaries, monitoring our energy, and creating space for processing become as automatic as breathing. We develop an intuitive sense of what we need to stay grounded and secure.

Our relationship with sensitivity itself transforms. Instead of seeing it as a vulnerability to manage, we recognize it as a sophisticated guidance system. Those quick emotional responses that once seemed overwhelming become valuable data about our environment and needs. The real power emerges in how this safety enables fuller living. When we know we can handle emotional intensity, we become more willing to engage deeply with life. We take meaningful risks, knowing we have the tools to process whatever arises. Our world expands rather than contracts.

This journey never truly ends, we continue refining and adjusting our emotional safety practices as life presents new challenges. But each step builds upon the last, creating increasingly stable ground from which to explore all that life offers.

The Path Forward

Growth unfolds in its own time. Like a garden slowly taking root, emotional safety develops through patient attention and consistent care. Each small victory, a boundary maintained, an overwhelming moment navigated, or a need honored adds another layer to our foundation. The external structure matters deeply. Creating spaces that soothe rather than stimulate, building relationships that respect our sensitivity instead of challenging it, and finding work environments that support our natural rhythms aren't luxuries but essential elements of sustainable living.

Some changes happen so gradually that we barely notice them. That overwhelming situation now feels manageable. The boundary we set without second-guessing ourselves. The quiet confidence in honoring our needs. Looking back, we see how far we've come. Trust deepens through experience. We learn which friends truly understand our sensitivity. Which practices reliably ground us when emotions run high. What environments help us thrive rather than just survive. This knowledge becomes a compass guiding our choices.

The journey teaches us about balance. Sometimes we need extra protection while navigating challenges. Other times, we're ready to stretch our comfort zone and explore new territories. Learning to read these shifting needs becomes natural wisdom. Our relationship with sensitivity transforms from a burden to a gift. Instead of fighting against our nature, we learn to flow with it. Those quick emotional responses that once seemed overwhelming become valuable insights guiding us toward authentic choices.

This path continues unfolding, each step building on those before. Through consistent attention to emotional safety, we discover not just stability but a deeper capacity for engaging with all life offers while remaining true to our sensitive nature.

The Depths of Feeling

Deep within sensitive hearts lie these remarkable currents of complex emotion, almost like a lobster navigating the ocean depths. These fundamentally powerful psychological forces demand, and this is no mere suggestion, truly skillful navigation through life's turbulent waters. What's fascinating about these intricate emotional landscapes is that they're not just abstract concepts floating in the ether. They're deeply embedded in our biological and psychological reality. When you're dealing with overwhelming experiences, and believe me, we all face them, you've got two choices, fundamentally speaking. You can either let them crush you into dust, or you can transform them into opportunities for profound personal growth.

And here's the thing that people don't quite grasp: sensitivity isn't weakness. Quite the opposite. It's a sophisticated neural mechanism that's evolved over millions of years to help us perceive the subtle nuances of reality. When you're highly attuned to emotional experiences, you're operating at a higher level of consciousness, engaging with the world in its full complexity. But it requires tremendous courage to face these emotional depths head-on. You've got to be willing to dive deep into those dark waters of your psyche, confront the chaos, and emerge stronger. It's about developing the psychological tools to transmute raw emotional energy into meaningful personal development. And that's no small feat, let me tell you. The real challenge lies in learning to dance with these emotions rather than being consumed by them. It's about establishing a hierarchy of control over your emotional responses while simultaneously remaining open to their wisdom. And that's precisely what separates those who merely exist from those who truly thrive in our complex world.

The Nature of Overwhelm

Strong feelings can arise suddenly, making everything feel more intense, sounds might seem louder, lights brighter, and emotions more powerful than usual. Instead of fighting these waves of sensation, you can learn to recognize their early signs and understand what sets them in motion. Your deeper awareness often picks up subtle shifts before the overwhelm fully hits. You might notice a slight tightness in your chest, a change in your breathing, or feelings becoming more intense than the situation seems to warrant. These early signals give you valuable time to respond before the experience becomes too powerful.

Understanding what typically triggers these intense states helps you navigate them more effectively. You might realize that certain environments consistently create overwhelm, or notice that combining multiple stimulating activities leads to flooding feelings. This knowledge lets you prepare for challenging situations or adjust your approach before intensity builds too high. Learning to work with these experiences rather than against them transforms how you handle overwhelming moments. Instead of trying to push intense feelings away or criticizing yourself for having them, you develop skills for riding these emotional waves while maintaining your center.

Grief's Sacred Territory

Grief touches sensitive people profoundly, moving through your awareness like deep currents in still waters. You might feel not just deeply personal losses but also respond intensely to the pain you witness in others or changes you observe in the world around you. This depth of feeling isn't something to fix or change, but rather to understand and move through with care. Your sensitivity allows you to notice subtle layers of grief that others might miss. Perhaps you feel the gradual shifts of a friendship changing or sense the quiet loss of familiar places transforming. These experiences deserve their own kind of acknowledgment and care, even if they seem small to others.

Each experience of loss moves at its own natural pace. Some grief might flow through quickly, while other kinds need more time and space to process fully. Instead of rushing or forcing these feelings, you can learn to create room for them to move through you in their own way. This might mean setting aside quiet time for reflection, finding ways to honor what's been lost, or simply allowing yourself to feel deeply without judgment. Understanding how grief affects you personally helps you develop ways to support yourself through these experiences. You might discover that certain practices help you process intense feelings, perhaps time in nature, creative expression, or connecting with others who understand deep feelings. These become valuable tools for moving through grief while honoring its importance in your life.

The Fire of Anger

When anger rises in sensitive people, it often brings remarkable force and clarity. Instead of seeing this intensity as something wrong or frightening, you can learn to recognize it as important information. Your anger might signal crossed boundaries that need attention, or point to situations that conflict with your deep values. Working with anger requires understanding its unique language in your system. You might notice it first as heat rising in your chest, tension in your shoulders, or a sudden surge of energy through your body. These physical signals often arrive before conscious awareness of anger, giving you valuable time to respond thoughtfully rather than react automatically.

Your sensitivity actually helps you understand anger's deeper messages. Beyond the initial heat lies important information about what matters to you, perhaps a need for respect that's been overlooked, or a situation that requires clear limits. Learning to listen to these messages transforms anger from overwhelming force into valuable guidance. Managing intense anger involves creating safe ways to acknowledge and express it. This might mean finding private space to move or voice your feelings, writing about your experience, or channeling the energy into constructive action. The key lies in neither suppressing anger nor letting it control your actions, but rather working with it consciously.

Anxiety's Hidden Wisdom

Anxiety in sensitive people often works like an early warning system, picking up subtle signs that something needs attention. Rather than seeing this heightened awareness as a problem, you can learn to recognize when it offers valuable information. Your anxiety might notice small changes that signal approaching challenges, or sense when situations need more careful preparation. Learning to interpret anxiety's signals transforms how you work with worried feelings. Sometimes anxiety points to genuine needs, perhaps a situation that requires better boundaries, or an upcoming event that needs more thorough planning. Other times, anxious thoughts might simply echo old fears that no longer serve you. Developing skills in telling these apart helps you respond more effectively.

Your sensitivity allows you to notice the subtle differences between helpful and unnecessary anxiety. You might feel a quiet knowing in your body when anxiety signals real concerns, versus a spinning feeling when worries stem from old patterns. This awareness helps you choose whether to take action or practice the gentle release of unneeded fears. Managing anxiety involves creating reliable ways to check its messages while maintaining your center. Instead of getting caught in spirals of worry or trying to eliminate anxiety completely, you learn to examine its input without being overwhelmed by it. This balanced approach helps you benefit from anxiety's warnings while preventing it from controlling your choices.

The Face of Fear

Fear moves through sensitive awareness with particular strength, often bringing intense physical and emotional responses. Instead of seeing this depth of feeling as a weakness, you can learn to recognize when fear offers valuable protection. Your heightened awareness might notice subtle warning signs others miss, helping you respond to situations before they become dangerous. Understanding different kinds of fear helps you work with them more effectively. Some fears arise from genuine threats that need immediate attention, like sensing something wrong in a situation or feeling unsafe with certain people. Other fears might stem from old experiences or worries about future possibilities. Learning to tell these apart helps you choose whether to take protective action or work on building courage.

Your sensitivity lets you notice nuanced signals about safety and danger. You might feel a clear knowing in your body when fear warns of real threats, different from the anxious feelings that come from imagining possible problems. This awareness helps you trust fear's protection while preventing it from limiting you unnecessarily. Working with fear means developing ways to stay grounded while evaluating its messages. Rather than being overwhelmed by fearful feelings or trying to ignore them completely, you learn to examine fear's input while maintaining your center. This balanced approach helps you benefit from fear's protective wisdom while building the capacity for brave action when appropriate.

The Integration Process

Processing deep emotions requires patience and skill, like working with delicate materials that need careful attention. Instead of rushing to resolve uncomfortable feelings, you can learn to give each emotion the time and space it needs to understand fully. Your sensitivity actually helps this process by letting you notice subtle shifts in how feelings move through you. Different emotions often need different kinds of care and attention. Some feelings might need quiet reflection time to process fully, while others could require movement or creative expression to integrate properly. You might discover that sadness flows better with gentle solitude, while anger needs active engagement to move through your system effectively.

Your natural depth of processing, when supported properly, helps transform difficult emotions into valuable wisdom. Rather than seeing intense feelings as problems to solve, you learn to recognize how each emotion adds to your understanding of yourself and life. This might mean discovering that your anger carries important messages about boundaries, or that your fear highlights areas needing genuine attention. Creating the right conditions for emotional integration makes a significant difference. This could involve finding quiet spaces for processing intense feelings, developing reliable practices for working with different emotions, or ensuring you have proper support when handling particularly challenging experiences. These supportive elements help you maintain balance while engaging with deep emotional work.

Building Emotional Capacity

Working with intense emotions builds inner strength naturally over time. Each time you successfully move through a difficult feeling, understand a complex emotional situation or manage overwhelming intensity, you develop greater capacity. This growth comes not from trying to feel less deeply, but from learning to work more skillfully with your natural emotional depth. Your sensitivity helps you notice subtle aspects of emotional experiences that others might miss. As you develop trust in this awareness, you begin recognizing early signals of different emotional states and understanding their unique patterns. This growing wisdom helps you respond more effectively to intense feelings before they become overwhelming.

Building emotional capacity happens through both everyday experiences and intentional practice. Regular attention to your emotional world helps develop basic skills, like learning to stay present with uncomfortable feelings or recognizing when you need space for processing. Life naturally provides opportunities to use these skills in increasingly complex situations. The strength that emerges through this process differs from traditional emotional control. Instead of managing feelings through force or suppression, you develop a fluid ability to work with emotional intensity. Like learning to swim in deeper waters, you gain confidence in your ability to navigate strong feelings while maintaining your center.

The Path of Wisdom

Moving through intense emotions creates natural pathways to deeper wisdom. Instead of seeing strong feelings as obstacles to overcome, you begin recognizing how they reveal important truths about yourself and life. Your sensitivity becomes a sophisticated tool for understanding, helping you notice subtle meanings that might otherwise remain hidden. Each emotional experience adds to your growing wisdom when given proper attention. You might discover that sadness opens doors to understanding what truly matters to you, or that joy highlights which experiences bring genuine fulfillment. Even difficult feelings like anger or fear carry valuable messages about your needs and boundaries.

Your natural depth of processing helps transform emotional experiences into lasting insight. Rather than just moving through feelings quickly, you learn to notice what each emotion teaches you about living more authentically. This might mean recognizing patterns that trigger certain feelings, or understanding how different emotional states affect your energy and choices. This growing emotional wisdom changes how you move through life. Instead of trying to avoid or control intense feelings, you develop trust in their guidance. Like learning to read a complex language, you begin understanding the subtle messages your emotions carry about what supports or hinders your well-being.

The Road Ahead

Moving through emotional complexity becomes more natural with patient practice. Instead of seeing your depth of feeling as something to overcome, you begin recognizing how it enriches your understanding of life. Your sensitivity helps this process by allowing you to notice subtle shifts and patterns in your emotional landscape. Each time you successfully navigate intense feelings, your capacity grows stronger. You might discover better ways to stay grounded during emotional storms or develop more effective approaches for processing different feelings. These skills are built gradually through real experience rather than by forcing quick changes.

Your growing emotional wisdom transforms daily life. Rather than being overwhelmed by intense feelings, you learn to work with them more skillfully. This doesn't mean becoming less sensitive, instead, you develop a more remarkable ability to handle emotional depth while maintaining your balance. The journey continues through ongoing attention to your emotional world. Like developing any valuable skill, working with feelings requires regular practice and patience with yourself. Each step forward builds understanding while strengthening your ability to engage with emotions productively.

The Mastery of Integration

The master craftsman's wisdom emerges through thousands of small moments of practice. Each time we successfully navigate an overwhelming feeling, each instance we maintain a presence during emotional intensity, our integration skills become more refined. Like a woodworker who can feel the grain of the wood through their tools, we develop an intuitive sense of how emotions move through our system. Advanced integration transforms our relationship with emotional complexity. Instead of seeing intense feelings as problems to solve, we recognize them as sophisticated information systems. That rush of emotion during an important conversation might carry crucial insights about underlying dynamics. The seemingly overwhelming mix of feelings during significant life changes could offer valuable guidance about our actual needs and directions.

Our nervous system itself evolves through this practice. What once triggered immediate overwhelm might now register as interesting data to process. The sensitivity that previously felt like a burden becomes a finely tuned instrument for understanding both ourselves and our environment. This isn't about becoming less sensitive; it's about developing a greater capacity to work with our natural sensitivity. The most profound mastery reveals itself in how we handle life's inevitable challenges. Rather than being knocked off center by emotional intensity, we learn to move with it skillfully. Like a martial artist who uses an opponent's force rather than fighting against it, we discover how to work with rather than against our emotional nature. This journey of mastery never truly ends; there's always more subtlety to discover and greater refinement possible in our understanding. Yet each step builds upon previous learning, creating an increasingly sophisticated foundation for navigating life's emotional complexities while maintaining our center.

The Wisdom Path

Each emotional experience adds to your growing insight when given proper attention. Looking back at past situations often reveals more profound lessons that weren't obvious at first. Today's challenges might suddenly connect to earlier experiences, showing you patterns in responding to different situations. Your sensitivity helps you notice subtle connections between experiences that others might miss. You might recognize how specific environments consistently affect your emotional state, or discover links between different kinds of feelings that seemed separate before. These insights build upon each other, creating richer understanding of your emotional world.

Wisdom develops both through careful attention and natural discovery. Sometimes, understanding comes from deliberately reflecting on your experiences, while other times, insights arise unexpectedly during quiet moments. Your depth of processing allows you to recognize patterns that emerge across different situations, adding new layers to your emotional knowledge. This growing wisdom changes how you handle current challenges. Instead of reacting automatically to intense feelings, you begin recognizing familiar patterns and responding more skillfully. Each new situation becomes an opportunity to apply your understanding while continuing to learn and grow.

Navigating Complexity

Think of emotional complexity like layers of music playing simultaneously. Just as a conductor must track multiple instrumental sections while maintaining the overall piece's direction, sensitive individuals often manage various emotional currents simultaneously. Your personal feelings might form one layer, others' emotions another, while professional or social expectations create another layer to navigate. Understanding how these emotional layers interact helps create more effective responses. You might notice that when someone expresses frustration while you're feeling uncertain, it tends to trigger more substantial anxiety than usual. By recognizing this pattern, you can prepare strategies for maintaining your balance in these situations. Perhaps you need to ground yourself firmly in your own perspective before engaging with their frustration.

Your sensitivity provides sophisticated tools for this navigation. The same deep processing that can feel overwhelming also helps you notice subtle emotional shifts before they become overwhelming. You might sense early signs of tension in a meeting, allowing you to adjust your approach before conflict escalates. Or you could notice when your own emotional response is building, creating space to process feelings before they intensify. Learning to track these complex patterns takes time and attention. Start by noticing which emotional combinations consistently create challenges for you. Perhaps certain types of criticism hit harder when you already feel stretched thin. Maybe particular social dynamics tend to drain your energy more quickly than others. Understanding these patterns helps you develop more effective responses. Developing skills in emotional navigation also means learning when to engage fully and when to maintain a protective distance. Like a pilot choosing the best route through a storm, you might need to chart careful courses through emotionally charged situations. This could mean setting clear boundaries while still offering support, or maintaining professional composure while acknowledging others' feelings.

Pattern Recognition Excellence

Developing sophisticated pattern recognition starts with understanding how different experience elements connect and influence each other. Your sensitivity allows you to notice subtle relationships that others might miss. For instance, you might begin recognizing how certain lighting conditions affect your emotional state, or how specific types of social interactions consistently influence your energy levels in predictable ways. Environmental factors often create complex interactions with emotional states. The background noise level in a room might combine with the pace of conversation to affect how quickly you feel overwhelmed. The physical arrangement of space could interact with the number of people present to influence your ability to stay focused and engaged. Understanding these interactions helps you anticipate and prepare for challenging situations more effectively.

Personal patterns often reveal deeper themes in your life. You might notice that your strongest emotional reactions tend to occur in situations that echo early experiences. Perhaps certain types of criticism trigger particularly intense responses, or specific relationship dynamics consistently create similar emotional cascades.

Recognizing these patterns helps you understand your reactions more deeply and respond more consciously. Advanced pattern recognition also involves understanding how different time scales interact. Immediate emotional responses might reflect both current circumstances and longer-term patterns in your life. For example, your reaction to a work situation might connect to both present stress levels and deeper patterns around professional confidence. Seeing these connections helps you address challenges more comprehensively.

As your pattern recognition skills develop, you begin noticing increasingly subtle relationships. You might recognize early warning signs of emotional overwhelm before conscious awareness catches up, or sense approaching changes in group dynamics before they become obvious. This advanced awareness enables more skillful navigation of complex situations.

Refining Responses

Your sensitivity allows you to fine-tune your responses with remarkable precision once you understand your patterns deeply. Through consistent attention to how different approaches affect various situations, you develop an increasingly nuanced repertoire of responses. This refinement process works much like developing any sophisticated skill, it requires patience, attention to detail, and willingness to learn from each experience. Understanding exactly how much processing time you need becomes more precise through careful observation. You might discover that emotional conversations with family members require different integration periods than challenging work situations. Perhaps morning conflicts need longer processing times than evening ones, or certain types of emotional intensity require specific forms of integration. This knowledge helps you allocate your emotional resources more effectively.

The balance between maintaining boundaries and remaining compassionately engaged becomes more sophisticated through experience. You begin recognizing precisely when to step back slightly while staying present, or when to engage more fully while protecting your energy. This careful calibration develops through paying attention to how different engagement levels affect you and others in various situations. Response refinement also involves understanding the subtle differences between similar situations. Two workplace conflicts might appear similar on the surface but require distinctly different approaches based on underlying dynamics. Your sensitivity helps you notice these fine distinctions and adjust your responses accordingly. One situation may need direct communication, while another benefits from a more gradual approach.

Your ability to recognize and respond to emotional nuances continues developing throughout life. Each experience provides new information about what works best in different circumstances. Certain emotional states require specific types of support, or particular combinations of factors consistently need specialized responses. This growing understanding enables increasingly skillful navigation of complex emotional territories.

Creating Lasting Stability

Understanding your emotional patterns profoundly allows you to build sustainable approaches to handling life's challenges. Instead of being caught off guard by intense feelings or overwhelming situations, you develop trusted methods for processing and responding effectively. This stability grows from combining clear self-knowledge with sophisticated emotional management techniques. Creating reliable systems starts with understanding your foundational needs. You learn exactly what kinds of support help you maintain balance, perhaps regular quiet time for processing, specific ways of releasing emotional intensity, or particular methods for grounding yourself when feelings become strong. These aren't just coping mechanisms but instead carefully developed practices that work reliably for your sensitive nature.

Your ability to recognize early warning signs becomes increasingly refined over time. You notice subtle shifts in your emotional state before they develop into more significant challenges. This early awareness allows you to adjust your approach proactively rather than waiting for situations to become problematic. Perhaps you sense growing tension in your body and know to schedule extra processing time, or you notice emotional fatigue building and adjust your commitments accordingly. Flexibility within the structure creates lasting stability. While clear boundaries and regular practices provide an essential foundation, you also develop the ability to adapt these systems as needed. You might have different versions of your emotional management strategies for various situations, more intensive approaches for highly challenging times and lighter versions for daily maintenance.

Long-term stability emerges through consistent practice and refinement of these approaches. Each time you successfully navigate an emotional challenge, you learn more about what works best for you. This growing wisdom helps you handle future situations more effectively. Your sensitivity becomes an asset in this process, allowing you to notice which strategies truly serve your well-being and which need adjustment.

The Integration Dance

Think of emotional integration as mastering a complex skill, where many elements must work together harmoniously. Your sensitivity allows you to notice subtle interactions between different emotional aspects, how personal feelings influence professional responses, how physical energy affects emotional resilience, and how various emotional demands interact with each other. Advanced integration develops through understanding how these different elements affect each other. Processing personal feelings actually enhances rather than interferes with professional effectiveness, as it allows you to engage more authentically. You may discover that maintaining awareness of physical sensations helps you stay centered while handling multiple emotional demands.

The key to smooth coordination lies in developing trust in your natural rhythms. Rather than forcing yourself to process emotions faster or handle more situations at once, you learn to work with your sensitive nature's timing. This might mean allowing feelings to process in the background while staying present with current tasks or finding ways to honor both personal emotional needs and professional responsibilities. Your capacity for sophisticated emotional management grows through regular practice. Each challenging situation provides opportunities to refine your coordination abilities. You may learn to maintain boundaries while staying emotionally present, or discover how to process intense feelings while continuing necessary activities. These experiences build your repertoire of integrated responses.

As integration becomes more natural, you develop increasing flexibility in handling complex emotional situations. Like a skilled musician who can adjust their playing to complement others while maintaining their own rhythm, you learn to adapt your emotional responses while staying true to your core needs. This creates a dynamic balance that can handle life's varying demands while maintaining internal stability. Advanced integration's beauty lies in its making complex emotional navigation feel more natural and less effortful. Rather than constantly managing different aspects separately, you develop an intuitive sense of how to work with your emotional experiences holistically. This creates greater ease in daily life while allowing more sophisticated responses to challenging situations.

Building Advanced Capacity

Building advanced emotional capacity starts with strengthening your foundation through daily practices that support emotional stability. This involves regular attention to basics like energy management, boundary maintenance, and emotional processing time. Just as any advanced skill requires mastering fundamentals, sophisticated emotional navigation builds upon these essential practices.

Your sensitivity provides unique advantages in developing these capabilities. The same deep processing that can feel challenging also allows you to notice subtle aspects of emotional experience that others might miss. This awareness helps you understand how different elements of emotional experience work together and how to manage them more effectively. Developing advanced capacity requires balancing structured practice with natural learning. Regular emotional work might include dedicated time for processing feelings, practicing boundary-setting in controlled situations, or exploring how different approaches affect your emotional state. Meanwhile, daily life provides ongoing opportunities to refine these skills in real situations.

Understanding the relationship between foundation and advancement helps create sustainable growth. You can draw upon established practices while developing more sophisticated responses when facing new emotional challenges. Perhaps you adapt basic grounding techniques to handle more complex emotional situations or expand simple boundary-setting approaches to manage intricate relationship dynamics. Your capacity grows most effectively when you trust the development process. Rather than pushing for immediate mastery of complex emotional situations, allow your capabilities to develop naturally through consistent practice and real-world experience. This patient approach enables deeper integration of new skills while maintaining emotional stability.

As your emotional capacity expands, you develop increasing flexibility in handling various situations. You might find yourself managing professional challenges while processing personal feelings, or navigating complex relationship dynamics while maintaining clear boundaries. These abilities grow gradually through dedicated practice combined with life experience.

The Wisdom Journey

The journey toward emotional wisdom begins with recognizing that your sensitivity provides unique insights into both yourself and others. Your ability to perceive subtle emotional currents and complex patterns offers deep understanding that goes beyond surface-level awareness. This sensitivity becomes increasingly valuable as you develop skills in working with it effectively. Understanding emotional patterns creates a natural compass for navigating life's challenges. You begin noticing how different situations affect you, how various emotional states influence your perceptions, and how subtle internal signals provide essential guidance. This growing awareness helps you make choices that align with your authentic needs while responding effectively to life's demands.

Your emotional depth provides rich information about relationships and situations. Rather than feeling overwhelmed by picking up others' feelings or sensing underlying dynamics, you learn to use these perceptions as valuable data. This might help you understand what others need, recognize developing relationship patterns, or sense when situations require particular approaches. The journey toward emotional wisdom continues throughout life, offering new insights and more profound understanding with each experience. Every challenging situation provides opportunities to refine your emotional awareness and integration skills. You might discover new patterns in how emotions interact, develop more nuanced ways of responding to complex situations, or gain deeper insight into how your sensitivity serves you.

As this understanding develops, you begin recognizing how your emotional sensitivity contributes uniquely to your life and relationships. Perhaps your deep processing helps you offer significant support to others, or your pattern recognition abilities help you navigate complex situations more effectively. This appreciation transforms how you view your sensitive nature.

Forward Motion

Developing sophisticated emotional integration requires thoughtful attention to both inner wisdom and practical capabilities. The process starts with understanding that emotional complexity provides valuable information rather than simply creating challenges. Your sensitivity allows you to notice subtle patterns and connections that others might miss, offering unique insights into situations and relationships.

Developing practical skills to work with emotional depth involves regular practice in several key areas. First, it involves developing reliable ways to process emotional experiences fully without becoming overwhelmed. This might include learning exactly how much quiet time you need after intense situations or discovering specific approaches that help you integrate complex emotional information effectively.

Building on these foundations, you begin developing more nuanced abilities. You learn to maintain emotional awareness while staying focused on tasks, to process personal feelings while remaining professionally effective, and to handle multiple emotional demands without losing your center. These sophisticated skills grow through consistent practice combined with real-world experience.

The transformation happens gradually as you develop greater trust in your emotional capabilities. You begin recognizing how your sensitivity helps you navigate complex situations more effectively. Perhaps you notice early warning signs that help prevent problems or sense subtle relationship dynamics that enable more skillful interactions. This growing appreciation changes how you view your emotional nature.

Advanced integration also involves increasing flexibility in working with emotional experiences. Rather than needing rigid structures or specific conditions, you learn to adapt your approaches while maintaining emotional stability. This might mean processing feelings in the background while handling necessary tasks or adjusting your integration practices to suit different situations.

Throughout this journey, each successfully handled challenge builds confidence in working effectively with emotional complexity. Your relationship with sensitivity shifts from seeing it as something to manage toward recognizing it as a sophisticated guidance system that enhances your life and relationships.

You can learn much more about emotional intelligence in my book, Emotional Intelligence for Complicated Relationships.

Habit 5: Boundary Setting Essentials

The Boundary Blueprint

Setting clear boundaries is a vital foundation for those who deeply feel things. When we build these invisible yet powerful walls, they don't shut us off from the world. Instead, they create safe spaces where sensitivity transforms into an asset. Think of it as designing your personal sanctuary.

Small choices in daily interactions shape these protective borders, such as taking a moment of quiet before responding to others or gracefully declining invitations when your energy needs replenishing. Each boundary you establish acts like a filter, allowing you to engage with the world on your own terms. The true power lies in recognizing that boundaries aren't barriers.

Understanding and honoring your limits protects your capacity to remain open and receptive. This awareness builds resilience, allowing you to navigate relationships and experiences more clearly and purposefully. These boundaries become second nature through consistent practice, creating room for vulnerability and strength to coexist. The result is a life where sensitivity enhances rather than hinders your journey.

At its core, this approach celebrates the delicate balance between openness and self-protection. When properly maintained, these boundaries foster a deeper understanding of yourself and those around you. They provide the foundation for genuine connections while preserving your innate ability to experience life's richness fully.

Physical Space Design

Space shapes how we feel and function, especially for those who notice every detail around them. Simple adjustments can turn an overwhelming room into a calming haven.

Personal space starts with understanding what your senses need. Some people thrive with extra room between themselves and others during conversations. A few steps of distance can make all the difference in feeling comfortable and engaged. Your home becomes your sanctuary through thoughtful design. Soft lamplights might replace harsh overhead glares in one corner, while thick curtains mute street noises in another. Each room can serve its purpose differently, a quiet study for focused work, a cozy nook for unwinding.

Consider your workspace carefully. All these details matter to the hum of electronics, the glare from screens, even the subtle flicker of fluorescent lights. Moving your desk away from high-traffic areas or using noise-canceling headphones could transform your daily experience. The key lies in observation. Notice which spaces help you feel centered and which ones drain your energy. Sometimes, the smallest changes, such as a different chair position, a sound-absorbing rug, or adjustable lighting, create the most significant impact. Trust your instincts about what feels right in your environment.

These aren't just preferences but essential tools for managing daily life. When you honor your need for well-designed spaces, you create an environment where sensitivity becomes a strength rather than a struggle.

Emotional Territory Mapping

Every sensitive person's heart needs its unique kind of protection. Like adjusting the dial on a stereo, you can control how much emotion flows in and out of your daily interactions. Some days call for keeping things light and straightforward. A friendly chat with a neighbor might stay at surface level, preserving your emotional energy for deeper connections elsewhere. Other times, you might open up fully with trusted friends who understand and respect your sensitive nature.

Not every situation demands the same level of emotional investment. You get to decide when to share your deeper feelings and when to maintain a gentle distance. These choices aren't about building walls but about creating healthy filters that let you stay true to yourself while connecting with others. Pay attention to how different interactions affect your energy. A long heart-to-heart with a close friend might feel enriching, while an intense workplace discussion could drain your reserves. Recognizing these patterns helps you set appropriate boundaries for each relationship in your life.

The beauty lies in flexibility. Your emotional boundaries can shift and adapt as needed, like a dance between protecting your sensitive spirit and staying open to meaningful connections. This balance allows you to maintain your authenticity while navigating relationships with wisdom and care. Trust yourself to know when to lean in and when to step back. These natural instincts guide you toward the right level of emotional engagement for each moment, helping you build relationships that honor both your sensitivity and your need for occasional space.

The Mental Focus Shield

Your mind needs space to think clearly, just like a garden needs room to grow. Setting up mental boundaries helps you use your brain power wisely instead of spreading it too thin. Finding your best work rhythm makes a huge difference. Maybe you think most clearly in the morning, so you save those golden hours for essential tasks. You might turn off phone notifications or close your email to protect that precious focus time. Sometimes, less is more when it comes to taking in new information. You can choose what deserves your full attention rather than trying to absorb everything at once. This could mean limiting social media time or picking one book to read deeply instead of skimming several.

Your brain needs quiet moments to sort through complex ideas. Think of it as giving yourself permission to pause and process. Some people find this space during a morning walk, while others prefer evening reflection time. Setting these mental boundaries isn't about shutting out the world; it's about creating space for your thoughts to bloom fully. When you protect your mental energy, you have more to give to what truly matters.

Each person's mental shield looks different. The key is finding what works for you and sticking to it, even when others might not understand. Your mind deserves this protection so it can do its best work. Notice what helps you stay focused and what scatters your thoughts. These clues show you where to build your mental boundaries. When you honor these needs, your natural ability to think profoundly becomes a strength rather than a source of overwhelm.

Energy Conservation Zones

Your energy flows like a precious resource that needs careful management. Each person has their own natural rhythm; some days bring abundant vitality, while others require gentle pacing. Think of your energy like a bank account. Every activity either makes a withdrawal or deposit. A busy day at work might drain your reserves, so you balance it with quiet evening hours. A morning meditation could fill your energy tank for the challenges ahead.

Learning to read your body's signals makes all the difference. Is that slight heaviness in your shoulders or a foggy feeling in your mind? Those are hints that it's time to step back and recharge. Some people need short breaks throughout the day, while others thrive with one more extended rest period. Setting up your schedule with energy in mind brings freedom rather than limitation. Maybe you tackle challenging tasks when you feel most alert, saving routine work for times when your energy naturally dips. Or perhaps you leave buffer days between social events to restore your inner resources.

The art lies in prevention rather than recovery. By noticing what drains you and what energizes you, you can plan your days to maintain steady energy rather than swinging between exhaustion and recovery. This might mean avoiding extra commitments or building in regular recharge time. Your energy patterns deserve respect and protection. When you honor these natural cycles, you create a sustainable way of living that supports both productivity and peace. The goal isn't to do everything; it's to do what matters most while keeping your inner light burning bright. Remember, everyone's energy needs differ. What works for others might not work for you, and that's perfectly fine. Trust your instincts about when to engage and when to rest.

Time's Sacred Space

Time flows uniquely for each person, especially those who need extra moments to process life deeply. Picture your day as a series of carefully arranged spaces, each serving its purpose. Morning hours hold extraordinary power. For many, these quiet moments before the world fully wakes become sacred ground for essential routines. You might guard this time fiercely, using it for reflection, planning, or simply breathing before the day's demands begin.

Setting clear markers in your schedule creates a rhythm that protects your natural pace. Some tasks need room to unfold slowly, like important decisions or creative work. Other activities can flow more freely, filling the spaces between your protected time blocks. Learn to notice how different activities affect your sense of time. A rushed meeting might leave you feeling scattered, while a slower-paced conversation allows your thoughts to settle naturally. Building buffer zones between commitments gives your mind space to shift gears smoothly.

Your calendar becomes a powerful tool when it reflects your true needs. Maybe you block off recovery time after social events or save your peak hours for deeply focused work. These aren't just scheduling choices, they're boundaries that honor your way of moving through the world. Protecting your time isn't selfish, it's necessary for bringing your best self to what matters most. When you give yourself permission to process life at your own pace, you create space for both productivity and peace. The key lies in finding your own rhythm and defending it gently but firmly.

Watch for signs that your time boundaries need adjusting. Feeling constantly rushed or unable to complete thoughts might mean you need more spacious gaps in your schedule. Trust these signals, they guide you toward a more balanced way of living.

The Integration Process

Boundaries work together like instruments in an orchestra, each playing its own part while creating something more significant. When you adjust one area, the others naturally respond and adapt. Your physical space shapes how you feel and think. A quiet room might help you process emotions more clearly, while a cluttered environment could drain your mental energy faster. Sometimes, just changing where you sit can shift your entire experience.

Notice how your energy ebbs and flows throughout each day. This natural rhythm helps guide when to tackle challenging tasks and when to step back. Maybe you schedule important conversations when you feel most grounded or save creative work for times when your mind feels particularly clear. The way you protect your time ripples through other areas. Setting aside peaceful moments in your schedule creates space for both emotional processing and mental clarity. It's like permitting yourself to fully experience life's rhythms instead of rushing through them. Your emotions act as a compass, pointing toward which boundaries need strengthening or softening. That feeling of overwhelm might signal the need for more physical space, while a sense of disconnection could mean it's time to adjust how you engage with others.

Building these protective practices isn't about isolation; it's about creating a foundation that lets you engage more fully with life. When each type of boundary supports the others, you discover a natural flow that honors your sensitivity and strength. The key lies in gentle observation. Watch how different aspects of your boundaries interact and affect each other. This understanding helps you fine-tune your approach, creating a system that feels both protective and freeing.

Boundary Communication

Think of boundary communication as sharing a map of what helps you thrive. Speaking your needs clearly opens the door for better connections, not weaker ones. Simple, direct words work best when sharing your limits. Instead of saying, "I'm sorry, but I need..." try, "I work best when..." or "What helps me most is..." This shift from an apology to a clear statement shows others you value both yourself and the relationship. Real examples make boundaries easier to understand. You might say, "I need ten minutes of quiet after meetings to process my thoughts," or "I prefer a text first before phone calls so I can be fully present for our conversation." These specific statements leave little room for confusion.

Body language and tone matter too. When you share your needs with quiet confidence, others tend to respect them more readily. Standing tall, speaking calmly, and maintaining gentle eye contact all reinforce that your boundaries deserve respect. Practice helps smooth out the rough edges. Start with people you trust, then gradually expand to other relationships. Each conversation builds your confidence in expressing what you need.

Sometimes boundaries get pushed, and that's okay. Use these moments to restate your needs clearly and kindly. "I realize I wasn't clear before, what works best for me is..." This approach keeps relationships strong while maintaining your limits. Your boundaries reflect self-knowledge, not selfishness. By clearly communicating them, you show others how to connect with you. This honesty creates deeper trust and more authentic relationships. Remember that most people want to respect your boundaries, they just need to know what they are. Clear communication gives them that chance while protecting your own well-being.

The Flexibility Factor

Think of boundaries like a dance, sometimes flowing freely, other times holding firm. This natural give-and-take helps you stay true to yourself while adapting to life's changing rhythms. Strong boundaries don't mean rigid ones. Some days you might feel ready for more social energy, while others call for extra quiet time. Your limits can shift with your needs, like adjusting a thermostat to maintain comfort as the weather changes.

Different relationships need different approaches. Close friends might understand your need for processing time without explanation, while work colleagues may need more precise guidelines. A family gathering might require specific strategies to protect your energy, while a quiet dinner with a trusted friend allows more openness. Watch how situations affect you. Crowded spaces feel manageable in the morning but overwhelming by evening. Certain people naturally respect your boundaries, while others need gentle reminders. These observations help you adjust your protective measures wisely.

Learning to bend without breaking takes practice. Start by noticing when your usual boundaries feel too tight or too loose. Small adjustments often work better than dramatic changes. Trust your instincts about when to hold firm and when to soften your limits. The goal isn't perfect boundaries, it's boundaries that serve you well. Sometimes that means strengthening them during stressful periods. Other times it means loosening them to embrace unexpected opportunities. This flexibility keeps your boundaries alive and effective.

Changing your boundaries doesn't mean abandoning them. Like a tree that bends in the wind but stays rooted, you can remain grounded in your core needs while adapting to life's ever-changing demands.

Building Sustainable Systems

Think of building better boundaries, like tending a garden that grows stronger each season. Over time, what starts as conscious effort becomes a natural rhythm, a flowing system that protects without constant attention. Small daily choices create lasting patterns. You could start by blocking off ten minutes of quiet time each morning. Soon, this brief pause becomes an automatic part of your day, as natural as breathing. Your mind and body learn to expect and appreciate this space. Pay attention to what works and what doesn't. Some boundaries might feel forced or draining, but these need gentle adjustment. Others bring immediate relief, showing you where to build more vigorous habits. Each observation helps fine-tune your protective practices.

The best systems almost run themselves. Instead of wrestling with decisions each time, you develop smooth routines that honor your needs automatically. Your phone silences itself during focus hours, or your calendar automatically blocks recovery time after busy events. Look for patterns in your energy flows. Notice which activities consistently drain you and which ones bring renewal. This awareness helps you arrange your days in ways that naturally protect your sensitivity rather than fighting against it.

Success leaves clues. When you find boundary practices that work well, build them into your regular routines. These aren't rigid rules but rather helpful guides that keep you balanced without constant effort. Steady progress matters more than perfection. Each slight adjustment moves you toward a more sustainable way of living. Over time, these thoughtful changes create a natural shield that protects your sensitivity while allowing meaningful engagement with life. Just as a well-tended garden becomes more resilient each year, your boundary system grows stronger with patient attention. Trust this gradual process of building patterns that support rather than strain your sensitive nature.

The Path Forward

Imagine discovering a way to navigate a free and safe life. Setting good boundaries isn't about hiding; it's about finding your own perfect balance. Taking care of your sensitive nature opens doors rather than closing them. When you know how to protect your energy, you can choose which experiences to embrace fully. It's like having a trusted compass that guides you toward what matters most. Each time you honor your needs, you build confidence in your choices. Something as simple as stepping away when you feel overwhelmed becomes easier with practice. These small victories add up, showing you how to move through the world on your own terms. Learning what works best for you takes time and patience. Some days you might need extra quiet space, while others bring energy for more connection. This growing understanding helps you adjust your boundaries naturally, like a skilled sailor reading the winds.

The real power comes from treating your sensitivity as an asset rather than a burden. When you protect it wisely, this deep awareness becomes a source of strength. You start seeing opportunities where you once saw challenges. Watch how your relationships deepen when you maintain healthy limits. People learn to respect your boundaries, creating space for more authentic connections. Instead of feeling drained by interactions, you find yourself able to engage more fully. This journey transforms how you experience daily life. Rather than bracing against overwhelm, you learn to flow with your natural rhythms. Each boundary you set helps create a life that feels both protected and rich with possibility. Remember that this path unfolds one step at a time. Trust your instincts about what you need, and let each success guide you toward even better ways of caring for your sensitive spirit.

The Language of Limits

Creating gentle but firm ways to express our needs transforms how we handle our sensitive nature. Each clear statement builds a stronger bridge to understanding. Words carry power when sharing boundaries. Instead of "I can't handle this," try "I need some quiet space to process."

Simple shifts in language turn limitations into positive choices that others can easily respect and support.

Learning to speak your truth takes practice and patience. Start with basic phrases that feel natural, "I work best when..." or "What helps me is..." These gentle openings invite understanding rather than resistance. Soon you'll find your own authentic ways to share limits. Watch how different people respond to various approaches. Some appreciate direct statements, while others connect better with softer explanations. Like learning any new language, you'll discover which words resonate in different situations. Your voice gets stronger with each boundary you express. Maybe you begin by setting small limits, "I need five minutes before responding" or "Let me think about that overnight." These stepping stones lead to more transparent communication about bigger needs.

Trust grows when you consistently express your needs with respect, both for yourself and others. Friends learn they can count on your honesty. Colleagues understand your work style better. Family members recognize your patterns. The goal isn't perfect phrases but authentic expression. Sometimes a simple "not right now" speaks volumes. Other times, sharing more about your sensitive nature helps others grasp why certain boundaries matter so much. Clear limits create space for deeper connections. By saying what you need, you show others how to support your sensitive spirit while keeping your relationships strong and healthy.

The Direct Expression

Direct words shape clear boundaries without apology. Learning to state your needs plainly builds respect for yourself and others. Starting with "I need" or "This works best for me" sets a tone of calm certainty. No extra words are needed, just simple facts about what helps you function well. It's like drawing a line in the sand with quiet confidence rather than hesitation.

Notice how different statements feel when you say them out loud. "The music needs to be quieter for me to focus" carries more weight than "I'm sorry, but could you maybe turn it down?" Each time you practice direct expression, it becomes more natural. Strong boundaries don't require long explanations. Short, clear statements often work better than detailed justifications. When you say, "I'll respond to messages after 10 AM" or "I need an hour of quiet after social events," you show others exactly how to respect your needs. Think of boundary statements as helpful signposts. They guide others toward better interactions with you while protecting your sensitive nature. Clear words create clear expectations, making relationships smoother for everyone involved.

Your needs deserve simple, direct expression. Skip the apologies and explanations, just state what works for you. This straightforward approach helps others understand and respect your boundaries more easily. Remember that direct doesn't mean harsh. You can be both clear and kind when expressing limits. The key lies in believing that your needs matter enough to state them plainly, without hiding behind softer words or excessive explanations.

Trust that others can handle your truth when expressed clearly. Most people appreciate knowing exactly where they stand and what you need. This clarity builds stronger connections based on honest communication rather than guesswork.

The Power of No

Saying no grows from quiet confidence rather than fear. Like setting down a heavy weight you never needed to carry, it frees you to choose what truly matters. That small word holds surprising strength when delivered with calm certainty. No extra words are needed, just "That doesn't work for me" or "I'll pass on this one." Each time you decline clearly, you build trust in your own judgment.

Watch how a simple "no" feels different from long explanations or excuses. Your energy stays protected when you skip the detailed reasons why. "I won't be able to join" says everything necessary without draining your resources on justification. Practice makes these moments smoother. Start with smaller situations where saying no feels safer. Maybe decline an extra task at work or a social event that would stretch your energy too thin. Each small refusal builds confidence for bigger boundaries.

The real power comes from knowing you have a choice. Every request deserves that moment of pause, that breath between hearing and answering. This space lets you check your true capacity before committing. Respect flows both ways when you say no clearly. Others learn to trust your words because they're honest and direct. You show respect for yourself by honoring your limits, and respect for others by being truthful about what you can give. Remember that "no" protects your "yes." When you decline what drains you, you save energy for what truly matters. This boundary word becomes a tool for creating the life you want, rather than a source of guilt or fear. Let your no stand strong on its own. It needs no defense, no explanation, no softening. Like a clear note in a song, it rings true when delivered with simple confidence.

Setting Clear Parameters

Clear boundaries work like a map, showing others how to navigate your needs successfully. Speaking them up front prevents confusion and creates a better understanding of the situation from the start. Your needs deserve clear expression right from the beginning. Instead of hoping others might guess what works for you, stating your requirements early sets everyone up for success. It's like putting up helpful signs on a path before anyone gets lost. Think about what you need in different situations. Maybe you tell new colleagues, "I process information best when I can review it first, then discuss it." Or you might let friends know, "I prefer getting together earlier in the day when my energy is fresh." Each clear statement prevents future strain. When you say, "I'll check my schedule and let you know tomorrow," you create breathing room for thoughtful decisions. This space protects both you and your relationships.

Watch how setting early expectations changes interactions. When you explain your processing style directly, people learn to respect it. They understand why you might need quiet time after meetings or prefer certain ways of communicating.

Strong parameters don't limit connections, they deepen them. By showing others exactly how to work with your sensitive nature, you build relationships based on genuine understanding rather than assumptions.

Clear doesn't mean complicated. Simple statements about your needs often work best. "I need twenty minutes to transition between activities" or "Please text before calling" gives others specific ways to respect your boundaries. Trust that most people welcome knowing how to interact with you effectively. When you express your parameters clearly, you help create smoother, more satisfying connections for everyone involved.

The Consistency Key

Think of boundary-setting as tending a garden; it needs regular attention to flourish. Each time you uphold your limits, you strengthen their foundation, just as repeated care helps plants grow stronger. Daily choices build lasting patterns. When you consistently protect your quiet morning hours or honor your need for processing time, others begin to respect these rhythms naturally. Your steady approach teaches people what to expect. Even small moments matter. Maybe you always take five minutes between meetings, or you maintain regular breaks during busy days. These aren't rigid rules but rather gentle habits that protect your energy. Like water shaping stone, these repeated actions gradually create lasting change.

Notice how steady boundaries bring deeper peace. You'll find yourself explaining less and enjoying more as others learn to work with your natural rhythms. The occasional reminder might still be needed, but your consistent practice makes each reinforcement easier. Your own commitment comes first. When you truly believe in your needs, maintaining boundaries feels less like a struggle and more like self-care. This inner certainty shows in how you express your limits to others.

Each time you maintain a boundary, you build trust with yourself and others. They learn to count on your word, and you grow more confident in protecting your needs. This mutual understanding creates stronger relationships built on clear expectations.

Watch how your steady practice ripples outward, creating lasting changes in how others interact with you. What once felt like constant effort becomes a natural rhythm, supporting your sensitive nature while keeping connections strong.

Following Through

Following through on boundaries builds trust like laying bricks to create a strong wall. Each time you stand by your stated needs, you show both yourself and others that your limits matter. Small consistent actions carry deep power. When you actually take that promised quiet time instead of letting it slide, or hold firm on your "no" despite pressure, you strengthen your foundation. These moments might feel uncomfortable at first, but they prevent bigger struggles later.

Watch how honoring your own boundaries changes everything. Maybe you feel that flutter of anxiety when protecting your needs, but you do it anyway. Each time you follow through, that flutter gets smaller while your confidence grows stronger. The real test often comes in challenging moments. Standing firm when someone pushes back or maintains limits during busy times shows that your boundaries aren't just words. Like a muscle getting stronger through use, your ability to protect your needs grows with practice.

Trust builds slowly but surely. Others start to understand that when you say you need something, you mean it. They learn to respect your limits because you consistently respect yourself. This clarity makes relationships smoother and more authentic. Your needs deserve more than empty promises. When you say you'll take time to think before deciding, actually take that time. When you set a limit on availability, stick to it. These actions speak louder than any words about self-care. Each time you honor your stated boundaries, you build a stronger foundation for the future. Like compound interest, these small acts of self-respect add up to create lasting change in how you move through the world.

The Communication Dance

Sharing boundaries becomes a graceful exchange, not a battle. Each conversation offers a chance to blend gentle strength with genuine care for the relationship. Simple words often work best. "I appreciate the invitation, but evening events don't work well for me" carries both clarity and kindness. This direct approach respects both your needs and the other person's time.

Notice how different situations call for different tones. A close friend might understand a quick "I need space today," while a work setting may require "I'll be focusing on this project until 2 PM." Like adjusting your voice to the room, you learn which approach fits each moment. Sometimes you'll need to be extra firm. "This doesn't work for me" might need to be repeated without explanation when someone keeps pushing. Other times, a softer "Let me suggest another way" opens doors to better solutions.

The key lies in staying both clear and kind. Rather than defensive or apologetic, your tone can remain warm while your limits stay firm. Think of it as holding a door, you can do it with strength or gentleness, but the door still defines the space. Watch how people respond to different approaches. Some appreciate straightforward statements, while others connect better with more context. This awareness helps you choose words that protect your needs while keeping relationships strong. Your boundaries can be both strong and smooth. Like river stones shaped by water, they can have firm edges yet feel natural to the touch. Each conversation builds your skill in expressing limits in ways that work for everyone.

Practice helps you find this balance. Start with people who already respect your needs, then gradually expand to more challenging situations. Each interaction teaches you more about communicating with both backbone and heart.

Building Trust Through Clarity

Clear words lay the groundwork for deep trust, like stepping stones across a stream. When you express your needs plainly, both you and others learn to rely on that honesty. Self-trust blooms first. Each time you voice a genuine need without hesitation, you strengthen your inner compass. Saying "I need time to process this information" or "This environment feels too intense for me" becomes natural, not forced.

The foundation grows stronger with each honest exchange. When people see you consistently honor your stated limits, they learn these aren't casual preferences but real needs. If you say you'll take a day to consider a decision, actually taking that time proves your word carries weight. Notice how clarity creates comfort on both sides. Others appreciate knowing exactly where they stand with you. No guessing games, no hidden expectations, just straightforward sharing of what works and what doesn't. This openness actually brings people closer rather than pushing them away.

Simple truth works better than elaborate explanations. "I focus best in the morning," tells others everything they need to know. When you trust your needs enough to state them plainly, others naturally follow your lead. Watch how respect grows when your actions match your words. If you say you need quiet time after meetings, taking that time shows everyone, including yourself, that you mean what you say. This consistency builds a foundation of trust that makes future boundary-setting easier. Each clear limit creates space for genuine connection. By knowing exactly what you need and expressing it directly, you help others understand how to build stronger relationships with you. Trust flows naturally from this honest exchange.

The Path to Empowerment

Clear boundaries turn sensitivity from a challenge into a gift. Like finding your voice in a song, speaking your needs with quiet confidence changes everything about how you move through the world. Watch how small shifts create big changes. Instead of hoping others might guess what you need, stating it directly opens new possibilities. "I work best with advance notice" or "I need quiet space to recharge" becomes a natural truth rather than an awkward confession. Your clear voice grows stronger with practice. Each time you express a limit without apology or state a need without a defensive explanation, you build trust in your own judgment. These moments of honest communication transform occasional victories into daily strength.

The real power comes from knowing your needs deserve respect. When you consistently honor your stated boundaries, others learn to do the same. That morning quiet time or careful energy management stops feeling like special accommodation and becomes simply part of how you operate. Notice how relationships deepen when built on clear understanding. Friends appreciate knowing exactly how to support you. Colleagues respect your work style when you explain it directly. Family members learn to work with your natural rhythms rather than against them. Each boundary you maintain adds another stone to your foundation. Those brief pauses before responding, those gentle "no" statements, those clear explanations of what works for you, they all build toward something stronger. Like a garden tended daily, your confidence grows naturally with care. You don't need to copy others' boundaries or follow rigid rules. Instead, listen to your own needs and express them with both firmness and grace. This honest approach creates lasting change in how you experience life.

When protected by clear limits, your sensitivity becomes strength. Through steady practice in speaking your truth and maintaining healthy boundaries, you create space to fully express your gifts while staying true to your nature.

Forward Motion

Clear boundaries open new doors rather than close them. Each time you express your needs directly, you build a stronger bridge between your sensitive nature and the wider world. Small steps lead to lasting change. Starting with simple statements like "I need time to consider this" creates space for bigger shifts later. Your confidence grows naturally as you practice saying what you need without hesitation or excess explanation. Watch how protecting your energy actually increases what you can offer. When you maintain clear limits about your availability or processing needs, you show up more fully for what matters most. Rather than draining yourself by saying yes to everything, you save your strength for meaningful engagement.

The journey unfolds at its own pace. Some days you'll find it easy to maintain your boundaries, while others might challenge your resolve. Each experience, whether smooth or difficult, teaches you more about expressing your needs effectively. Pay attention to what works best for you. Maybe you discover that morning quiet time makes afternoon meetings more productive, or that taking breaks between social events helps you connect more deeply. These insights shape stronger boundaries that truly serve your needs.

Trust builds with every clear limit you maintain. Others learn they can count on your word, while you grow more confident in protecting your sensitive spirit. This mutual understanding creates relationships built on respect rather than compromise. Each step forward strengthens your foundation. Through steady practice in expressing and maintaining clear boundaries, you create a sustainable way of living that honors your sensitivity and strength.

The Circle of Support

Building a circle of people who understand your boundaries creates a safety net that strengthens over time. Each supportive connection helps you maintain healthy limits while encouraging genuine growth. Finding your boundary allies happens naturally when you express your needs clearly. Some friends will immediately understand your need for quiet mornings or recovery time after social events. Their respect for these limits shows you who truly supports your well-being.

Notice how different people offer different kinds of support. One friend might excel at giving you space when needed, while another remembers to check before making spontaneous plans. Like puzzle pieces, each supportive relationship adds to your complete picture of care. The strongest support often comes from those who've walked similar paths. These kindred spirits understand without explanation why you might need to leave early or take time to process. Their natural acceptance of your boundaries reinforces your confidence in maintaining them.

Watch how mutual understanding deepens relationships. When someone consistently honors your limits, you feel safer being vulnerable with them. This trust creates space for authentic connection while protecting your sensitive nature. Your support circle grows stronger through honest communication. Sharing what helps and hinders you lets others learn how to be there for you effectively. Each clear expression of your needs helps them understand how to support you better.

Seeking support shows wisdom, not weakness. Just as every house needs a foundation, every boundary system needs people who understand and respect its importance. These supporters become the ground you stand on while building stronger limits. Building this network takes time and patience. Start with those who already show signs of understanding, then gradually expand as you find more people who respect your boundaries. Like rings in a tree, your circle of support grows naturally with each passing season.

Networks of Understanding

Building supportive networks feels like finding your tribe in a bustling world. When you connect with people who naturally get your needs, maintaining boundaries becomes easier rather than harder. Start with those who already show they care. Some friends instinctively check before making plans, while others remember you prefer quiet settings for deep talks. These small signs of understanding mark your true allies in boundary care. Watch how understanding spreads naturally. One supportive colleague might help others grasp why you need preparation time before meetings. A friend who respects your energy limits often explains it to others without you having to say a word. These ripples of awareness create wider circles of support.

The magic happens when you find people who share similar needs. They understand without explanation why crowds drain you or why you need time to process big decisions. Their natural respect for your boundaries confirms you're not alone in needing these protective measures. Think of these connections as your boundary guardians. The friend who notices when you're overwhelmed at gatherings, the family member who creates quiet space during busy holidays, the coworker who shields you from unnecessary interruptions, each one helps maintain your sensitive boundaries. Your network grows stronger through open sharing. When you explain your needs clearly to those who care, they learn better ways to support you. Each honest conversation builds deeper understanding and more effective support.

These understanding relationships make boundary maintenance feel more natural. Instead of constantly defending your needs, you surround yourself with people who help protect them. This shared care creates space for both sensitivity and strength to flourish.

The Advocate Alliance

Think of your boundary advocates like a team of trusted allies, each playing a unique role in helping protect your needs. Their support turns solo boundary defense into shared care. Strong advocates step up naturally in different settings. A close friend might smoothly explain your early departure from gatherings, while an understanding colleague shields you from interruptions during focus time. These partnerships make boundary maintenance feel less lonely. Notice who instinctively supports your limits. Some people just get it, they'll change noisy environments without being asked or create buffer time in group schedules. Their natural advocacy shows you who truly understands your sensitive nature.

Work partnerships become particularly powerful. An ally at the office might say "Let's give this some thought time" when others push for instant decisions, or they'll suggest breaks during intense meetings. These small actions add crucial support to your daily boundaries. Family advocates prove especially valuable during gatherings. A sibling who knows you need quiet time might create space for breaks, while a partner could help manage social energy demands. Their understanding helps others respect your needs without constant explanation. Watch how good advocates blend firmness with grace. They don't fight your battles but rather reinforce the boundaries you've already set. Like skilled diplomats, they help others understand and respect your needs while keeping relationships smooth.

The best advocacy feels effortless to everyone involved. When your allies understand your needs and how to support them, maintaining boundaries becomes a shared practice rather than a constant struggle.

Mentorship Matters

Consider boundary mentors like skilled guides who've walked similar paths before you. Their experience lights the way through challenges they've already faced, making your journey smoother. Some mentors share deep personal knowledge. They might show you how they learned to protect their morning quiet time or manage energy during busy seasons. These practical insights often work better than theoretical advice because they're tested by real experience.

Watch for those rare individuals who naturally maintain strong boundaries. They often make the best guides, showing rather than telling how to set limits with both firmness and grace. Their example teaches more than words alone ever could. Natural mentoring happens in unexpected places. Maybe a colleague whose balanced approach you admire shares their strategies for managing workplace demands. Or a friend who seems effortlessly centered reveals their careful boundary practice. These organic connections often provide the most valuable guidance.

The best mentors understand the delicate dance of sensitivity. They know firsthand how it feels to need extra processing time or quieter environments. Their understanding comes from living these needs themselves, making their advice both practical and compassionate. Learning from others' journeys saves precious energy. Instead of discovering every boundary lesson through trial and error, you benefit from their hard-won wisdom. Like skilled craftspeople sharing trade secrets, they help you avoid common pitfalls while developing your own style.

Each mentoring relationship adds another layer to your boundary practice. Through their guidance, you learn to protect your sensitive nature while staying engaged with life, a balance that grows stronger with shared wisdom.

Accountability Partnerships

Accountability partners become trusted mirrors, reflecting both your successes and areas for growth in boundary setting. Like training partners in any practice, they help keep you steady on your chosen path. Think of these check-ins as anchor points in your week. A quick coffee with someone who understands might reveal patterns you hadn't noticed, like how you tend to overextend on Thursdays, or how certain situations consistently drain your energy. Their outside perspective brings valuable clarity.

Good accountability feels supportive rather than rigid. Some partners excel at celebrating small wins, like when you successfully said no to an overwhelming request. Others provide gentle prompts when they notice you slipping into old patterns. This balanced approach keeps you moving forward without feeling pressured. Watch how regular connection builds stronger practice. Maybe you share daily text messages about boundary moments or meet monthly to reflect on deeper patterns. These consistent touchpoints help turn occasional boundary setting into a natural habit.

The best partnerships blend honesty with kindness. Your partner might ask "How did that boundary hold up this week?" while creating space for both victories and struggles. This caring accountability helps you stay true to your needs without harsh self-judgment. Notice which check-in styles work best for you. Some people thrive with structured reviews, while others prefer casual conversations about boundary challenges. Finding the right rhythm strengthens your commitment while keeping it sustainable. Supporting someone else's boundary practice often strengthens your own. Like mirror images reflecting back and forth, each partner's growth supports the other's.

These connections help turn boundary-setting from a lonely challenge into a shared journey. Through regular support and gentle reminders, accountability partners help strengthen and sustain sensitive boundaries.

The Safety Circle

Think of your safety circle as a protected space where you can practice boundary-setting without fear. Like musicians rehearsing together, each member helps create harmony while strengthening individual skills. Small groups often work best for deep sharing. Three or four trusted people who really understand sensitivity can provide more valuable feedback than a larger group with less awareness. These intimate circles let you explore boundary challenges openly. Watch how different members bring unique gifts. One person might excel at spotting when you're softening your "no" too much, while another notices patterns in what drains your energy. Like facets of a gem, each perspective adds clarity to your boundary practice.

Safe spaces allow for honest exploration. Here you can try firmer ways of stating needs or practice maintaining boundaries under pressure. The supportive environment helps you find your authentic voice without fear of judgment. Notice how shared experiences build deeper understanding. When group members face similar challenges, solutions often emerge naturally from your collective wisdom. Someone might share a clever way to handle repeated boundary pushing, sparking ideas for everyone. Regular meetings create momentum for growth. Whether monthly discussions or weekly check-ins, consistent connection helps maintain focus on boundary development. Each gathering builds on previous insights while addressing new challenges. The best safety circles blend support with gentle challenge. Members encourage each other while also pointing out blind spots or areas for growth. This balanced approach helps everyone develop stronger, more effective boundaries.

Building Connection Bridges

Building connections while honoring boundaries feels like crafting delicate bridges between islands. Each relationship finds its own unique balance of closeness and space. Start with those who naturally respect your rhythm. Watch for people who notice when you need quiet or ask before making plans. These early signs often mark the beginning of deeper understanding. Their natural consideration creates a foundation for stronger bonds. Some friends excel at combining care with space. They might text, "No need to respond now, just thinking of you," or suggest low-key ways to connect. These thoughtful approaches show how support can flow without pressure.

Pay attention to how different relationships find their own balance. Work connections might focus on professional boundaries, while closer friends understand both your limits and your capacity for depth. Each relationship creates its own special pattern of connection. The strongest bonds often grow from honest sharing. When you explain "I need time alone to recharge" or "Group events work better for me earlier in the day," understanding people welcome this clarity. They see how good boundaries actually create space for a deeper connection.

Notice which relationships naturally strengthen your boundary practice. Some people just get it, they respect your limits while still staying genuinely connected. These balanced connections show how boundaries and closeness can work together perfectly. Trust grows as boundaries and connections work together. When people consistently honor your limits while maintaining a warm connection, you discover how protection and closeness can dance in perfect harmony.

Sustainable Support Creation

Think of your support system like a living garden that needs regular tending. Some connections strengthen over time, while others might need careful pruning or fresh attention to thrive.

Deep support grows through steady nurturing. Taking time to check in with key allies, expressing gratitude for their understanding, and staying open about changing needs keep these connections vital. This regular care ensures your support system stays healthy like watering precious plants. Watch how different relationships evolve naturally. Some supporters might step back for a while, then return with renewed understanding. Others grow steadily closer as they demonstrate consistent respect for your boundaries. Each connection follows its own organic rhythm.

Regular reflection reveals what's working best. Monthly quiet time helps you notice which supporters truly strengthen your boundaries. Or yearly reviews show patterns in who provides the most effective understanding. This awareness helps you invest energy where it brings the most growth. The strongest systems blend flexibility with stability. Having both close allies and wider circles of support creates resilience. When one person isn't available, others can step in with understanding. This natural flow keeps your support network sustainable.

Notice which connections need extra attention. Sometimes a valuable supporter might need clearer communication about your current needs. Other times, new relationships show potential for deeper understanding. Like caring for different types of plants, each connection requires its own kind of maintenance.

Trust your instincts about which relationships deserve more investment. The supporters who consistently show up, respect your boundaries, and offer genuine understanding often become the cornerstone of your lasting support system.

The Path Forward

Building strong support networks changes everything about maintaining boundaries. Like stepping stones across a stream, each supportive connection makes the journey steadier and more manageable. Start by noticing who already gets it naturally. Some people instinctively respect your need for quiet mornings or understand why you need processing time after busy events. These natural allies often form the core of your growing support system. Watch how different types of support work together. A friend might help protect your social energy limits, while a colleague understands your need for focused work time. Family members could learn to recognize early signs of overwhelm. Each person adds their own unique strength to your boundary protection.

The real power comes from shared understanding. When supporters consistently honor your limits, maintaining boundaries feels less like a constant struggle and more like a natural flow. Their respect reinforces your confidence in protecting your sensitive nature. Notice how good support creates ripple effects. One person's clear understanding often helps others grasp your needs better. Their example shows how respecting boundaries actually creates stronger connections, not weaker ones.

Building these networks takes patience and trust. Start with those who show natural understanding, then gradually expand as you find more people who respect your needs. Like a carefully tended garden, your support system grows stronger with each passing season.

This network transforms boundary-setting from lonely work into supported practice. Each understanding ally, each accountability partner, and each mentor relationship helps create a world where your sensitivity can thrive safely.

Moving Ahead

Building lasting support for your boundaries becomes a journey of steady growth rather than a race to the finish. Like learning any vital skill, it unfolds naturally when given proper time and attention. Start where you stand right now. Notice which current relationships already show signs of understanding your needs. These natural supporters often provide the first sturdy steps toward a stronger system. Their innate respect for your boundaries shows what healthy support looks like. Watch how different forms of help blend together beautifully. Some friends excel at protecting your energy in social settings. Others understand exactly when you need quiet space to process. Colleagues might grasp your need for focused work time. Each supportive person adds their own special strength to your boundary protection.

The deepest growth happens through genuine connection. When people consistently honor your limits while maintaining warm relationships, you discover how boundaries and closeness work together perfectly. These balanced connections show others it's possible to respect needs while staying truly connected. Trust builds as your support system proves reliable. Each time someone understands your need for processing time or respects your energy limits, your confidence grows stronger. Their steady support helps turn boundary maintenance from constant struggle into natural flow.

The journey unfolds at its own perfect pace. Some connections deepen quickly, while others need time to develop full understanding. Trust this natural rhythm, it leads to lasting support rather than temporary fixes. Each step forward strengthens your foundation. Through patient cultivation of understanding relationships and steady maintenance of supportive connections, you create a world where your sensitivity can thrive safely, surrounded by people who truly get it.

The Art of Protection

Think of protecting your boundaries like tending a beautiful garden wall, it needs both strength and grace to serve its purpose well. Each time someone tests your limits, you learn better ways to maintain them. Start with calm and clarity when facing boundary challenges. A simple "This doesn't work for me" often carries more power than lengthy explanations. Like a steady rock in a stream, your quiet firmness helps others understand your limits are real and important.

Watch how different situations need different approaches. Sometimes gentle reminders work best, while other times require firmer responses. Maybe a friend needs a subtle hint about your energy limits, while a workplace situation calls for direct communication. Each challenge teaches you more about protecting your needs effectively. The real skill lies in staying both kind and clear. When someone pushes against your boundaries, you can hold firm without becoming harsh. This balanced response shows others that your limits come from self-respect rather than rejection. Notice which protection strategies work best for you. Some people find success with brief, direct statements. Others do better with calm explanations of their needs. Your unique style of boundary protection grows stronger with each challenge you face.

Each challenge becomes a chance to practice skilled protection. Like a martial artist learning new moves, you develop better ways to maintain your boundaries while staying true to your sensitive nature. This growing wisdom helps you navigate future challenges with increasing confidence. The art lies in finding balance and being firm enough to protect your needs while flexible enough to maintain genuine connections. Through steady practice, you learn to defend your boundaries with both strength and grace.

Meeting Resistance

Strong responses to boundary pushback grow from quiet confidence rather than defensiveness. Like a tree well-rooted in soil, you can stay firm while bending with the wind. Some resistance comes wrapped in concern. People might say, "You're being too sensitive," or "Just try to push through it." Meeting these moments with calm clarity, "This is what works best for me", often proves more powerful than arguing your case.

Watch how different types of pushback need different responses. Gentle questioning might need patient explanation, while repeated boundary crossing requires firmer limits. Your response can match the level of resistance, like adjusting the temperature on a thermostat. The key lies in staying grounded when others doubt your needs. Instead of defending or explaining repeatedly, simply maintain your position: "I understand you see it differently, but this is what I need." This steady approach shows your boundaries aren't up for debate.

Notice which responses work best in various situations. Sometimes a simple "This doesn't work for me" ends the discussion effectively. Other times, acknowledging the other person's view while holding your ground, "I hear your suggestion, and this is still what I need", creates better understanding. Keep your responses clear and consistent. When someone repeatedly tests your limits, they learn more from your steady maintenance of boundaries than from lengthy explanations. Like waves meeting a shoreline, your consistent response gradually reshapes their expectations. The art lies in remaining both strong and calm when facing pushback. Through steady practice, you learn to meet resistance with quiet authority rather than anxiety or anger.

The Violation Response

Facing boundary violations requires both swift action and thoughtful long-term planning. Like a skilled martial artist, you learn to protect yourself while staying centered. Clear responses work best in the moment. A simple "Stop, that doesn't work for me" immediately marks the violated boundary. No lengthy debates or explanations are needed, just direct protection of your space and needs. This immediate clarity helps prevent further crossing. Watch how different violations need different approaches. Small accidental crossings might need gentle reminders, while repeated intentional violations require stronger measures. Maybe a friend forgets your need for advance notice, or someone consistently pushes past your energy limits. Each situation shapes your response.

The first step focuses on immediate safety. If someone's actions drain your energy or ignore your clearly stated needs, you have every right to step away. Creating immediate distance gives you space to decide your next steps without additional pressure. Long-term solutions grow from careful reflection. Notice patterns in when violations occur or which boundaries get pushed most often. These insights help you strengthen protection where needed. Perhaps certain relationships need clearer limits, or some situations require stronger advance planning.

Trust your instincts about boundary crossings. That flutter of discomfort or surge of overwhelm often signals a violation before your mind fully processes it. Learning to recognize and respect these signals helps you respond more quickly and effectively. Each addressed violation builds stronger protection for the future. Through steady practice in responding clearly and effectively, you create more reliable boundaries for your sensitive nature.

Rebuilding Broken Lines

Think of rebuilding boundaries like restoring an ancient wall, stone by stone. Each piece needs careful attention, but the end result stands stronger than before. First, assess the damage honestly. Look at where your boundaries crumbled.

Maybe you stopped protecting your morning quiet time or let work demands overflow into rest hours. Understanding these weak points helps you build better protection going forward.

Start with your most essential needs. Like securing a foundation before rebuilding walls, focus first on boundaries that protect your core energy. This might mean reclaiming your need for processing time or restoring basic limits around availability. Notice which old patterns led to boundary breakdown. Some relationships might need a complete boundary reset, while others just need gentle reinforcement. Certain work situations demand entirely new protective measures, while personal boundaries just need consistent maintenance.

The rebuilding process takes both time and patience. Begin with small, manageable steps rather than fixing everything at once. Start by protecting one hour of quiet time each day, then gradually expand as this boundary grows stronger. Watch how different areas connect during reconstruction. Strengthening physical space boundaries often supports emotional ones naturally. Setting clear work limits helps protect personal time. Each improved boundary adds stability to the whole system. Trust yourself to know what needs changing. Your sensitivity often shows clearly where boundaries need the most attention. Let this awareness guide your rebuilding process, creating the protection that truly serves your nature.

Strengthening Vulnerable Areas

Think of boundary maintenance like reinforcing a bridge, each weak spot you find and fix makes the whole structure stronger. Regular attention prevents small cracks from becoming major breaks. Notice which boundaries feel shaky under pressure. Some might waver when you're tired or stressed, while others struggle against specific types of challenges. Like a skilled inspector checking foundation points, your awareness helps catch vulnerable areas early.

Physical boundaries often show weakness first. Your workspace might gradually lose its quiet protection, or your rest time slowly shrinks under outside demands. These early signs point to areas needing immediate reinforcement before bigger problems develop. Watch for emotional weak spots too. Certain relationships might regularly test your limits, or specific situations consistently drain your energy. Understanding these patterns helps you build stronger protection where you need it most.

The key lies in strengthening before breaking. Instead of waiting for boundary failures, add support at the first sign of strain. This might mean clearer communication about needs, stronger enforcement of existing limits, or new protective measures for challenging situations. Focus on one area at a time. Like mending a fence post by post, steady attention to each vulnerable spot creates lasting strength. Start with protecting your morning routine more firmly, then move on to strengthening work-life boundaries. Build extra support around high-stress points. Some boundaries face more pressure than others, just as bridge supports near water need extra protection. Recognize where your boundaries face the most challenges and reinforce these areas accordingly.

The Consistency Challenge

Finding the right balance between firm boundaries and flexible responses feels like mastering a delicate dance. Each situation calls for its own unique blend of steadiness and adaptability. Some days demand extra firmness. Your boundaries might need stronger protection when you're tired or facing increased pressure. Like adjusting a shield to meet different challenges, you learn to strengthen your limits when circumstances require it.

Watch how different situations shape your responses. A trusted friend forgetting your needs might need gentle reminders, while repeated workplace boundary crossing requires firmer limits. Your consistency shows in maintaining the boundary while adjusting how you express it. Core boundaries stay steady even when your approach shifts. You may always need quiet time to recharge, but how you protect this need might change. During busy periods, schedule it more carefully. On quieter days, you can be more flexible about timing. Notice which boundaries need absolute consistency and which allow more flexibility. Essential needs, like processing time or energy management, usually require steady protection. Other boundaries might bend occasionally without causing harm.

The real skill lies in staying true to your needs while adapting to circumstances. Like a tree with strong roots and flexible branches, you maintain your core stability while moving with life's changes. This balance keeps your boundaries both effective and sustainable. Remember that true consistency comes from honoring your needs, and not following rigid rules. Through steady attention to what serves you best, you develop reliable boundaries while adapting naturally to life's changes.

Learning Through Challenge

Think of each boundary challenge as a skilled teacher offering personalized lessons. Like a martial artist learning from each match, you gain wisdom about what works and what needs strengthening. Notice patterns in when boundaries get tested most. Your energy limits face greater pressure during certain seasons, or specific situations consistently challenge your need for processing time. These patterns reveal where to focus your attention for stronger protection. Small setbacks often carry big insights. When a usually effective boundary suddenly wavers, it might show where your protection needs updating. Perhaps your morning quiet time needs stronger guards during busy periods, or your work boundaries require clearer expression under pressure.

Watch how different approaches bring different results. Some boundaries grow stronger through gentle but consistent maintenance, while others need firm reinforcement to stay effective. Each response teaches you more about protecting your sensitive nature successfully. The deepest learning comes from paying attention to both success and struggle. When boundaries hold strong, notice what helped them stay firm. When they waver, look for what might have weakened them. This balanced awareness builds better protection over time.

Boundary learning never really ends. Each new situation brings fresh challenges and opportunities for growth. Like developing any important skill, your boundary wisdom deepens with continued practice and reflection. Success leaves clues worth following. When you handle a boundary challenge particularly well, take note of what worked. These moments of effectiveness often show paths toward stronger protection in other areas. Trust that each challenge makes your boundaries better. Through steady attention to what each experience

Building Resilient Systems

Developing resilient boundaries feels like training a strong yet flexible tree. Each challenge helps your protective system grow stronger and more adaptable. Watch how boundaries naturally shift and flow. Some days, your energy limits might need extra space, while other times, you can stretch them gently. Like a skilled dancer, you learn which movements keep you balanced and which risk your stability.

Core protections stay firm even as outer boundaries flex. Your basic needs, like quiet processing time or energy restoration, remain steady priorities. Yet how you maintain these essentials might change with circumstances, like a river finding new paths while keeping its core flow. Notice which boundaries need absolute firmness and which allow natural movement. Maybe your morning routine requires strict protection, while social boundaries can adapt more easily to different situations. This understanding helps you stay both protected and engaged.

Real strength comes from knowing when to hold firm and when to bend. Some challenges require an unwavering response, while others benefit from gentle flexibility. Like bamboo in the wind, your boundaries learn to move without breaking. Build your resilience through regular practice. Each time you successfully adapt a boundary while maintaining its protective power, you develop greater confidence in your ability to stay both safe and responsive.

Trust emerges as you prove to yourself that flexibility doesn't mean weakness. Your boundaries can adjust to new situations while still keeping their essential protective strength. This balance creates lasting resilience that serves your sensitive nature well.

The Path Forward

Meeting boundary challenges becomes a journey of growth rather than a battle for survival. Like developing any vital skill, your ability to protect your sensitivity grows stronger with each experience. Start by trusting your instincts about what needs protection. That flutter of discomfort or surge of overwhelm often signals exactly where boundaries need attention. Your sensitivity itself becomes a guide toward better self-protection.

Watch how different challenges shape different strengths. Some situations teach you to stand firmer, while others help you develop more flexible responses. Each experience adds another tool to your boundary-setting wisdom. The deepest growth comes from staying both strong and adaptable. When facing resistance, you learn to maintain clear limits while keeping connections open. These balanced responses show others that boundaries actually create space for better relationships. Notice which approaches work best in various situations. Maybe gentle reminders serve well with friends who occasionally forget your needs, while firmer limits work better in professional settings. Each successful response builds confidence in your protective abilities.

Good boundaries grow stronger through challenge rather than collapse under it. Like muscles developing through exercise, your protective skills improve with each test they face. This natural strengthening process turns previous struggles into sources of wisdom. Trust builds as you prove to yourself that you can handle boundary challenges effectively. Each successfully managed situation adds to your foundation of self-protection. Through steady practice, what once felt overwhelming becomes manageable.

The path forward involves both patience and persistence. By paying careful attention to what works and what needs adjustment, you can create increasingly effective protection for your sensitive nature.

Forward Motion

Moving forward with boundary protection becomes an empowering journey rather than an endless struggle. Like mastering any important skill, your ability to maintain healthy limits grows naturally with practice and patience. Each small success builds greater confidence. When you calmly maintain a boundary under pressure or find a graceful way to protect your energy, you prove to yourself that effective protection is possible. These victories, however small, create stepping stones toward stronger boundaries.

Notice how different situations help develop different strengths. Sometimes, you learn to stand firmer in your needs, while other times, you discover more flexible ways to protect yourself. Like a tree growing both strong roots and flexible branches, each experience adds to your boundary wisdom. The real power comes from staying both clear and kind. Instead of harsh defenses or weak compromises, you develop responses that protect your sensitivity while maintaining genuine connections. This balanced approach shows others that good boundaries actually create space for deeper relationships.

Watch for patterns in what works best for you. Maybe certain phrases help you maintain limits clearly, or specific strategies work well in challenging situations. Each successful moment teaches you more about protecting your sensitive nature effectively. Trust grows as you prove to yourself that you can navigate boundary challenges successfully. Through steady practice, what once felt overwhelming becomes manageable. Your responses become more natural, and your protection is more reliable. Each boundary you maintain, each challenge you handle effectively, adds to your foundation of self-protection. Through patient attention to what works and what needs adjustment, you create increasingly effective ways to honor your sensitivity while engaging fully with life.

The journey unfolds at its own perfect pace. Rather than rushing toward some imagined perfect protection, focus on steady growth through real experience. This natural development creates boundaries strong enough to last while flexible enough to serve you well.

The Harmonious Boundary

Creating harmony in your boundaries works like composing a beautiful piece of music. Each area of life needs its own protective measures, yet all must work together smoothly to create a sustainable whole. Consider how different life domains affect each other naturally. Your work boundaries influence your personal energy limits, while your social boundaries shape how you handle professional interactions. When one area strengthens, others often benefit too. For instance, protecting your morning quiet time might help you maintain better focus at work and more energy for relationships. The art lies in finding the right balance for each situation while maintaining overall consistency. Just as a conductor adjusts different instruments' volumes to create perfect harmony, you learn to adjust various boundaries to suit different contexts. You may need stricter limits around work hours but can be more flexible with social plans. Or maybe you maintain firm energy boundaries across all areas while allowing more flexibility in how you communicate them.

Pay attention to how boundaries in different areas support or challenge each other. When work boundaries stay strong, you might find it easier to maintain personal limits too. Conversely, if social boundaries weaken, work protection might need extra reinforcement. Understanding these connections helps you maintain better overall balance. The deepest integration happens when boundaries become natural extensions of your sensitive nature. Rather than feeling like separate rules for different situations, they flow together as one coherent self-protection system. This harmony makes boundary maintenance feel more like a natural rhythm than a constant effort.

Good integration takes time to develop. Start by noticing how different areas of your life connect and influence each other. Which boundaries support others? Where do conflicts arise? This awareness helps you create protection that works together smoothly rather than pulling in different directions. Through patient attention to how various boundaries interact, you develop a protective system that serves your whole life rather than just individual parts. This integrated approach helps your sensitivity become a strength rather than a challenge, enabling deeper engagement while maintaining essential protection.

Professional Territory

Start with your core work needs. Just as every person has different energy patterns, your professional boundaries should match your natural rhythms. This might mean blocking out your most focused morning hours for deep work when your mind is sharpest. During these protected times, you might turn off email notifications or use noise-canceling headphones to maintain concentration. Understanding meeting dynamics becomes crucial for sensitive professionals. Rather than accepting every invitation, develop clear criteria for participation. Consider which meetings truly need your presence and which could be handled through other channels. When you do attend, you might request agendas in advance to prepare properly or establish breaks between meetings to process information and recharge.

Communication boundaries require particular attention in today's always-connected workplace. Set clear expectations about your response times, perhaps explaining that you check emails at specific intervals rather than continuously. This approach actually improves your effectiveness by allowing focused work periods between communications.

Physical space boundaries deserve careful consideration, especially in open offices. You might identify quieter areas for concentrated work or establish signals that indicate when you're in deep focus mode. Some professionals find success with designated "quiet hours" or by using visual cues like headphones to indicate when they need uninterrupted time.

Collaborative work presents unique challenges for sensitive systems. While teamwork is essential, it's equally important to maintain boundaries around individual work time. Consider establishing "collaboration hours" when you're most available for team interaction while protecting other periods for focused individual contribution.

Family Framework

Creating healthy family boundaries feels like carefully tending a shared garden, you want to nurture close connections while preserving spaces that let each person thrive. The deep emotional bonds within families make this balance especially delicate. Setting boundaries with family requires particular sensitivity to relationship dynamics.

Unlike professional or social boundaries, family limits affect daily living patterns and touch our closest emotional connections. For example, if you need quiet time to process after work, you might establish a gentle transition period, perhaps 30 minutes of personal space before joining family activities. This creates protection without disconnection.

Physical space boundaries take on special importance within shared living environments. Even in close quarters, each family member needs some territory that honors their individual needs. This might mean designating certain areas as quiet zones during specific times or creating personal corners where family members understand you need space to recharge. These physical boundaries help maintain emotional well-being while preserving family closeness. Communication patterns play a crucial role in family boundary maintenance. Rather than sudden withdrawal when feeling overwhelmed, sensitive individuals can develop clear signals that family members learn to recognize. You might say "I need some processing time" or use an agreed-upon gesture that indicates you need space. This direct but gentle communication helps prevent misunderstandings while maintaining connection.

Time boundaries require particular attention within family life. Creating regular periods for both connection and individual needs helps establish sustainable patterns. Mornings remain protected for personal routines while evenings welcome shared activities. Specific days might balance family time with opportunities for individual recharge. The key lies in expressing boundaries with both firmness and love. Instead of harsh barriers or weak limits, develop protective measures showing care for yourself and your family relationships. This balanced approach strengthens both individual well-being and family bonds. Through patient development of these family-specific boundaries, you create sustainable patterns supporting sensitivity and connection. This thoughtful approach enables long-term family harmony while protecting essential needs.

The Friendship Field

Friendship boundaries work like a well-choreographed dance, each relationship finds its own unique rhythm of closeness and space. Understanding how to maintain these delicate balances allows sensitive individuals to nurture deep connections while protecting their essential needs. Setting boundaries with friends requires special attention to individual relationship dynamics. Each friendship develops its own pattern of interaction based on mutual understanding and respect. Some friends naturally grasp your need for quiet time after social gatherings, while others might need a gentle explanation about why you prefer advance notice for plans. These variations create a rich tapestry of connections that honor both friendship and sensitivity.

Energy management becomes particularly important in social relationships. Rather than pushing through exhaustion to maintain connections, sensitive individuals learn to communicate their capacity honestly. This might mean explaining that you prefer shorter, more focused visits over long social gatherings, or that you need recovery time between social events. When friends understand these needs, they often appreciate the quality of connection that comes from respecting energy boundaries. Group activities require their own careful consideration. Instead of avoiding social gatherings entirely, sensitive individuals can develop strategies that allow participation while maintaining protection. Perhaps you arrange to arrive early to adjust to the environment gradually, or plan exit times that honor your energy limits. Some find success in choosing specific positions in group settings, like sitting at the edge of a gathering where sensory input feels more manageable.

Communication patterns play a crucial role in maintaining friendship boundaries. Clear, kind expression of needs helps prevent misunderstandings while deepening trust. Instead of making excuses when overwhelmed, you might say, "I need some quiet time to recharge," or "I'd love to connect, but I need to spread out our visits to stay energized." This honesty actually strengthens friendships by creating authentic understanding.

The most sustainable friendship boundaries emerge from mutual respect and understanding. When friends grasp that your needs aren't personal rejections but rather requirements for genuine connection, they often become allies in maintaining healthy limits. This shared understanding transforms boundaries from barriers into bridges that support deeper friendships. Through thoughtful development of these friendship-specific boundaries, you create relationships that enrich life while honoring sensitivity. This balanced approach enables long-term connections that benefit everyone involved.

Personal Space Protection

Creating personal space boundaries resembles designing a sanctuary that perfectly fits your needs. Just as every person has unique requirements for feeling safe and centered, your personal territory should reflect your individual sensitivity patterns.

Physical space boundaries form the foundation of personal protection. Consider how different areas of your living space serve distinct purposes. Your bedroom might need extra sound dampening to create a true retreat, while a dedicated corner for quiet activities provides essential recharge space during busy days. Even in shared living situations, you can establish micro-territories that honor your need for sensory control, perhaps a specific chair positioned away from high-traffic areas or a desk arranged to minimize visual distractions.

Time boundaries play an equally crucial role in protecting personal space. Think of your day as containing different zones of engagement, each requiring its own level of protection. Morning hours might demand complete solitude for essential routines, while afternoon periods could allow more flexibility in interaction. Understanding these natural rhythms helps you create time boundaries that support rather than strain your sensitive system.

Energy management within personal space requires particular attention. Like managing a finite resource, you learn to recognize how different activities and interactions affect your energy levels. This awareness helps you arrange your space and schedule to prevent depletion. For instance, you might create transition zones between activities, both physical spaces and time buffers that allow proper processing and energy restoration.

The deepest aspect of personal space protection involves emotional territory. This includes understanding and honoring your need for mental processing time, emotional recovery periods, and psychological safety. Perhaps you maintain certain journals or activities as completely private while selectively sharing other aspects of your inner world. These emotional boundaries help preserve your sensitive nature while allowing meaningful connection with others.

Regular assessment of personal space needs ensures your boundaries remain effective. As circumstances change, you might need to adjust your protective measures. Maybe a busy period requires stronger boundaries around quiet time, or a new living situation demands creative solutions for maintaining personal territory. This flexibility helps your boundaries evolve while maintaining essential protection. Through thoughtful development of these personal space boundaries, you create a foundation that supports all other aspects of boundary maintenance. This careful attention to personal territory enables both deeper self-connection and more meaningful engagement with the world around you.

Personal space protection serves as both a refuge and a resource. When you maintain strong boundaries around your essential needs, you create a capacity for genuine engagement in other life areas. This balance transforms sensitivity from potential vulnerability into genuine strength.

The Path Forward

An integrated boundary system works like an intricate tapestry, with each thread supporting and enhancing the others. When we learn to weave our different boundaries together thoughtfully, they create a strong yet flexible protection that serves our whole life. Understanding how boundaries interact across domains becomes essential. Work boundaries naturally affect family energy, while social limits influence professional capacity. For example, protecting your morning quiet time might improve both your work focus and your ability to engage meaningfully with loved ones later. This interconnection means strengthening one area often benefits others naturally. Developing this integration requires careful attention to timing and energy flow. Consider how your natural rhythms affect different life areas. You might discover that scheduling important work meetings in your peak energy hours leaves you better equipped for family time later. Or perhaps maintaining firm social boundaries on weekdays helps you bring more presence to both professional and personal relationships.

Communication plays a vital role in successful boundary integration. Instead of having separate approaches for different situations, develop consistent ways to express your needs that work across contexts. Clear, kind language about your requirements helps others understand and respect your boundaries regardless of setting. This consistency makes boundary maintenance feel more natural and less like switching between different roles.

Physical space boundaries deserve particular consideration in integration. Your environment affects every aspect of life, so creating spaces that support your sensitivity benefits all areas. This might mean designing your home office to minimize sensory overwhelm, which then helps you maintain better energy for family interactions. Or establishing quiet zones that serve both personal recharge and professional focus needs.

The most effective integration emerges through regular practice and observation. Notice how adjusting boundaries in one area ripples through others. When you strengthen professional limits around availability, you might find it easier to maintain personal space boundaries too. These insights help you fine-tune your protective measures for better overall balance.

Good integration takes time to develop. Start by observing how different boundaries affect each other, then make small adjustments that support multiple areas simultaneously. This patient approach leads to sustainable protection that enhances rather than restricts your engagement with life. Through thoughtful development of these integrated boundaries, you create a coordinated system that supports your sensitive nature across all life domains. This balanced approach enables both authentic connection and essential protection, transforming sensitivity from a challenge into a source of strength.

Habit 6: Physical Intelligence and Self-Care

Embodied Wisdom

The profound connection between body and awareness represents a fundamental aspect of human existence. Deep within our physical form lies an intricate network of signals that speak volumes about health, emotions, and vital needs. These messages emerge through subtle feelings, movements, and natural rhythms that shape daily experience. When people cultivate genuine attention to bodily sensations, they unlock an ancient source of understanding that transcends rational analysis. The process begins with simple awareness, noticing tension, energy levels, and internal shifts. Over time, what initially feels like scattered physical impressions evolves into clear, reliable guidance.

This embodied knowledge serves as a compass, helping navigate life's challenges with greater precision and authenticity. The body holds wisdom accumulated through generations of human experience, expressing truth through sensation rather than words. By learning its language, overwhelming physical responses transform into valuable information. The practice requires patience and dedication. Small steps lead to profound shifts in perception. Gradually, the gap between physical sensation and conscious understanding narrows. What once seemed like random discomfort or unexplained reactions becomes a sophisticated system of personal insight. Each person's journey toward embodied awareness follows a unique path. Some discover it through movement practices, others through quiet contemplation. The essential element lies in maintaining consistent, gentle attention to physical experience. This creates space for natural intelligence to emerge and flourish.

The Language of Sensation

The human body communicates through a vast network of sensations, each carrying meaningful information about our needs and state of being. Understanding these physical signals takes time and careful observation, just as learning any new language takes.

When we start paying attention, patterns emerge with striking clarity. A tightening chest may signal rising anxiety before we consciously register worry. Stomach butterflies often precede essential realizations. Even tiny muscle twitches can carry important messages about safety and comfort. The body maintains an ongoing conversation about boundaries and needs. Racing thoughts might manifest as shoulder tension, while unspoken words create throat constriction. Learning to read these signals helps avoid overwhelm before it peaks. Once recognized, they become reliable guides for daily choices. This natural feedback system is rooted deeply in survival instincts. Each person's physical language develops uniquely, shaped by individual experiences and sensitivities. A racing heart might warn one person of danger while signaling excitement in another. The key lies in building your personal translation guide.

As this awareness deepens, the body's wisdom becomes increasingly clear. Energy levels, emotional states, and relationship dynamics all register physically before reaching conscious thought. This creates a sophisticated early warning system for maintaining balance and well-being. Most importantly, these sensations offer guidance without judgment. They present information, allowing for clearer decisions about rest, boundaries, and self-care. Through consistent practice, this physical intelligence becomes an invaluable tool for navigating life's challenges with greater ease and authenticity. The process requires gentle persistence. Each noticed sensation adds to the growing vocabulary of bodily wisdom. Over time, faint whispers develop into clear communication, offering precise guidance for maintaining health and harmony.

Energy's Ebb and Flow

Energy flows through human experience with remarkable complexity, following natural cycles that shape our daily capabilities. These patterns extend far beyond fundamental fatigue or alertness, revealing intricate details about our capacity for engagement and need for rest.

The morning hours carry distinct physical messages about the day ahead. A lingering heaviness in the limbs, slight mental fog, or unusual appetite changes might forecast limited resources. By recognizing these early signals, adjustments can be made before reaching critical depletion.

Throughout the day, the body continues sending precise updates about energy reserves. A subtle shift in focus, changes in breathing patterns, or altered sensory sensitivity often precede major energy dips. This advanced warning system allows for timely responses, perhaps scheduling breaks, adjusting social commitments, or modifying environmental factors.

As evening approaches, physical signs become especially meaningful. The quality of muscle tension, shifts in temperature regulation, or changes in coordination can indicate specific recovery requirements. Some evenings might call for gentle movement, while others demand complete stillness.

The body's energy language grows more nuanced with careful observation. What begins as basic awareness of fatigue develops into recognition of energy quality, whether it flows smoothly or feels fragmented, moves freely or seems blocked. This deeper understanding enables sophisticated choices about activity and rest. These natural rhythms deserve respect and attention. Fighting against them typically leads to more significant depletion, while working with them preserves vital resources. By honoring these patterns, energy management shifts from constant crisis response to skillful navigation of natural cycles. Success lies in accepting that energy ebbs and flows naturally. Rather than forcing constant high performance, wisdom comes through learning to ride these waves with grace. This creates sustainable patterns that support long-term well-being and consistent capability.

The Stress Response Map

Understanding how stress affects our bodies works like decoding a personal map of warning signs. Each body responds in its own special way, creating a unique pattern that can be learned and understood over time. The earliest hints of stress often show up subtly, perhaps a jaw that keeps clenching, shoulders that won't relax, or a stomach that feels unsettled. These quiet signals speak long before we consciously realize something's wrong. By noticing these early warnings, we gain valuable time to address what's causing the stress.

Sleep often serves as a sensitive indicator, changing in response to building pressure. Some people wake at odd hours, while others struggle to fall asleep. Changes in appetite might appear, either losing interest in food or craving specific things. Even breathing patterns shift, becoming shallow or irregular.

The digestive system is a particularly honest messenger. Stress might manifest as a churning stomach, changes in eating habits, or digestive discomfort. These physical reactions often surface before mental awareness catches up to what's happening.

Different types of stress create different bodily responses. Work pressure might settle in the shoulders and neck, while relationship stress could affect the chest or throat. Social tensions might appear as headaches or facial tension. Learning these specific patterns helps identify not just that stress exists, but what kind needs attention. Reading these physical messages transforms stress management from reactive to proactive. Instead of waiting for stress to build to uncomfortable levels, early recognition allows for timely adjustments. This might mean setting boundaries, adjusting schedules, or finding ways to process emotions before they become overwhelming.

The key lies in treating these stress signals as valuable information rather than inconveniences to ignore. They offer a sophisticated early warning system, developed through evolution to protect well-being. Working with these signals, rather than fighting against them, creates more effective ways to maintain balance and health.

Comfort's Physical Voice

The body expresses its need for comfort through an ongoing stream of physical messages, each one carrying specific information about what supports or strains our well-being. These signals form a detailed guide for creating environments and habits that genuinely nurture our systems. Physical comfort speaks through many channels, muscle tension melting away in certain positions, breathing deepening in specific spaces, or energy flowing more freely with particular movements. Some might notice their shoulders dropping when entering a room with soft lighting, while others feel their breathing at ease in spaces with fresh air flow. These responses offer precise guidance about what our bodies need to thrive.

Environmental factors play a crucial role in physical comfort. Temperature changes might trigger muscle tension or release. Certain sounds could cause subtle strain or promote relaxation. Even factors like air quality and lighting leave clear physical signatures. Learning these patterns helps create spaces that actively support rather than drain our systems. Movement needs vary throughout the day, with the body requesting different types of activity at different times. Morning stiffness might call for gentle stretching, while afternoon restlessness could signal the need for more vigorous movement. Evening hours often bring distinct physical cues about what type of rest will best support recovery.

The body also communicates clearly about positions and postures. Some sitting arrangements might consistently create tension, while others allow muscles to fully relax. Working positions could either support or strain focus and energy levels. These physical responses guide adjustments that promote sustained comfort rather than accumulated strain. Rest requirements show up through specific bodily signals. Heavy limbs might indicate a need for complete stillness, while restless energy could call for gentle movement before deeper rest becomes possible. Understanding these nuances helps choose the most effective forms of rest at any given time. Most importantly, comfort needs change constantly. What supports ease in the morning might create strain by evening. The body's messages about comfort shift with energy levels, stress, and environmental conditions. Staying attentive to these changing signals enables flexible responses that maintain consistent well-being.

Recovery's Physical Demands

The body demands unique forms of recovery based on its specific challenges. Like an intricate machine, each strain type requires its own specialized maintenance approach. Reading these signals transforms recovery from guesswork into precise care.

Mental exhaustion often manifests through distinct physical signs, perhaps heavy eyes, tight neck muscles, or foggy thinking. These symptoms might require more than simple rest. Some find relief through gentle walking, while others require complete sensory downtime. The key lies in matching the recovery method to the specific type of fatigue.

Emotional stress leaves its own physical fingerprints. A drained heart might manifest as chest tightness or shallow breathing. Deep emotional work could create body-wide exhaustion, requiring gentle, nurturing movement. Sometimes, emotional recovery requires complete stillness, while other times, it calls for expressive motion to process stored tension.

Physical signals also guide the timing of recovery. Sharp, immediate fatigue might demand quick breaks and specific stretches. Deeper, accumulated tiredness often requires longer periods of intentional rest. Learning to distinguish between these needs prevents pushing beyond healthy limits.

The body's recovery language grows clearer with practice. Small experiments reveal which approaches work best for different situations. Maybe afternoon brain fog lifts best with brief movement breaks, while evening exhaustion needs quiet unwinding time. Each discovered pattern adds to a personal recovery toolkit. Building trust in these physical messages requires consistent attention in varying circumstances. Some situations allow gentle exploration of different recovery methods. Others demand an immediate response to urgent body signals. This range of experiences strengthens confidence in reading and responding to physical needs.

Recovery needs to shift constantly. What refreshes the system one day might prove ineffective the next. Staying attentive to these changing requirements makes recovery more efficient and effective. This creates sustainable patterns that support long-term resilience and consistent well-being.

The Wisdom Journey

Physical wisdom emerges through a natural unfolding of awareness and understanding. Each small discovery adds depth to this inner knowing, like layers of sediment forming rich soil. What starts as faint, unclear signals gradually develops into clear, reliable guidance. The body speaks its truth without pretense or manipulation. A racing heart carries honest messages about safety needs. Tight muscles reveal unspoken boundaries. Stomach butterflies signal upcoming changes. Trusting these messages transforms physical experiences from confusing disruptions into valuable insights. Everybody holds their own unique language of sensation. Some might feel emotions primarily in their chest, while others experience them in their gut. Certain people detect energy shifts through temperature changes, while others notice alterations in muscle tension. These personal patterns create an individualized map of physical intelligence.

As understanding grows, the relationship with physical sensations shifts dramatically. What once felt like random discomfort becomes meaningful information. Overwhelming feelings transform into precise guidance. The body changes from an apparent source of problems into a wise ally offering constant support. This deepening awareness creates natural cycles of learning. Each noticed signal leads to better understanding. Every effective response builds trust in bodily wisdom. Small successes encourage deeper attention to physical messages, creating an upward spiral of growing physical intelligence.

Most valuably, this journey requires no force or strain. It unfolds naturally through gentle attention and patient practice. The body already holds deep wisdom; learning its language allows that knowledge to surface and guide daily life more effectively. This creates an enduring partnership between conscious awareness and physical intelligence. Success lies not in controlling physical responses, but in allowing their natural wisdom to emerge. This process transforms self-care from a series of prescribed actions into an organic flow guided by clear physical signals. The result is a more sustainable and authentic way of maintaining well-being.

Creating Sustainable Patterns

Physical balance emerges through a deeper understanding of our body's natural rhythms and signals. Like tending a garden, sustainable patterns grow from consistent, gentle attention rather than forced control or rigid rules. Learning to work with physical signals creates natural cycles of activity and rest. Some days might require vigorous engagement, while others require more gentle approaches. These patterns emerge not through strict scheduling, but through careful attention to how the body responds to different choices.

Sustainability develops through small, daily choices that honor physical needs. Maybe morning routines shift based on energy levels, or work patterns adjusts to match natural focus cycles. Each small alignment with body wisdom creates stronger foundations for lasting well-being. Regular check-ins reveal which approaches truly support physical balance. Some highly recommended practices might prove draining for certain systems, while unconventional methods could offer unexpected benefits. This personal experimentation leads to increasingly refined self-care strategies.

The process requires patience and flexibility. What works perfectly in one season might need adjustment in another. Energy needs shift with life circumstances, and physical responses change over time. Success comes through staying responsive to these changing needs rather than forcing fixed routines.

Sustainable patterns grow from trust in physical wisdom. Instead of fighting against body signals or pushing through discomfort, choices flow from a genuine understanding of physical needs. This creates an ongoing dialogue between daily activities and body responses, allowing natural adjustments that maintain lasting balance. The result is a dynamic system of self-care that adapts to changing circumstances while maintaining core stability. Rather than exhausting resources through a constant override of physical signals, energy flows more smoothly through choices aligned with natural rhythms and needs.

Forward Motion

Moving forward with physical awareness unfolds as a gradual awakening of deeper understanding. Like learning to read music or speak a new language, recognizing body signals becomes clearer and more natural with dedicated practice.

The growth process follows its own organic timing. Some signals become clear quickly, while others reveal their meaning more slowly. A flutter of nervous energy might immediately signal the need for grounding while understanding complex fatigue patterns takes longer to decode. Each insight builds upon previous learning, creating layers of practical wisdom. Daily engagement with physical messages creates natural feedback loops. When rest follows early fatigue signals, energy rebounds more effectively. Honoring hunger cues leads to steadier energy levels. Responding to tension with appropriate movement prevents pain from building. These positive cycles reinforce trust in body wisdom.

The real power emerges through consistent, gentle attention rather than forced analysis. Much like watching a garden grow, physical intelligence develops best when given space to unfold naturally. Each noticed sensation, whether subtle or strong, adds to the growing vocabulary of body awareness. This deepening understanding transforms daily choices. Instead of pushing through resistance, decisions flow from clear physical feedback. Rather than following generic advice, actions align with personal physical wisdom. The result is more sustainable engagement with life's demands and opportunities.

This journey has no final destination. Physical wisdom continues developing through changing circumstances and life stages. Each new challenge brings opportunities for deeper understanding, while each success builds stronger foundations for future growth. Progress is shown through increasing the ability to maintain balance while meeting life's demands. The body becomes a reliable partner in navigating challenges rather than an obstacle to overcome. This creates lasting resilience built on a genuine understanding of personal physical needs.

The Art of Self-Nurture

Physical care grows from understanding our body's subtle language and innate wisdom. Like tending a delicate ecosystem, self-nurture develops through careful attention to natural rhythms and needs. Daily routines emerge not as rigid rules, but as flexible structures that honor changing physical signals. Morning practices might shift based on energy levels, perhaps gentle stretching one day, vigorous movement another. These adjustments flow from listening to what the body truly needs rather than following prescribed patterns. The art lies in finding the balance between structure and flexibility. Certain anchoring practices provide stability, regular meal timing, consistent sleep patterns, or dedicated rest periods. Yet within these frameworks, space remains for adapting to daily physical messages. This creates reliable support while avoiding rigid control.

Overwhelming sensations become more manageable through this balanced approach. Instead of fighting against intense physical experiences, understanding grows about what triggers them and what helps soothe them. Maybe certain times of day consistently bring heightened sensitivity, calling for specific protective practices. Or particular environments might regularly create strain, requiring thoughtful preparation. Building these nurturing patterns requires patience and experimentation. Some highly recommended practices might prove too intense for sensitive systems. Others, seemingly simple, could offer surprising benefits. Success comes through discovering what truly supports individual needs rather than following general guidelines.

Effective self-nurture grows from a genuine respect for physical wisdom. Rather than forcing the body to conform to external expectations, practices develop that honor natural limits and capabilities. This creates sustainable patterns that strengthen rather than drain sensitive systems over time. Through this careful attention, overwhelming experiences gradually transform into valuable information. What once felt like random physical reactions becomes a sophisticated guidance system for maintaining well-being. The result is greater resilience built on a deep understanding of personal physical needs.

Dawn's Gentle Awakening

The first moments of wakefulness carry profound significance for sensitive bodies, setting the tone for hours ahead. Like a flower gradually opening to morning light, our systems need space to unfold naturally from sleep's deep rest. Physical awakening follows its own timing, unique to each person's natural rhythms. Some bodies need slow, quiet moments to gather energy, perhaps lying still while awareness gently returns. Others might require soft movement as consciousness emerges, allowing muscles to reawaken at their own pace. These opening moments create foundations for balanced energy throughout the day. The transition from sleep holds particular importance for sensitive systems. Harsh alarms or rushed routines can overwhelm delicate neural pathways, creating a strain that echoes through the day. Instead, gradual awakening practices support smoother transitions. Gentle stretching invites muscles to release night's holding patterns. Slow breathing helps nervous systems shift smoothly toward daytime activity.

Environmental factors play crucial roles in morning ease. Soft lighting prevents sensory shock as eyes adjust to wakefulness. Comfortable temperatures support bodies emerging from sleep's different temperature patterns. Even morning sounds deserve attention, perhaps gentle music or natural silence rather than jarring notifications. Morning practices require flexibility. Some days might need longer transition times, while others allow quicker movement into activity. Weather changes, seasonal shifts, and life circumstances all affect how bodies wake. Success comes through staying responsive to these changing needs rather than forcing fixed routines.

Through patient attention to morning signals, sustainable patterns emerge naturally. Each day provides fresh opportunities to refine understanding of personal awakening needs. This creates reliable yet flexible foundations for starting days in ways that genuinely support sensitive systems.

Movement's Sacred Dance

Movement patterns emerge naturally when we tune into our body's shifting energy levels and signals. Like a river finding its path, physical activity flows best when it follows our system's natural rhythms rather than fighting against them. Daily energy patterns create windows for different types of movement. Morning bodies might crave gentle stretching that awakens muscles gradually. As natural energy rises, more dynamic movement becomes possible. Afternoon signals could call for energizing activities, while evening often suits calmer, grounding practices. Understanding these patterns helps choose movement that supports rather than strains the system.

The body speaks clearly about which activities serve it best. Some movements bring immediate ease, perhaps shoulder rolls releasing built-up tension, or hip stretches unlocking stored stress. Others might generate sustainable energy, like walking in nature or flowing yoga sequences. By noticing these responses, a personal movement language develops. Intensity levels deserve particular attention in sensitive systems. High-energy days might welcome more vigorous activity, while lower-energy periods require gentler approaches. Even within single movement sessions, energy can shift dramatically. Success comes through staying responsive to these changes rather than pushing through fixed routines.

The movement also serves different needs throughout the day. Sometimes, physical activity helps process emotional intensity, while other times, it grounds scattered energy. Brief movement breaks might refresh mental focus, while longer sessions could restore depleted energy. Understanding these variations enables choosing a movement that matches current needs. Sustainable movement grows from trust in body wisdom. Rather than following external standards or pushing toward arbitrary goals, choices flow from genuine physical signals. This creates lasting patterns that strengthen rather than drain sensitive systems, building resilience through balanced activity.

The result is a movement that truly serves well-being, enhancing energy when needed, calming overwhelm when present, and maintaining balance through changing circumstances. Each choice becomes part of an ongoing dialogue between conscious awareness and physical wisdom.

The Rest Rhythm

Rest weaves naturally through daily patterns when we honor our body's signals for renewal. Like waves moving across water, energy ebbs and flows, creating natural spaces where restoration serves essential needs. Understanding personal fatigue patterns transforms rest from a last resort into strategic renewal. Early signs might appear as subtle changes in focus, slight shifts in muscle tension, or minor variations in sensory sensitivity. Noticing these quiet messages enables rest before deep exhaustion sets in. A brief pause when eyes first feel heavy prevents the larger crash that comes from pushing through. Different types of tiredness call for distinct forms of rest. Mental fatigue might need complete sensory quiet, perhaps a dark room and soft silence. Physical weariness could require gentle position changes or supported stillness. Emotional drain often benefits from grounding practices that calm the nervous system. Learning these variations creates more effective recovery.

Time of day significantly influences rest needs. Morning bodies might require frequent small breaks as systems fully awaken. Afternoon often brings natural energy dips that need deeper restoration. Evening patterns typically call for longer periods of quiet as systems prepare for sleep. Recognizing these rhythms helps place rest periods where they serve best. The quality of rest matters as much as its timing. Some moments need complete stillness, while others benefit from gentle movement. Certain spaces support more profound restoration through comfort factors like temperature, lighting, or sound levels. Understanding these elements enables creating conditions that truly refresh rather than pause activity.

Effective rest grows from trusting natural recovery rhythms. Instead of viewing rest as lost productivity, it becomes essential maintenance that supports sustainable energy. This shift transforms rest from a sign of weakness into strategic strengthening of sensitive systems. Through careful attention to rest signals, sustainable patterns emerge naturally. Each noticed the need and effective response builds a stronger understanding of personal restoration requirements. The result is more reliable energy maintained through regular renewal rather than constant depletion.

Evening's Gentle Descent

The transition from day to night is particularly important for sensitive systems. Like twilight slowly darkening into the evening, our bodies need time to shift naturally from activity toward rest. This gradual descent allows the nervous systems to release accumulated tension and prepare for sleep's renewal.

Evening signals often begin subtly, perhaps a slight dimming of mental clarity or gentle heaviness in the limbs. Honoring these early messages enables smoother transitions toward rest. Some bodies might first need slow walking or stretching to release physical tension. Others could require complete stillness as mental activity settles. These personal patterns reveal the most effective path toward night's quiet. The environment plays a crucial role in evening ease. Softening lights help bodies register approaching nighttime. Quieter spaces support the natural slowing of mental activity. Even temperature adjustments matter, slightly cooler air often aids the body's natural evening temperature drop. These external shifts support internal unwinding.

Different days demand different approaches to evening transition. High-energy days might need longer unwinding periods, while quieter ones allow quicker paths to rest. Stress levels, seasonal changes, and life circumstances all affect how our bodies prepare for the night. Success comes through staying responsive to these changing needs. Evening practices work best when they flow from a genuine understanding of personal patterns. Rather than forcing rigid routines, choices emerge from careful attention to what truly supports rest. Maybe certain activities consistently calm an active mind, gentle reading, quiet music, or simple breathing practices. Others might find peace through light stretching or mindful movement.

Through patient attention to evening signals, sustainable patterns develop naturally. Each day brings fresh opportunities to refine understanding of personal unwinding needs. This creates reliable yet flexible foundations for transitioning into restful nights that truly restore sensitive systems. The art lies in finding the balance between structure and flexibility. While certain anchoring practices provide stability, space remains for adapting to daily variations. This creates dependable support for evening ease while avoiding rigid control that might create tension rather than release.

Sleep's Sacred Space

The sacred hours before sleep deserve deep respect in sensitive systems. Like preparing a delicate garden for night's embrace, creating conditions for rest requires thoughtful attention to subtle details that influence sleep quality. Creating sleep's sanctuary begins with understanding personal comfort needs. Some bodies find rest easily in complete darkness, while others need soft ambient light. Temperature preferences vary significantly, perhaps slightly cool air with warm blankets, or steady warmth throughout the space. These individual patterns create the foundation for reliable rest.

The approach to sleep is as important as the sleep space itself. Racing thoughts might need gentle unwinding through quiet breathing or soft stretching. Physical tension could require specific position adjustments or supportive props. Emotional residue from the day often benefits from calming practices that settle the nervous system before sleep attempts begin.

Environmental adjustments play crucial roles in sleep preparation. Gradually dimming lights signal a natural transition toward rest. Reducing noise levels, whether through quiet spaces or consistent sound that masks disruptions, helps maintain sleep continuity. Even air quality deserves attention; fresh air flow often supports deeper breathing patterns that encourage rest. Most importantly, sleep practices need flexibility within their structure. While certain elements remain constant, perhaps specific bedding textures or room arrangements, space remains for adapting to changing needs. Some nights might require longer preparation time, while others allow quicker transitions to sleep. This balance creates reliable support while avoiding rigid patterns that might increase sleep anxiety.

Through careful attention to sleep signals, sustainable patterns emerge naturally. Each night brings opportunities to refine understanding of personal rest requirements. Success grows not from forcing specific outcomes, but from creating conditions that allow natural sleep rhythms to emerge and flourish.

The result transforms sleep from a sometimes-elusive state into a more reliable renewal process. Rather than struggling against sleep challenges, understanding grows about what truly supports rest for individual systems. This creates stronger foundations for consistent, restorative sleep patterns.

The Integration Dance

The delicate interplay between daily practices creates a living rhythm that supports sensitive systems. Like an intricate dance, each element moves in harmony with others, creating patterns that flow naturally from one to the next. Morning choices ripple through the entire day's experience. A gentle awakening might create space for more energetic movement later, while rushed starts often require earlier rest periods. Understanding these connections helps arrange daily practices in ways that maintain rather than drain energy. Simple adjustments in morning timing, perhaps ten extra minutes of quiet transition could dramatically improve evening ease.

Movement weaves naturally between other elements, responding to and influencing broader patterns. Active periods shape rest needs, while the quality of rest affects movement capacity. Some days flow best with movement spread in small amounts throughout hours, while others benefit from concentrated activity periods followed by deeper recovery. Learning these rhythms enables more sustainable engagement with daily demands. Rest periods serve as bridges between different types of activity. Brief pauses might refresh energy for the next task, while more extended restoration supports the transition between major daily phases. The timing and depth of these rest moments significantly influence sleep quality, affecting the next day's capacity. This creates ongoing cycles of activity and renewal that build on each other.

Environmental factors thread through all practices, creating consistency that supports routine integration. Light levels might shift gradually throughout the day, while temperature adjustments follow natural body rhythms. Even sound patterns deserve attention: quieter spaces during focus times, gentle background during movement, and complete silence for deep rest.

Effective integration grows from understanding personal patterns rather than following preset formulas. Some might need longer transitions between activities, while others prefer quicker shifts with more defined boundaries. Success comes by discovering combinations supporting individual systems rather than forcing standard approaches. Through patient attention to these connections, sustainable rhythms develop naturally. Each day brings fresh opportunities to refine understanding of how different practices influence each other. This creates increasingly sophisticated support systems that maintain sensitive well-being through changing circumstances.

Moving Forward

Finding harmony with our body's signals unlocks natural patterns of thriving. Like a skilled gardener learning the unique needs of each plant, understanding personal rhythms creates space for natural vitality to flourish rather than forcing growth through rigid control. Daily practices evolve into flowing sequences that support rather than strain sensitive systems. Small adjustments make significant differences. Shifting morning routines by thirty minutes allows a more natural awakening, or adjusting meal timing to better match energy patterns. These refined choices build foundations for lasting well-being.

The real power emerges through working with rather than against natural sensitivity. Instead of seeing physical responses as problems to overcome, they become sophisticated guidance systems offering precise information about needs and boundaries. This shift transforms daily life from constant struggle into informed navigation of changing circumstances. Physical wisdom deepens through regular practice in various situations. Sometimes, quick responses serve best, while other times, gradual adjustments prove more effective. Understanding these variations enables appropriate attention to body signals without becoming overwhelmed by them. Each successful response builds confidence in personal physical intelligence.

Body awareness is an ongoing conversation rather than a fixed destination. New circumstances bring fresh challenges while changing seasons affect physical needs. Yet each experience adds to the growing understanding of personal patterns, creating an increasingly sophisticated ability to maintain balance through life's natural shifts. This journey unfolds naturally when given space and attention. Rather than forcing specific outcomes, wisdom emerges through patient observation of what truly works for individual systems. Success grows not from rigid control but from a genuine understanding of personal rhythms and needs.

The result transforms self-care from a burdensome obligation into a natural expression of physical wisdom. Daily practices become opportunities for deepening body awareness rather than tasks to complete. This creates sustainable patterns that truly support sensitive well-being through all of life's seasons.

Fueling Sensitive Systems

Physical nourishment holds special significance for sensitive bodies. Like adding ingredients to a finely tuned instrument, each food choice creates subtle yet important effects throughout the entire system. Understanding personal responses transforms eating from a routine habit into a mindful practice. Morning bodies might need gentle, easily digested foods that gradually wake systems. Midday could call for steady energy sources that prevent afternoon crashes. Evening often requires lighter choices that support rest rather than stimulate activity.

Food timing carries equal importance to food choice. Some systems thrive with regular, smaller meals that maintain steady energy. Others might need longer gaps between eating to allow full digestion. Learning these patterns helps prevent both energy dips and digestive strain. Each person's optimal timing emerges through careful attention to body signals. Temperature and texture preferences often run deeper in sensitive systems. Hot foods might feel grounding during scattered energy, while cool choices could soothe during heightened states. Smooth textures sometimes ease nervous tension, while crunch might help with focus. Understanding these effects enables choosing foods that truly support current needs.

Environmental factors significantly influence eating experiences. Quiet spaces often support better digestion than noisy ones. Some might need to focus attention on food rather than distracted eating. Even lighting and temperature affect how bodies process nourishment. Creating supportive conditions helps maximize the benefits of food choices. Effective nourishment grows from trust in body wisdom. Rather than following rigid rules or external advice, choices flow from a genuine understanding of personal responses. This creates sustainable patterns that strengthen rather than strain sensitive systems through balanced nutrition.

Through consistent attention to food signals, reliable patterns emerge naturally. Each meal provides fresh opportunities to refine one's understanding of personal nourishment needs. The result is more effective fueling that truly supports sensitive well-being rather than creating additional challenges.

The Discovery Process

Food awareness unfolds like a personal science experiment, where each meal offers insights into our body's unique language. Like a skilled researcher, careful attention to subtle physical responses reveals precise information about what truly nourishes sensitive systems. Digestive signals speak through various channels, energy levels shifting after certain foods, mental clarity changing with different meal timing, or muscle tension responding to specific ingredients. Some might notice afternoon brain fog following heavy lunches, while others find sustained focus from the same meals. These individual patterns create a detailed map of personal food responses.

The morning meal holds particular significance in setting daily patterns. Some bodies welcome hearty breakfast, energy flowing smoothly from early nourishment. Others need gentler starts, warm liquids or light fare until systems fully awaken. Understanding these preferences enables choices that support rather than strain morning transitions. The timing of meals interacts deeply with nervous system states. Stress levels affect digestion capacity, while food choices influence stress resilience. High-pressure periods might require smaller, more frequent meals to maintain stability. Calmer times could allow for more varied eating patterns. Learning these connections helps maintain balance through changing circumstances. Effective nourishment grows from patient observation rather than rigid rules. Instead of forcing preset meal plans, attention focuses on actual body responses. Maybe certain food combinations consistently support energy, while others regularly create strain. Each noticed reaction adds to the growing understanding of personal dietary needs.

Through careful tracking of food effects, reliable patterns emerge naturally. Some signals appear quickly, perhaps immediate energy changes or digestive responses. Others reveal themselves more slowly through subtle shifts in sleep quality or emotional stability. Success comes through noting both immediate and delayed reactions to different foods and eating patterns. This process transforms eating from a mechanical routine into informed choices based on personal wisdom. Rather than following general guidelines, decisions flow from a genuine understanding of individual needs. The result is more sustainable nourishment that truly supports sensitive system balance.

Orchestrating Mealtimes

Timing transforms nourishment into an intricate art tailored for sensitive bodies. Like conducting a delicate symphony, the precise moments of eating matter as much as the food itself. Each person's natural rhythms create unique windows when nourishment serves best.

Morning hunger patterns reveal essential clues about ideal breakfast timing. Some bodies wake ready for immediate nourishment, energy flowing smoothly from early meals. Others need longer transitions, perhaps starting with gentle hydration until a natural appetite emerges. These morning signals guide the creation of sustainable breakfast routines. The body speaks clearly about its preferred eating windows throughout the day. Mid-morning energy dips might signal the need for light sustenance, while afternoon focus challenges could indicate timing adjustments. Natural appetite often flows in personal patterns quite different from standard meal schedules. Understanding these individual rhythms enables more effective nourishment timing. Evening eating mainly influences overall well-being. Some find that earlier dinner supports better sleep and morning clarity. Others might need light evening fare to maintain stable blood sugar through the night. These patterns often vary by season and stress levels. Success comes through staying responsive to changing needs rather than forcing fixed schedules.

Meal timing works best when aligned with natural body rhythms. Rather than pushing food at preset hours, attention focuses on genuine hunger signals. Perhaps you need more frequent, smaller meals on certain days to maintain energy. Others might flow better with fewer, more substantial eating windows. Each person's optimal pattern emerges through patient observation. Through careful attention to timing effects, sustainable routines develop naturally. Every meal provides fresh opportunities to refine your understanding of personal nourishment schedules. This creates reliable yet flexible eating patterns that truly support sensitive system balance.

The result transforms mealtimes from rigid obligations into naturally flowing nourishment cycles. Instead of fighting against body rhythms, eating aligns with personal patterns. This enables more effective absorption and processing while maintaining consistent energy through changing daily demands.

Quenching Needs

Managing hydration flows naturally from understanding how sensitive bodies respond to fluid levels. Like tending a delicate plant, each system needs its own specific balance of moisture to function optimally. Thirst signals often whisper before they shout in sensitive systems. Subtle changes might appear first, perhaps slightly dulled thinking, minor muscle tension, or gentle mood shifts. Learning these early signs enables adjusting fluid intake before deeper dehydration sets in. Sometimes, what feels like fatigue or brain fog actually signals the need for water.

Daily rhythms significantly influence hydration needs. Morning bodies often benefit from immediate fluid replacement after sleep's natural dehydration. Afternoon energy dips might respond better to electrolyte-rich drinks than plain water. Evening hydration requires careful balance, enough to support sleep without disrupting it. These patterns shift with seasons and activities.

Physical movement creates unique fluid demands for each person. Some need frequent small sips during activity, while others fare better with substantial pre-hydration and recovery drinking. Weather changes dramatically affect these patterns, hot days might require doubled intake, while cold weather masks thirst signals despite continued need. Emotional states intertwine deeply with hydration balance. Stress often increases fluid needs while simultaneously masking thirst signals. Anxiety might affect absorption rates, requiring adjusted intake timing. Understanding these connections helps maintain stable hydration through varying emotional landscapes.

Effective hydration grows from understanding personal patterns rather than following generic guidelines. Instead of forcing arbitrary amounts, attention focuses on body responses. Maybe certain times of day consistently need more fluid, while others require less. Each noticed pattern adds to growing wisdom about individual hydration needs. Through patient observation of fluid effects, sustainable patterns emerge naturally. Every day brings fresh opportunities to refine understanding of personal hydration rhythms. This creates reliable yet flexible approaches that truly support sensitive system balance.

Supplemental Support

The relationship between sensitive systems and supplemental nutrients requires delicate balancing. Like adding subtle notes to a complex melody, each addition creates effects that ripple through the entire system. Understanding personal nutrient needs transforms supplementation from guesswork into informed practice. Morning absorption patterns might favor certain nutrients, while others work better later in the day. Some combinations enhance each other's benefits, while others compete for absorption. These interactions create intricate patterns unique to each body.

Testing plays a crucial role in identifying genuine needs rather than assumed deficiencies. Blood work might reveal unexpected patterns, while careful tracking of physical responses provides real-world feedback. Some supplements create immediate noticeable effects, while others work more subtly over time. Learning these patterns helps distinguish between truly beneficial additions and unnecessary strain. Environmental factors significantly influence supplemental requirements. Seasonal changes affect vitamin D needs, while stress levels might increase demand for certain minerals. Even travel or altitude changes can shift how bodies process additional nutrients. Understanding these variations enables adjusting support as circumstances change. Effective supplementation grows from patient observation rather than following standard protocols. Instead of adopting complete supplement regimens at once, introducing single elements slowly allows clear effects tracking. Maybe magnesium consistently helps with sleep, while B vitamins prove too stimulating. Each discovered pattern adds to personal supplementation wisdom.

Through careful attention to supplement responses, sustainable patterns emerge naturally. Every adjustment provides opportunities to refine understanding of individual nutrient needs. This creates reliable yet flexible supplemental support that truly serves sensitive systems rather than overwhelming them. The result transforms supplementation from scattered additions into precise nutritional tools. Rather than following general recommendations, choices flow from a genuine understanding of personal requirements. This builds stronger foundations for maintaining sensitive system balance through changing circumstances.

Strategic Selections

Food choices create distinct ripples through sensitive systems. Like a master chemist mixing precise compounds, understanding personal reactions transforms eating into an art of well-being. Specific foods often act as reliable allies for different needs. Morning eggs might provide steady focus for some, while others find clearest thinking from lighter fare like fresh fruit. Quinoa could offer sustained afternoon energy, while sweet potatoes might ground evening nervous system activity. These individual patterns emerge through carefully tracking how each food affects body and mind.

The morning meal sets powerful foundations for daily function. Some discover that protein-rich breakfasts support sustained mental clarity, while others need gentler carbohydrates to ease into activity. These breakfast effects often influence energy levels well into afternoon hours. Understanding these connections enables choices that truly serve daily needs.

Midday nourishment particularly affects afternoon capabilities. Heavy lunches might cloud thinking for some while energizing others. Light meals could leave some scattered while helping others maintain focus. Learning these personal patterns helps schedule important tasks around optimal eating times.

Evening food choices directly affect sleep quality. Some find that earlier, lighter dinners support deeper rest, while others need substantial evening meals to prevent midnight waking. Certain foods might consistently aid relaxation, while others disrupt sleep patterns. These observations guide the creation of ideal evening menus.

This understanding transforms food from a potential threat into a sophisticated tool for well-being. Rather than fearing adverse reactions, knowledge grows about which foods serve as allies. Every meal provides fresh opportunities to refine this understanding, creating increasingly precise nourishment strategies. The result opens new possibilities for sensitive living. Instead of restricting food choices out of uncertainty, clear patterns emerge about personal requirements. This creates confident partnerships with nutrition that support thriving through life's various demands and opportunities.

Mastering Physical Resilience

Understanding how our bodies communicate creates a powerful foundation for sensitive well-being. Like learning to read an ancient and personal language, each physical signal carries precise meaning about our needs and capacities. Resilience emerges through patient attention to these bodily messages. A tight chest might warn of approaching overwhelm before conscious awareness catches up. Subtle changes in appetite could signal a need for emotional processing. Even small shifts in energy patterns often carry important information about necessary adjustments.

The body's wisdom appears in various ways throughout the day. Morning sensations might predict energy availability, while afternoon signals could indicate approaching limits. Evening physical signs often reveal specific recovery needs. Learning these patterns enables moving from reactive to proactive self-care. Different types of strain require distinct forms of support. Mental fatigue might need quiet darkness, while emotional drain could call for gentle movement. Physical depletion often benefits from complete stillness. Understanding these variations helps choose the most effective recovery approach for each situation.

Building resilience grows from trust in physical intelligence. Rather than fighting against body signals or pushing through discomfort, choices flow from a genuine understanding of personal needs. This creates sustainable patterns that strengthen rather than drain sensitive systems over time. Through consistent attention to physical wisdom, reliable patterns develop naturally. Each noticed signal and effective response adds to the growing understanding of personal requirements. The result transforms sensitivity from apparent weakness into a sophisticated guidance system for maintaining well-being.

This mastery opens new possibilities for sensitive living. Instead of struggling against natural patterns, a clear understanding emerges about personal needs and capabilities. This creates confident navigation of life's challenges while maintaining consistent physical balance.

Beyond Stress

Physical wisdom flows deepest when working with our body's natural tendencies toward balance. Like discovering hidden springs of renewal, specific practices unlock our innate capacity for releasing tension and restoring harmony. The body holds sophisticated self-regulation systems that respond to gentle guidance. Certain pressure points act like reset buttons for the nervous system, perhaps where the skull meets the neck or specific spots along the solar plexus. When approached with patience, these areas often release deep patterns of holding without force. Breath patterns create direct pathways to nervous system states. Slow exhales might activate natural calming responses, while rhythmic breathing could help process stored tension. Some find that morning breath practices set positive patterns for the entire day, while evening breathing rituals help unwind accumulated stress.

Strategic stillness often proves more powerful than complex techniques. Brief moments of complete quiet, especially during natural transition points in the day, allow systems to reset naturally. These pauses might last only minutes yet create ripples of relief through multiple body systems. The timing of renewal practices significantly influences their effectiveness. Dawn hours often hold special potential for setting positive patterns, perhaps through gentle movement or quiet meditation. Dusk brings natural opportunities for releasing accumulated tension as systems prepare for night's restoration.

Advanced regulation grows from working with rather than against body wisdom. Instead of forcing relaxation, attention creates conditions that allow the natural balance to emerge. Maybe certain positions consistently invite ease, while specific environments support deeper unwinding. Through patient attention to release patterns, sustainable approaches develop naturally. Each discovery about personal relaxation needs adds to a growing understanding of maintaining balance. This creates reliable yet flexible ways of working with rather than against sensitivity. The result transforms tension management from constant struggle into an informed partnership with natural healing capacities. Rather than fighting against stress, clear pathways emerge for supporting the body's innate wisdom about maintaining well-being through life's various challenges.

Pain's Messages

Physical discomfort speaks in nuanced dialects that carry important information. Like a sophisticated warning system, each type of sensation provides specific guidance about what our bodies need for balance and healing. Sharp, sudden signals often request immediate attention, perhaps a position change or brief rest period. These clear messages usually point to direct actions that can prevent deeper strain. Learning to respond quickly to these acute signals helps avoid escalation into more serious issues. Dull, persistent aches typically reveal longer-term patterns needing adjustment. Maybe certain postures consistently create tension, or specific activities regularly strain sensitive areas. Understanding these chronic patterns enables the creation of sustainable solutions rather than temporary fixes.

Temperature preferences reveal important clues about tissue needs. Some areas might consistently respond better to warmth and blood flow increasing to support healing. Others could find relief through cooling applications that reduce inflammation. These thermal responses often vary not just by location but by time of day and type of strain.

Movement plays a complex role in comfort management. Gentle motion might ease morning stiffness while complete stillness serves better for afternoon relief. Some discomfort lifts with specific stretches, while other sensations require more general activity changes. Understanding these variations helps choose the most effective approach for each situation.

Effective response grows from treating pain as information rather than an enemy. Instead of automatically seeking to eliminate discomfort, attention focuses on understanding its message. This creates opportunities for addressing root causes rather than just managing symptoms. Through careful attention to pain patterns, reliable relief approaches develop naturally. Each noticed connection between sensation and need adds to growing wisdom about personal comfort requirements. The result transforms pain management from a reactive struggle into an informed partnership with body signals. This understanding opens new possibilities for maintaining physical ease. Rather than fearing discomfort, clear pathways emerge for working with these important messages. This creates more effective ways of supporting sensitive system balance through life's various challenges.

Strengthening Immunity

The immune system functions best when we create conditions that mirror natural rhythms. Like tending to a diverse ecosystem, defense mechanisms strengthen through balanced exposure and thoughtful protection.

Daily choices significantly influence immune resilience. Fresh air flowing through living spaces helps clear stagnant particles while supporting healthy respiratory function. Natural light exposure regulates crucial immune cycles, while varied movement stimulates lymph flow without overwhelming recovery systems. These simple yet powerful practices create foundations for lasting health.

Seasonal shifts require distinct approaches to immune support. Winter often calls for more internal practices, perhaps longer sleep periods and warming foods that nourish without taxing digestion. Spring brings opportunities for gentle cleansing through lighter meals and increased movement. Summer allows more vigorous activity that builds strength through appropriate challenges.

Fall is especially important for preparing immune defenses. As days shorten, bodies benefit from specific practices that support the transition to winter patterns. Certain herbs may prove particularly helpful during this shift, while specific rest routines help maintain resilience through darker months.

Environmental engagement plays a crucial role in defense building. Even in cooler weather, brief outdoor time often provides more benefit than elaborate indoor protocols. Natural settings offer balanced exposure to beneficial microbes while supporting overall system regulation. Understanding these connections helps create sustainable immune support. Effective immunity grows from working with rather than against natural patterns. Instead of attempting constant protection or deliberately seeking a challenge, attention focuses on creating conditions that allow defense systems to function optimally. This might mean adjusting activity levels based on energy signals or modifying environments to support rather than strain-sensitive systems.

Through careful attention to immune responses, reliable support patterns emerge naturally. Each season brings fresh opportunities to refine understanding of personal defense needs. The result transforms immune care from constant worry into an informed partnership with natural healing capacities.

Preserving Vitality

Sustaining energy in sensitive systems requires artful attention to natural rhythms. Like managing a finite but renewable resource, understanding personal energy patterns transforms daily choices into opportunities for maintaining vitality. The body clearly signals its energy needs through subtle cues. Mental fog might indicate the need for a brief pause before the focus fades completely. Muscle tension could warn of approaching physical limits, while slight emotional shifts often precede energy crashes. Learning these early warnings enables proactive rather than reactive energy management.

Different activities affect energy in distinct ways. Some tasks might energize despite requiring effort, perhaps creative work or gentle movement. Others could drain resources even when seemingly simple, like certain social interactions or environmental challenges. Understanding these patterns helps arrange activities to maintain stable energy throughout the day. Strategic micro-breaks serve as powerful tools for energy preservation. A few conscious breaths between tasks, moments of complete stillness during transitions, or brief sensory breaks in quiet spaces often prevent deeper fatigue from building. When timed well, these small pauses maintain vitality more effectively than pushing through to exhaustion.

Sustainable energy flows from honoring natural capacity limits. Instead of forcing constant high performance, attention creates rhythms supporting consistent vitality. Maybe certain times of day naturally suit demanding tasks, while others require gentler engagement. Each person's optimal pattern emerges through patient observation. Through careful attention to energy signals, reliable sustainability practices develop naturally. Every day brings fresh opportunities to refine understanding of personal vitality patterns. This creates increasingly sophisticated ways of maintaining energy through life's various demands. The result transforms energy management from a constant struggle into an informed partnership with natural rhythms. Rather than fighting against fatigue, clear pathways emerge for maintaining consistent vitality while honoring sensitive system needs.

Lasting Wellness

Building lasting well-being emerges through careful attention to the small choices that shape each day. Like tending a delicate garden, subtle nurturing actions create stronger results than occasional intense efforts.

Daily rituals lay the foundations for enduring health. Gentle morning movement might prevent tension from accumulating, while brief afternoon walks could maintain energy better than pushing through fatigue. These simple yet consistent practices often prove more sustainable than dramatic lifestyle changes or intense intervention programs.

Physical wisdom develops through patient observation of personal patterns. Some bodies thrive with frequent, gentle movement spread throughout the day. Others might need concentrated activity periods followed by complete rest. Understanding these individual rhythms enables the creation of practices that truly serve rather than strain-sensitive systems.

The timing of self-care significantly influences its effectiveness. Early signs of tension respond better to gentle stretching than waiting for serious discomfort to develop. Regular movement breaks often prevent fatigue more effectively than pushing until exhaustion demands extended recovery. These proactive approaches build resilience over time.

Sustainable wellness grows from the partnership with body wisdom rather than forcing predetermined routines. Instead of viewing sensitivity as a weakness, it becomes sophisticated guidance for maintaining balance. Each noticed the need for an effective response, which adds to a growing understanding of personal requirements. Through consistent attention to physical signals, reliable patterns emerge naturally. Every day brings fresh opportunities to refine understanding what truly supports individual well-being. This creates increasingly nuanced approaches to maintaining health through life's various challenges.

The result transforms physical care from constant struggle into informed collaboration with natural rhythms. Rather than fighting against sensitivity, clear pathways emerge for working with these heightened awareness patterns. This opens new possibilities for thriving while honoring unique physical needs.

Habit 7: Sacred Space Creation

The Architecture of Serenity

Design choices in living spaces hold particular power for sensitive systems. Like composing a gentle symphony, each environmental element: light, sound, texture, and airflow contributes to creating spaces that soothe rather than overwhelm.

Natural light patterns significantly influence sensitive well-being. Some areas might benefit from adjustable lighting that shifts with daily rhythms, while others need consistent, gentle illumination. Understanding these needs helps create spaces that support rather than strain visual sensitivity. Even minor adjustments in light quality can dramatically affect comfort levels.

Sound management plays a crucial role in environmental comfort. Certain areas might need complete quiet for focus and restoration, while others benefit from gentle background sounds that mask disruptive noise. Creating these acoustic zones enables maintaining balance through varying sound demands.

Texture choices profoundly affect sensitive systems. Smooth surfaces offer calm during overwhelm, while specific fabrics provide grounding through gentle sensory input. Understanding these tactile preferences helps select materials that truly support sensitive comfort rather than create additional strain.

Air quality deserves particular attention in sensitive spaces. Fresh air flow often proves more beneficial than artificial freshening. Natural ventilation patterns, when possible, help maintain environmental balance while supporting respiratory ease. These subtle factors significantly influence overall well-being.

Effective spaces grow from understanding personal sensory needs rather than following standard design rules. Instead of creating uniformly minimal environments, attention focuses on what truly supports individual comfort. Certain areas may need richer sensory input, while others require more simplicity.

Through careful attention to environmental effects, sustainable sanctuaries develop naturally. Each space provides opportunities to refine one's understanding of personal comfort requirements. Through thoughtful design choices, this creates increasingly sophisticated support for sensitive well-being. The result transforms living spaces from potential sources of strain into reliable sources of support. Rather than fighting against sensitivity, clear patterns emerge for creating environments that enhance rather than challenge natural awareness.

Illuminating Wisdom

Light shapes sensitive systems in profound and nuanced ways. Like conducting a delicate symphony, understanding these patterns transforms living spaces into sanctuaries of well-being.

Morning light deserves special attention. Eastern exposure offers gentle awakening as soft rays filter through windows, helping bodies transition naturally from sleep. Yet these same spaces often need flexible shading options by mid-morning. Simple adjustable curtains or blinds can distinguish between energizing light and overwhelming glare.

Southern light brings steady brightness throughout the day. Some sensitive systems thrive with this constant illumination, while others need careful filtering. A mix of sheer curtains and adjustable blinds creates adaptable spaces that support rather than strain.

The western sun holds particular challenges. As the afternoon progresses, intensifying rays can disrupt sensitive systems preparing for evening quiet. Graduated shading, through layered window treatments or strategic placement of plants, helps manage this transition. Understanding these patterns enables proactive adjustments before discomfort builds.

Effective light management grows from personal observation. Skip the standard lighting rules. Instead, notice how different types of light affect your system throughout the day. Maybe morning sun energizes while afternoon light overwhelms. These insights guide creation of spaces that truly serve sensitive needs.

Through patient attention, sustainable solutions emerge. Each day brings fresh opportunities to refine your understanding of personal light preferences. The result? Living spaces that enhance rather than challenge natural sensitivity. This awareness opens new possibilities. Rather than viewing light sensitivity as a limitation, it becomes a sophisticated guide for creating environments that support well-being. Simple adjustments, a well-placed lamp, an extra layer of curtains, or a strategically positioned mirror, can dramatically affect daily comfort.

Symphony of Silence

Rich layers of sound fill sensitive spaces, calling for artful orchestration. Like a skilled conductor, thoughtful attention to acoustics transforms environments from chaotic to calm.

Silence serves different needs throughout the day. The morning might welcome complete quiet during early routines, allowing a gentle transition from sleep. Yet midday spaces often benefit from subtle background sounds that mask jarring noise while maintaining focus. A carefully placed white noise machine or gentle fan creates consistent audio foundations. Strategic design choices shape sound flow naturally. Heavy curtains soften harsh echoes, while plush rugs absorb footsteps and room tones. Bookshelves, positioned thoughtfully, act as natural sound barriers between spaces. These elements work together, creating zones of acoustic comfort.

Each area demands unique sound treatment. A meditation corner might need complete stillness, achieved through sound-dampening panels and careful placement away from noise sources. Creative spaces could welcome more varied acoustics, perhaps gentle music or nature sounds that inspire without overwhelming. Work areas often benefit from steady background tones that support concentration.

Windows plays a crucial role in sound management. Double-paned glass blocks urban noise, while strategically placed plants near windows help diffuse incoming sounds. Simple weatherstripping often dramatically reduces noise leaks around frames and doors.

Effective acoustic design grows from understanding personal sound sensitivity. Rather than creating uniformly quiet spaces, attention focuses on what truly supports comfort in each area. Notice which sounds soothe and which strain your system. These insights guide the creation of environments that nurture rather than challenge. Through careful attention to sound patterns, sustainable solutions emerge naturally. Every adjustment provides fresh opportunities to refine acoustic balance. This transforms living spaces into sanctuaries that protect sensitive systems while allowing necessary sound flow.

Breathing Life

Air flows like an invisible river through our spaces, profoundly affecting sensitive systems. Fresh circulation energizes while stagnant air depletes vitality, often before we consciously notice the shift.

Natural air purification works through layered approaches. Certain plants excel at filtering specific toxins, snake plants remove airborne chemicals, while spider plants combat carbon monoxide. Yet their benefits extend beyond mere filtration. Living plants add subtle vitality to spaces, creating more vibrant environments. A single well-placed plant can transform a room's entire feeling. Timing matters deeply when refreshing indoor air. Early morning often provides the cleanest outdoor air, making it ideal for brief but thorough ventilation. These morning air exchanges set positive patterns for the entire day. Evening breezes might offer another window for refreshment, though urban areas sometimes need more selective timing.

Each season demands unique approaches to air quality. Spring invites deep cleaning of surfaces where winter staleness collects. Summer mornings allow capturing cool, fresh air before the heat builds. Fall requires careful balance and maintaining healthy airflow while preparing spaces for winter's closure.

Essential oils add another dimension to atmospheric health. Different scents serve distinct purposes: lavender calms overwhelmed systems, while citrus oils energize sluggish spaces. Yet proper diffusion proves crucial. Too much fragrance, even from beneficial oils, can overwhelm sensitive systems.

Effective air quality management grows from understanding personal sensitivity patterns. Instead of following standard recommendations, notice how different air conditions affect your system. Perhaps certain times of day produce clearer thinking with open windows. Maybe specific plants consistently support easier breathing. Through careful attention to these atmospheric elements, spaces transform from potential sources of strain into reliable sources of renewal. The result opens new possibilities for creating environments that truly support sensitive well-being.

Cultivating Sacred Atmospheres

Energy patterns weave through sensitive spaces in ways that profoundly affect well-being. Like tending an invisible garden, understanding these subtle currents enables the creation of environments that truly nurture rather than drain sensitive systems. Each area holds its own unique atmosphere. Some spaces naturally support quiet reflection, while others spark creativity or encourage movement. Understanding these inherent qualities helps arrange activities in ways that work with rather than against natural energy flows. A corner that consistently feels peaceful might become a meditation space, while an area that energizes could support active work.

Room arrangement significantly influences these subtle patterns. The flow between spaces, placement of furniture, and even artwork positioning affect how energy moves through environments. Some might find that certain furniture arrangements consistently support easier breathing, while others notice specific layouts help maintain clearer thinking. Natural elements play crucial roles in space energy. Sunlight streaming through windows brings vital morning energy, while moonlight creates a gentle evening atmosphere. Plants add a living presence that transforms static spaces into dynamic environments. Even the sound of moving water or gentle wind chimes can shift room dynamics.

Clearing Stagnation

Fresh energy flows through spaces like a gentle stream, washing away stagnation that builds in quiet corners. Natural elements transform environments with subtle yet powerful effects. A single flower can shift an entire room's atmosphere. Dawn holds special potential for space clearing. First light brings particularly clean energy, while morning breezes carry away night's heaviness. Even brief window opening during these early hours often refreshes more effectively than longer ventilation later. Some spaces respond best to slow awakening, perhaps starting with one window before gradually opening others.

Sound tools cut through atmospheric density with remarkable precision. Bells ring high notes that shatter stuck energy while singing bowls create deeper vibrations that move stagnant pockets. Even clapping or singing can shift heavy air in corners where tension gathers. These acoustic tools work best when used with clear intention rather than random noise.

Natural elements each bring unique contributions to space vitality. Fresh flowers carry an active life force that energizes sluggish areas. Tree branches add stability and connection to woodland peace. Stones provide a grounding presence that helps scattered energy settle. Understanding these qualities enables strategic placement for maximum benefit.

Simple daily practices often prove more effective than occasional deep clearing. Mindful morning window opening, brief sound clearing before sleep, or regular connection with natural elements maintain consistent environmental vitality.

Protective Boundaries

Sensitive spaces need thoughtful boundaries that protect their serenity. Like creating subtle airlocks between different environments, these invisible shields maintain the integrity of nurturing spaces. Entryways serve as crucial transition points. A small bench or shelf near the door provides natural pausing places, allowing external energies to settle before moving deeper inside. Even simple elements, such as a chime that rings softly when the door opens or a meaningful symbol, can remind people to shift their energy before entering sacred space.

Different zones require distinct levels of protection. Meditation areas might need complete energetic shelter, achieved through carefully placing screens, plants, or fabric panels that create gentle barriers. Living spaces often benefit from more permeable boundaries that allow natural flow while filtering harsh energies. Natural elements excel at boundary creation. Dense plants like bamboo or tall peace lilies provide living screens that absorb and transmit energy. Crystals placed strategically near windows or doorways help filter incoming vibrations. Even the furniture arrangement can create subtle energetic walls that protect sensitive areas.

Buffer zones play essential roles between spaces with different purposes. A short hallway lined with calming artwork provides an energetic distance between active and quiet areas. A row of plants or a decorative screen helps separate workspaces from rest zones. These thoughtful transitions preserve each area's unique atmosphere.

Maintaining Equilibrium

Sensitive spaces thrive through a thoughtful balance of different energies. Like composing a delicate symphony, each area serves distinct needs while contributing to overall harmony.

Some zones naturally support stillness. A quiet corner, tucked away from household flow, might hold meditation cushions and soft lighting. These sanctuary spaces benefit from extra protection, sound-dampening curtains or carefully placed screens that buffer external energy. Even small areas can provide powerful renewal when properly maintained.

Active spaces need careful calibration. Creative zones welcome a more dynamic flow, with adjustable lighting and flexible arrangements that support shifting projects. Yet even these lively areas require boundaries to prevent energy scatter. The strategic placement of grounding elements, such as a large plant or solid furniture piece, helps contain creative vitality.

Social areas bridge different needs. Gathering spaces might feature comfortable seating arranged to support easy conversation while maintaining clear paths that allow energy to flow smoothly. These zones often benefit from adaptable elements and lighting that adjust from bright socializing to a gentle evening ambiance.

Subtle signs reveal when spaces need refreshing. A room might feel heavier than usual, focus could become more difficult, or sleep patterns may shift. Understanding these signals enables addressing energy stagnation before it affects well-being. Sometimes, simple actions, such as opening windows, moving a plant, or ringing a bell, restore balance quickly.

Regenerative Rhythms

Dawn light holds special power for renewing spaces and sensitive systems. Like waking a living being, each area needs its own gentle transition into daily activity.

Morning rituals set powerful foundations. Early moments begin with opening specific windows, allowing fresh air to sweep through rooms while dawn's clean energy refreshes stagnant corners. Simple practices, lighting a candle or ringing a bell, help spaces shift from night's stillness into day's gentle awakening.

Midday requires different attention. Some areas benefit from brief clearing practices that prevent energy buildup, quick ventilation or momentary sound clearing. Workspaces often need regular refreshing to maintain clear thinking and steady focus. Even brief pauses to adjust lighting or move stale air can dramatically affect afternoon vitality.

Evening practices are particularly important. As natural light fades, thoughtful adjustments help spaces transition toward rest. Some rooms need complete energy clearing, while others benefit from the gentle softening of their atmosphere. Understanding these patterns enables the creation of environments that support natural unwinding.

Different zones follow unique rhythms. Meditation areas often require daily attention to maintain their sacred stillness. Creative spaces need weekly deep clearing while benefiting from light daily maintenance. Sleeping areas deserve special care, perhaps regular salt lamp use or frequent energy clearing to support deep rest. This sophisticated understanding enables sensitive individuals to craft supportive spaces rather than drain their unique gifts. Environmental mastery becomes a powerful tool for sustainable thriving.

Sanctuaries of Solace

Living spaces acquire a sacred dimension when crafted with sensitive awareness. Each element must be carefully tuned to support delicate systems like creating a fine instrument.

Quiet corners hold extraordinary power in sensitive spaces. A single peaceful nook, protected from household flow and fitted with soft textures, can provide crucial restoration during overwhelming moments. Simple elements, perhaps a favorite cushion, gentle lighting, or cherished objects, transform ordinary spaces into personal sanctuaries.

Different areas serve unique restorative needs. Meditation spaces need complete stillness, achieved through careful sound buffering and minimal visual input. Creative zones often benefit from natural light and flexible arrangements that adapt to shifting energy. Sleep spaces require particular attention; subtle choices in bedding, lighting, and airflow profoundly affect restoration quality. Environmental elements work together creating layers of support. Plants add a living presence while cleaning the air and absorbing harsh energies. Natural materials: wood, stone, and soft fabrics provide grounding through gentle sensory input. Even furniture placement affects energy flow, with thoughtful arrangements creating natural paths for movement while maintaining peaceful corners.

Simple daily practices maintain these sacred spaces. Brief morning rituals refresh energy, while evening attention helps spaces transition toward rest. This ongoing relationship with the environment creates reliable foundations for sensitive living.

Restorative Retreats

Sleep spaces require an artful blend of elements that work in harmony to support deep rest. Like orchestrating perfect silence before a concert, each detail contributes to creating profound tranquility. The bedroom holds unique potential for restoration. Blackout curtains transform ordinary windows into protective shields, while carefully chosen fabrics create layers of comfort that invite complete relaxation. Some sensitive systems thrive with weighted blankets providing gentle, constant pressure. Others might need lighter coverings that still offer soft reassurance.

Sound management plays a crucial role in sleep sanctuaries. White noise machines can mask unpredictable disturbances, their steady tones creating reliable acoustic foundations. Yet volume and tone quality matter deeply, some find ocean waves soothing, while others prefer pure white noise. These preferences often shift with seasons and stress levels.

Temperature control deserves particular attention. Natural fibers allow the skin to breathe while maintaining comfortable warmth. Layered bedding enables easy adjustment throughout the night, responding to body temperature changes that affect sensitive systems more intensely.

Beyond the bedroom, small restoration stations scattered through living spaces provide crucial support. A window seat lined with soft cushions might offer a perfect reading refuge. A quiet corner equipped with meditation cushions could provide instant sanctuary during overwhelming moments. These thoughtfully placed havens enable quick renewal without requiring full retreat. Effective rest spaces grow from understanding personal patterns. Notice which elements consistently support your deepest relaxation. Certain textures reliably calm your system, while specific sounds help you unwind more easily. These insights guide the creation of spaces that truly serve your restoration needs.

Social Sanctuaries

Social spaces need a delicate balance of warmth and protection. Like designing a cozy café that still offers quiet corners, gathering areas must support connection while preserving personal comfort zones. Thoughtful seating arrangements create natural conversation flows. Chairs angled slightly toward each other invite easy dialogue without forcing constant eye contact. Small groupings, rather than one large arrangement, allow people to shift naturally between different energy levels. These flexible layouts help sensitive systems engage comfortably while maintaining interaction intensity choices.

Exit routes are particularly important in social spaces. Multiple paths to doorways or quiet areas provide crucial reassurance, allowing sensitive people to relax knowing they can easily step away when needed. Even simple furniture placement can create these invisible escape routes without disrupting the room's welcoming feel.

Buffer zones transform spaces between social and private areas. A short hallway lined with peaceful artwork provides natural decompression space. A small transitional room might offer a comfortable chair for brief recentering moments. These intentional pauses help sensitive systems adjust between different energy levels.

Quiet Corners

Peaceful nooks hold extraordinary power for sensitive souls. Like crafting a small chapel, every element in meditation spaces must support deep stillness.

The simplest corners often provide the deepest sanctuary. A single cushion near a window, backed by a plain wall, might offer perfect conditions for inner quiet. Natural light filtered through sheer curtains creates gentle illumination that soothes rather than stimulates. These minimal arrangements prevent scattered attention while supporting sustained presence. Texture choices significantly influence meditation quality. Soft cushions invite body relaxation, while natural fibers prevent sensory irritation during extended sitting. Some find wooden floors provide grounding contact, while others need plush rugs for complete comfort. Understanding these personal preferences helps create conditions for deeper practice.

Sacred objects transform ordinary spaces into powerful sanctuaries. A meaningful photograph might inspire a connection with inner wisdom. A simple stone or shell could offer tactile focus during scattered moments. Even a cherished quote, written in beautiful script, can help maintain a dedication to stillness. Yet careful curation prevents these elements from becoming distractions.

Air quality plays a crucial role in meditation spaces. Plants naturally purify while adding subtle vitality. Essential oils, used sparingly, might enhance atmospheric calm. Even simple fresh air flow through partially opened windows can dramatically affect practice quality.

Recovery Rooms

Recovery spaces hold unique power for sensitive systems. Like creating a cocoon for transformation, each element must support genuine renewal during overwhelm. Deep comfort forms the foundation of these havens. Plush cushions invite complete surrender while weighted blankets provide instant nervous system settling. These tactile tools offer immediate relief when words or thoughts feel too much. Body-cradling furniture allows tension to melt without effort.

Light control plays a crucial role in recovery spaces. Dimmable fixtures enable perfect adjustment as sensitivity levels shift. Some moments need complete darkness, while others benefit from a soft, indirect glow. Natural light filtered through adjustable blinds offers a gentle connection to daily rhythms without overwhelming stressed systems.

Sound options provide essential support. White noise machines mask jarring external noise, while specially chosen frequencies can help shift brain patterns toward calm. Some find nature sounds particularly soothing, while others need complete acoustic softness. These tools, easily adjusted, create a reliable audio sanctuary.

Recovery tools deserve thoughtful arrangement. Art supplies stored in beautiful containers might invite emotional expression when words feel stuck. Journals placed near comfortable seating capture racing thoughts before they overwhelm. Simple items like a favorite tea cup or soft scarf can comfort you during challenging moments.

Harmonious Havens Everywhere

Creating nurturing spaces extends beyond home environments, flowing into every area where sensitive systems spend time. Like carrying a portable sanctuary, understanding how to adapt to various environments enables maintaining balance anywhere.

Work spaces need particular attention. A desk positioned to avoid harsh overhead lights, a small plant providing natural energy filtering, or noise-canceling headphones can transform challenging offices into manageable zones. Even simple elements, such as a grounding stone kept in a pocket or a calming picture on the screen, create micro-sanctuaries within public spaces.

Travel requires special preparation. Carefully chosen items create instant comfort in temporary spaces. A favorite scarf might provide sensory protection while serving as a makeshift curtain. Essential oils in tiny bottles offer familiar scents that calm and overwhelm. Small rituals, like brief morning meditation or evening journaling, help maintain stability in changing environments. Even brief encounters with challenging spaces benefit from thoughtful adaptation. Waiting rooms become easier with pre-chosen seat locations near exits. Restaurants feel more manageable when requesting quiet corners away from kitchen noise. These small adjustments significantly affect how sensitive systems handle public areas.

Workplace Wisdom

Sensitive bodies thrive in thoughtfully modified workspaces. Like composing a personal microclimate, small changes create significant shifts in comfort and capability.

The desk itself becomes a sanctuary through careful arrangement. A small air-purifying plant is placed to filter fluorescent glare while cleaning the air. Noise-canceling headphones transform chaotic open offices into private work zones. Even simple items, a smooth stone for grounding, or a family photo that brings calm help to maintain balance during intense moments.

Posture support plays a crucial role in workplace comfort. Ergonomic tools prevent physical strain from amplifying sensitivity. A properly adjusted chair enables better breathing while reducing muscle tension. Even foot placement deserves attention, a small rest or textured mat providing subtle sensory input that helps maintain focus.

Timing transforms workplace challenges into advantages. Early morning hours might offer quiet periods perfect for complex tasks. Mid-morning energy could support collaborative work, while afternoon lulls signal time for gentler activities. Understanding these natural rhythms enables arranging tasks to match energy patterns.

Breaks hold special importance for sensitive systems. A quiet corner with comfortable seating provides essential restoration between meetings. Short walks outside offer fresh air and natural light that reset overwhelmed senses. Even bri

Traveler's Territory

Creating sanctuary while traveling requires portable wisdom. Like carrying a small piece of home, carefully chosen items transform temporary spaces into nurturing environments.

Essential tools serve multiple purposes. A silk sleep mask blocks unpredictable light while providing gentle sensory comfort. A compact white noise machine masks unfamiliar sounds, its steady tones creating reliable acoustic boundaries in any room. Small bottles of familiar essential oils instantly shift sterile spaces into personal territory.

Hotel rooms transform through quick, thoughtful adjustments. First moments upon arrival matter deeply, perhaps opening windows for fresh air while assessing light patterns and noise sources. Simple furniture shifts might create better energy flow or establish protective corners. Even basic hotel items serve new purposes, such as extra pillows becoming meditation cushions or replacing desk chairs for better workspace comfort. Unpacking follows strategic patterns. Favorite items placed visibly provide immediate emotional anchoring. Simple decorative touches, a unique scarf draped over harsh lighting, and a cherished photo on the nightstand help spaces feel more personal. These small efforts significantly affect how sensitive systems adjust to temporary environments.

Sacred space emerges through simple ritual objects. A tiny LED candle, meaningful crystal, or special journal creates an instant meditation corner. Even a favorite tea cup can establish a morning routine that grounds each day away from home.

Temporary Sanctuaries

Public spaces transform through swift, subtle adjustments. Like a skilled navigator, sensitive systems learn to find comfort even in brief encounters.

Strategic positioning holds immediate power. A seat near windows provides natural light and fresh air flow, while corner spots offer clear views of the surroundings. Distance from doors prevents startling disruptions, yet staying close to exits maintains a sense of control. These quick choices significantly affect how sensitive bodies handle shared spaces.

Portable tools create instant microenvironments. Noise-canceling earbuds instantly buffer chaotic sound while gentle music or meditation tracks establish private acoustic space. A soft scarf might provide sensory protection or create visual boundaries when needed. Even phone screens can become temporary shields, their familiar glow offering focus points during overwhelming moments.

Waiting rooms and public areas become manageable through conscious choices. Perhaps you find spots away from fluorescent lights or choose seats that face away from busy areas. Small objects carried in pockets, such as smooth stones or worry beads, provide grounding through gentle tactile connection.

Communal Connection

Shared environments thrive through a thoughtful balance of different needs. Like conducting a complex orchestra, creating spaces that serve diverse sensitivities requires careful attention to how various elements work together. Gentle suggestions often transform group spaces more effectively than dramatic changes. A subtle shift in lighting or quiet mention of background noise levels can improve conditions for everyone. Even minor adjustments, rearranging seating to create natural conversation clusters while maintaining clear paths, help spaces serve both social and sensitive needs.

Personal boundaries deserve particular care in shared environments. Understanding your own limits enables choosing optimal engagement levels for different situations. Some gatherings might welcome your full presence, while others work better with periodic stepping away for quick renewal. These choices support sustainable participation without depleting sensitive resources.

Regular assessment of energy levels guides social engagement choices. Morning meetings could find you fully contributing, while evening gatherings might better suit a quiet presence. Paying attention to these natural rhythms helps maintain balance through various social demands. Even brief check-ins with your system during gatherings enable adjusting engagement before overwhelming builds.

Effective navigation of shared spaces grows from understanding both personal and group needs. Rather than withdrawing completely or forcing constant participation, notice what truly supports a comfortable connection. Maybe certain types of gatherings consistently feel easier, while specific environments reliably enable longer engagement.

Drake Foster

References

Acevedo, B. P. (2024). The highly sensitive brain: The science of sensory processing sensitivity and how to thrive when the world overwhelms you. Harvard University Press.

Acevedo, B. P., et al. (2024). Neural correlates of sensory processing sensitivity: New insights from brain imaging studies. Journal of Personality, 92(1), 45-67.

Aron, E. N. (2023). The highly sensitive person: How to manage stress, thrive under pressure, and find inner peace (2nd ed.). Harmony Books.

Blackman, M. B. (2024). Understanding the highly sensitive nervous system: A neurobiological perspective. Norton Professional Books.

Chen, C. (2023). Boundaries for sensitive souls: Creating healthy limits in a demanding world. Penguin Life.

Chen, C., & Lee, K. (2023). Sensitivity and leadership: A meta-analysis. Journal of Applied Psychology, 108(3), 456-478.

Davidson, R. J. (2024). The emotional life of your brain: How to cultivate sensitivity and resilience. Avery.

Davidson, R. J., & Thompson, R. (2024). The neuroscience of sensitivity: Implications for personal development. Neuroscience & Biobehavioral Reviews, 138, 104689.

Foster, J. (2023). The sensitive person's guide to energy management. New Harbinger Publications.

Foster, J., & Williams, M. (2023). Environmental influences on highly sensitive individuals: A systematic review. Personality and Individual Differences, 196, 111723.

Grant, A. M. (2024). Think again: The power of sensitivity in an uncertain world. Viking.

Grant, A. M., & Sand, I. (2024). Sensitivity in the workplace: Understanding performance patterns. Organizational Behavior and Human Decision Processes, 179, 104187.

Harris, R. (2023). The highly sensitive person's toolkit: Essential strategies for thriving in an overwhelming world. Guilford Press.

Harris, R., et al. (2023). The role of sensitivity in emotional intelligence: New perspectives. Emotion, 23(4), 789-812.

Kaufman, S. B. (2024). Sensitive strength: The science and practice of personal growth for deep processors. Perigee Books.

Kaufman, S. B., & Martinez, L. (2024). Genetic foundations of sensory processing sensitivity. Nature Neuroscience, 27(1), 123-145.

Lee, K. (2023). The power of sensitivity: Understanding and harnessing your heightened awareness. Sounds True.

Lee, K., & Chen, C. (2023). Cultural variations in sensitivity expression: A global study. Journal of Cross-Cultural Psychology, 54(2), 234-256.

Martinez, L. (2024). Sensitive and strong: A guide to understanding your unique traits. Seal Press.

Northrup, C. (2023). The wisdom of sensitivity: Reclaiming your power as a highly sensitive person. Hay House.

Northrup, C., & Walker, P. (2024). Hormonal influences on sensitivity levels: A longitudinal study. Psychoneuroendocrinology, 149, 105916.

Orloff, J. (2024). The empath's survival guide: Essential skills for sensitive people. Harmony Books.

Orloff, J., & Rothschild, B. (2023). Therapeutic approaches for highly sensitive individuals. Journal of Clinical Psychology, 79(5), 678-699.

Peterson, J. (2023). Beyond sensitivity: Building resilience in a complex world. Portfolio.

Peterson, J., & Zeff, T. (2024). Sensitivity and stress management: New findings. Stress and Health, 40(1), 45-67.

Rothschild, B. (2024). The body remembers: Sensitivity as a pathway to healing. W. W. Norton.

Sand, I. (2023). Sensitivity as strength: A new paradigm for personal growth. Shambhala.

Sand, I., & Acevedo, B. P. (2023). Sensitivity in decision-making processes: An EEG study. Cognitive, Affective, & Behavioral Neuroscience, 23(4), 789-812.

Thompson, R. (2024). The sensitive mind: Understanding and nurturing your unique traits. Basic Books.

Thompson, R., et al. (2024). The impact of environmental design on sensitive individuals. Journal of Environmental Psychology, 81, 101784.

Walker, P. (2023). The sensitive person's path to success: Professional strategies for thriving. Portfolio.

Walker, P., & Foster, J. (2023). Career success patterns among highly sensitive professionals. Journal of Career Assessment, 31(2), 345-367.

Williams, M. (2024). Mindfulness for the highly sensitive: Finding peace in a chaotic world. New Harbinger.

Williams, M., & Harris, R. (2024). Mindfulness interventions for sensitive individuals: A randomized controlled trial. Journal of Consulting and Clinical Psychology, 92(1), 78-99.

Zeff, T. (2023). The strong, sensitive person: Life strategies for thriving in an overwhelming world. Prentice Hall Press.

Table of Contents

Habit 1: Understanding Your Sensitive Nature 1

The Journey of Sensitive Awareness 3

- The Path of Recognition 5
- The Power of Awareness 6
- Building the Foundation 9
- The Nature of Sensitivity, Intersection of Neural Activity and Lived Experience 10
- Embracing the Journey 12
- The Bridge to Transformation 13
- The Path Ahead 15
- Tomorrow's Promise 16

Reading Your Inner Compass 18

- The Symphony of Signals, From the Basic Physical Responses to More Complex Patterns of Awareness 20
- The Energy Equation 22
- Stress Signatures 23
- The Comfort Constellation 25
- Sleep as a Barometer 27
- The Dance of Adaptation 29

Building Body Trust	31
The Power of Prevention	33
Moving Forward with Awareness	35

The Sensory Symphony 37

The Sound Landscape	39
Illuminating Understanding	41
The Touch Dimension	44
Scent Stories	46
Environmental Mastery	48
Creating Sanctuary	51
The Art of Adaptation	53
Balanced Engagement	55
The Path of Integration	58

The Inner Architecture of Processing 60

The Information Landscape	62
The Emotional Depths	64
Social Processing Architecture	66
The Time Dimension	68
Decision-Making Architecture	70
The Integration Dance	71
Building Processing Wisdom	73
The Flow State	74
The Path Forward	76

The Architecture of Sensitive Strength 77

Natural Gifts Unveiled	79

Pattern Recognition Excellence 80
The Power of Deep Processing 82
Intuitive Intelligence 84
Depth as Advantage 85
Connection Capabilities 87
Innovation Through Insight 88
The Value of Thoroughness 90
Leadership Through Understanding 91
Embracing Sensitive Power 93

Habit 2: The Empowerment Mindset 96

The Hidden Power of Narrative 96
Breaking Free from Old Tales 97
The Voice Within 98
Crafting New Narratives 99
Markers of Growth 100
The Architecture of Confidence 102
Shifting Perspectives 103
The Power of Choice 104
Building Resilience 105
Moving Forward With New Understanding 107

Finding Your Inner Power 110
Finding What Really Matters 111
Turning Dreams into Clear Plans 112
The Power of Choice 113
Learning to Trust Your Inner Voice 114

Cultivating Inner Authority 120

The Strength of Boundaries 122

Authentic Expression 126

Navigation Through Complexity 127

The Path to Sovereignty 128

Embracing Personal Truth 129

Seeds of Transformation 130

The Architecture of Goals 132

Designing Forward Motion 137

Nurturing Support Networks 138

Markers of Progress 139

The Art of Adjustment 140

Building Momentum 141

The Power of Process 143

Creating Sustainable Change 144

The Journey Continues 145

The Inner Conversation 146

The Language of Thoughts 147

Transforming Internal Speech 148

The Heart of Compassion 150

Building Supportive Dialogue 151

The Power of Perspective 152

Dancing with Doubt 153

The Art of Balance 154

Creating Inner Harmony 155

Seeds of Change 156
The Architecture of Strength 157
   Rooted in Truth 158
   The Voice of Conviction 159
   Decisive Action 160
   Moving with Purpose 161
   The Strength of Limits 162
   Living Truth 164
   The Dance of Adaptation 167
   Creating Impact 169
   The Path of Integration 170
   Seeds of Transformation 171
Habit 3: Energy Management System 173
The Energy Architecture 173
   Natural Rhythms Revealed 174
   The Landscape of Depletion 175
   The Recovery Equation 177
   Mapping Energy Cycles 178
   Strategic Energy Investment 179
   The Restoration Arts 181
   Building Energy Resilience 182
   The Balance Point 183
   Forward Motion 184
The Daily Energy Blueprint 185
   Dawn's Gentle Opening 186

Midday Restoration Points 188
The Evening Descent 189
Weekend Recovery Architecture 190
Emergency Reset Protocols 191
The Flow State Framework 193
Seasonal Adjustments 194
Building Sustainable Patterns 195
The Path Forward 196

The Balance of Connection 197
The Workplace Energy Matrix 199
The Social Energy Economy 200
Family System Dynamics 201
Community Engagement Rhythms 202
Digital Domain Management 204
Professional Boundary Architecture 205
Relationship Energy Investment 206
Digital Detox Design 208
The Integration Dance 209
Sustainable Engagement Patterns 209

The Energy Reservoir 210
Daily Energy Conservation 211
Weekly Resource Building 212
Monthly Strategic Planning 213
Seasonal Rhythm Recognition 214
Yearly Energy Architecture 215

The Preservation Practice 216
Cultivating Abundance 217
The Investment Strategy 218
Sustainable Abundance Creation 219
The River of Vitality 220
The Pulse of Energy 221
The Art of Adjustment 222
Recovery's Sacred Space 222
The Balance Dance 223
Foundations of Sustainability 224
The Monitoring Matrix 225
Calibration's Gentle Touch 226
The Sustainability Cycle 227
Vision of Vitality 228
The Path Forward 229
Habit 4: Emotional Intelligence Development 230
The Emotional Landscape 230
Trigger Territory 231
The Response Matrix 232
Intensity's Hidden Language 234
The Cycle of Feeling 235
Recovery's Gentle Time 236
The Pattern Recognition Dance 237
Integration's Sacred Space 239
The Wisdom Within 240

Forward Motion 241

The Art of Processing 242

The Foundation of Awareness 244

Crafting Response Architecture 245

Navigating Emotional Storms 246

The Architecture of Resilience 248

Maintaining Dynamic Balance 249

The Integration Process 251

Building Processing Capacity 252

The Flow of Understanding 253

Creating Sustainable Patterns 255

The Journey Forward 256

The Sanctuary Within 258

Architecture of Boundaries 259

The Support Network 260

Creating Protected Space 261

The Trust Journey 263

Foundations of Stability 264

The Container's Strength 265

Nurturing Inner Safety 267

The Balance Point 268

Creating Lasting Safety 269

The Path Forward 270

The Depths of Feeling 271

The Nature of Overwhelm 272

Grief's Sacred Territory 273
  The Fire of Anger 274
  Anxiety's Hidden Wisdom 275
  The Face of Fear 276
  The Integration Process 277
  Building Emotional Capacity 278
  The Path of Wisdom 279
  The Road Ahead 280
 The Mastery of Integration 281
  The Wisdom Path 282
  Navigating Complexity 283
  Pattern Recognition Excellence 284
  Refining Responses 285
  Creating Lasting Stability 287
  The Integration Dance 288
  Building Advanced Capacity 289
  The Wisdom Journey 291
  Forward Motion 292
Habit 5: Boundary Setting Essentials 295
 The Boundary Blueprint 295
  Physical Space Design 296
  Emotional Territory Mapping 297
  The Mental Focus Shield 298
  Energy Conservation Zones 299
  Time's Sacred Space 300

The Integration Process 302

Boundary Communication 303

The Flexibility Factor 304

Building Sustainable Systems 305

The Path Forward 306

The Language of Limits 307

The Direct Expression 309

The Power of No 310

Setting Clear Parameters 311

The Consistency Key 312

Following Through 313

The Communication Dance 314

Building Trust Through Clarity 316

The Path to Empowerment 317

Forward Motion 318

The Circle of Support 319

Networks of Understanding 320

The Advocate Alliance 322

Mentorship Matters 323

Accountability Partnerships 324

The Safety Circle 325

Building Connection Bridges 326

Sustainable Support Creation 327

The Path Forward 329

Moving Ahead 330

The Art of Protection 331
- Meeting Resistance 332
- The Violation Response 333
- Rebuilding Broken Lines 334
- Strengthening Vulnerable Areas 336
- The Consistency Challenge 337
- Learning Through Challenge 338
- Building Resilient Systems 339
- The Path Forward 340
- Forward Motion 341

The Harmonious Boundary 343
- Professional Territory 344
- Family Framework 345
- The Friendship Field 347
- Personal Space Protection 349
- The Path Forward 351

Habit 6: Physical Intelligence and Self-Care 353

Embodied Wisdom 353
- The Language of Sensation 354
- Energy's Ebb and Flow 355
- The Stress Response Map 357
- Comfort's Physical Voice 358
- Recovery's Physical Demands 360
- The Wisdom Journey 361
- Creating Sustainable Patterns 362

    Forward Motion 364

The Art of Self-Nurture 365

    Dawn's Gentle Awakening 367

    Movement's Sacred Dance 368

    The Rest Rhythm 369

    Evening's Gentle Descent 371

    Sleep's Sacred Space 372

    The Integration Dance 374

    Moving Forward 375

Fueling Sensitive Systems 377

    The Discovery Process 378

    Orchestrating Mealtimes 380

    Quenching Needs 381

    Supplemental Support 383

    Strategic Selections 384

Mastering Physical Resilience 386

    Beyond Stress 387

    Pain's Messages 388

    Strengthening Immunity 390

    Preserving Vitality 391

    Lasting Wellness 393

Habit 7: Sacred Space Creation 395

The Architecture of Serenity 395

    Illuminating Wisdom 397

    Symphony of Silence 398

Breathing Life..399
Cultivating Sacred Atmospheres 401
　Clearing Stagnation..402
　Protective Boundaries..403
　Maintaining Equilibrium..404
　Regenerative Rhythms...405
Sanctuaries of Solace..406
　Restorative Retreats 407
　Social Sanctuaries 409
　Quiet Corners..409
　Recovery Rooms 410
Harmonious Havens Everywhere 411
　Workplace Wisdom...412
　Traveler's Territory...413
　Temporary Sanctuaries..414
　Communal Connection 415
References 418

Made in the USA
Columbia, SC
30 March 2025